RISE OF THE
ROCKET GIRLS

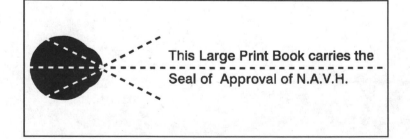

This Large Print Book carries the
Seal of Approval of N.A.V.H.

RISE OF THE ROCKET GIRLS

THE WOMEN WHO PROPELLED US, FROM MISSILES TO THE MOON TO MARS

NATHALIA HOLT

THORNDIKE PRESS
A part of Gale, Cengage Learning

GALE
CENGAGE Learning

Farmington Hills, Mich • San Francisco • New York • Waterville, Maine
Meriden, Conn • Mason, Ohio • Chicago

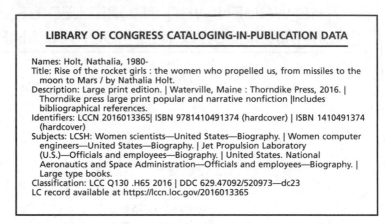

LIBRARY OF CONGRESS CATALOGING-IN-PUBLICATION DATA

Names: Holt, Nathalia, 1980-
Title: Rise of the rocket girls : the women who propelled us, from missiles to the moon to Mars / by Nathalia Holt.
Description: Large print edition. | Waterville, Maine : Thorndike Press, 2016. | Thorndike press large print popular and narrative nonfiction |Includes bibliographical references.
Identifiers: LCCN 2016013365| ISBN 9781410491374 (hardcover) | ISBN 1410491374 (hardcover)
Subjects: LCSH: Women scientists—United States—Biography. | Women computer engineers—United States—Biography. | Jet Propulsion Laboratory (U.S.)—Officials and employees—Biography. | United States. National Aeronautics and Space Administration—Officials and employees—Biography. | Large type books.
Classification: LCC Q130 .H65 2016 | DDC 629.47092/520973—dc23
LC record available at https://lccn.loc.gov/2016013365

Published in 2016 by arrangement with Little, Brown and Company, a division of Hachette Books Group, Inc.

For Larkin and our little rocket girls,
Eleanor and Philippa

CONTENTS

7

I did not come to NASA to make history.

— Sally Ride

Why do we, the solar sails,
fragile as a feather's frond,
silently seek to sail so far?
We walk the air from here to planet out
  beyond
Because we're more than fond of life and
  what we are.

— Ray Bradbury and Jonathan V. Post
To Sail Beyond the Sun

PREFACE

"Lily?" I suggested, pointing to a name I'd scribbled on a damp cocktail napkin. My husband shook his head no. I pressed the pen to my lips and concentrated, trying to balance my pregnant belly while perched on the wobbly edge of a bar stool. It was the summer of 2010, and my husband and I were trying to come up with names for our daughter's December arrival. Sitting in a bar in Cambridge, Massachusetts, we brainstormed names, each writing them down privately on a napkin before showing the other, as if we were on some bizarre game show: *Name Your Baby!* We weren't having much luck. We both have unusual first names — Nathalia and Larkin — so we wanted to find one that wouldn't subject our daughter to a lifetime of odd nicknames. When Larkin wrote down *Eleanor,* I immediately rejected it. It sounded so old-fashioned. I couldn't imagine naming my daughter that. But as the months went by and my belly grew, the name grew on me too. We started coming up with middle names. I suggested *Frances,* a fitting tribute to Larkin's mother, who had passed away seven years earlier.

Like any modern mother-to-be, I researched the names we were dreaming up on the Internet. When I plugged in *Eleanor Frances,* I was surprised to find, buried in history, an Eleanor Francis Helin, born November 12, 1932. She was a scientist at NASA's Jet Propulsion Laboratory, in charge of the program that tracked asteroids nearing Earth. Like the scientists we so often see personified in movies such as *Armageddon,* she hunted the asteroids that get a little too close to home. During her time at NASA, she discovered an impressive number of asteroids and comets — more than eight hundred. This was the kind of woman I wanted my daughter to share her name with. My search came up with an old black-and-white photo of her, blond bouffant hair curling at her shoulders, a timid smile as she held up an astronomy award for her asteroid discoveries. Exactly how long had this woman worked at NASA? I wondered. Did women even work at NASA as scientists during the 1950s?

Unfortunately it looked like I might never find out. Helin had passed away a year before, in 2009. When my daughter was born, in the last hours of December 14, 2010, we named her Eleanor Frances, in part for a woman I had never met but whose story I couldn't stop thinking about.

My continued obsession with Eleanor Francis Helin ("Glo" to her friends) led me to uncover the stories of a group of women intriguingly known as "the human computers" at the Jet Propulsion Lab in Pasadena, California. These women, recruited in the 1940s and 1950s, were responsible for all the critical calculations at JPL that powered early missiles, rocketed heavy bombers over the Pacific, launched America's first satellite, guided lunar missions and planetary explorations, and even navigate Mars rovers today. My search unearthed a 1950s picture of the group, the women working at their desks. The image was crisp, yet the archivists at NASA knew only a few of the women's names and weren't sure what had become of them. It seemed their stories had been lost in the shuffle of history.

While we tend to think of the role women played during the early years at NASA as secretarial, these women were the antithesis of that assumption. These young female engineers shaped much of our history and the technology we have today. They became the earliest computer programmers at NASA. One of them still works there, the longest-serving woman of the American space program. Their stories give us an inside look at pivotal moments in American history, from a perspective never before told.

Since the cold night my Eleanor Frances was born, I've thought of these women often — particularly when the mood is intense. In my years as a microbiologist, I've tinkered with broken breast pumps in remote research stations in South Africa, watched my toddler run down darkened laboratory halls, and held in my hands raw data that shimmered with beauty. At each moment, I'm brought back to the women who dealt with similar struggles and triumphs a half century ago. How did they handle the sometimes awkward, sometimes wonderful challenges of being a woman, a mother, and a scientist all at once? There was only one way to find out: I'd have to ask them.

January 1958
Launch Day

The young woman's heart was pounding. Her palms were sweaty as she gripped the pencil. She quickly scribbled down the numbers coming across the Teletype. She had been awake for more than sixteen hours but felt no fatigue. Instead, the experience seemed to be heightening her senses. Behind her she could sense Richard Feynman, the famous physicist, peeking at her graph paper. He stood looking over her shoulder, occasionally sighing. She knew that her every move was being carefully watched, her calculations closely studied. Her work would inform mission control if the first American satellite would be a success or a crushing failure.

Hours earlier, before the satellite had been launched, her boyfriend had wished her luck. He hadn't quite gotten used to the fact that his girlfriend worked late nights as an integral part of the American space program. Before leaving, he gave her a quick kiss. "I love you even if the dang thing falls in the ocean," he said with a smile.

Now, hours later, the worry that the satellite had crashed into the sea was real. They should have detected its signal by now. With each passing second they were inching closer to catastrophic failure. The numbers raced in from tracking stations across the globe. With each new measurement, she calculated the path of the satellite. If it didn't hit the right velocity, if it didn't make its trajectory, America would be left with egg on its face, even further behind the Soviets. Her pride was similarly tied to the fate of the satellite. She'd been here at the Jet Propulsion Laboratory from its earliest days, helping to design the rockets powering the tube-shaped spacecraft that was no heavier than a toddler. Now the project's ultimate fate was hers to reveal.

As she plotted a curved line across the orange graph paper, she realized the trajectory was coming close to the point of no return. If the satellite passed this point, it would leave the atmosphere, begin circling the globe, and become the first American space-success story. The future of space exploration rested on this moment. But the young woman tried not to think of this.

16

Instead, she focused on the paper in front of her, with its long lines of numbers. When she calculated that the satellite had left Earth's atmosphere, the critical juncture, she kept quiet. She made no comment but couldn't help letting a smile come to her lips.

"Why are you smiling?" Feynman said, his voice irritated as the moments crept by. Until the signal came through in California, after the satellite had completed a spin around Earth, they couldn't be sure the satellite would stay up. Everyone was on edge as they waited for the confirmation of a few faint beeps, proof that they'd made it.

The pounding of the Teletype filled her ears. The numbers came in. Suddenly the satellite's signal came through loud and clear, breaking its long silence. She confirmed her calculations before marking down the updated position on the graph paper.

"She made it!" she said triumphantly, twisting around in her seat to see the reaction. Behind her, a room of her colleagues, almost all men, broke into cheers. Ahead of her, the future stretched out, as limitless as space itself.

■ ■ ■ ■

PART I
1940s

■ ■ ■ ■

Barby Canright

Macie Roberts

Barbara Lewis (later Paulson)

Chapter 1
Up, Up, and Away

The first noise she heard was a low-pitched growl. Next came the explosion. Then the grating sound of metal grinding on metal came as loud as a thunderstorm. Barbara Canright whirled around to see a car-size piece of twisted steel teetering dangerously on the roof of the building above her. With her eyes fixed on the looming accident, the seconds slowed down as she stood frozen in place. Filled with a sudden terror, she hurried away, her heels clicking on the red-brick paths of the California Institute of Technology campus. A blur of faces surrounded her, all gawking at the scene, unsure of exactly what they were witnessing. But Barbara, known by everyone as Barby, knew what the thing falling from the sky was.

From a safe distance she watched as the warped hunks of metal rained down on the sidewalk. One after another, a platform, a rocket motor, and a pendulum fell to their doom. The homemade scientific equipment landed in a heap resembling little more than trash to the onlookers. Yet Barby could value its worth. She gasped when a piece of the building followed the debris to the ground, the bricks breaking apart into powdered clay. When the dust settled, the campus seemed impossibly quiet. As Barby moved away from the scene, the students around her were whispering; it was as if after so much noise, they hesitated to add a decibel.

Barby often had lunch with her husband in the afternoons. She'd escape the shackles of her typewriter and walk across the campus, drinking in the fresh air and the Southern California sunshine. Yet this March day in 1939 was unusually overcast. It was a foreboding beginning to the experiments that a team of men, known as the Suicide Squad, would run that day.

The group drew attention the way a circus attracts a crowd, with outlandish stunts and an eccentric appeal. It all started with three young men: Frank Malina, Jack Parsons, and Ed Forman. Hardly anyone thought of them as scientists. Perhaps this was because only Frank was a student at the university. It was difficult for those first meeting him to guess his age. He had the exuberance of a boy but the thinning hair of middle age. Despite his retreating hairline, he was twenty-six years old, the same age as Ed, and he shared a birthday with Jack, who was just two years younger. Together they tackled rocketry with all the bravado of youth.

Ed and Jack had been best friends since attending Washington Junior High School in Pasadena. Jack was the chemist in the trio. He grew up on the posh "Millionaire's Mile" in Pasadena with the expectation that, despite his poor performance in school, he would attend college. The Great Depression changed his destiny, leaving his family and his career prospects desolate. Ed, on the other hand, was from humble origins. His background in a working-class Pasadena family gave him experience in cobbling parts together. The machinist of the group, he made the modest equipment they had go a long way. The two bonded over a love of science fiction and rockets. It was this passion that led them to Frank.

For Barby and her husband, Richard, the group held no mystique; they were simply their friends. They met on the Caltech campus, where the Suicide Squad, despite the nonstudent status of two of their members, spent all their free time tinkering with rockets. As they sat around a wicker-and-glass table on the Canrights' patio, their imaginations fired late into the night with only the moon keeping track of their hours as it rose in the sky. The California moon seemed impossibly big. Barby had never seen one like it back home in Ohio, where in the warmth of the summer nights, everyone hid behind screened porches to shelter from the mosquitoes that descended at twilight.

In the sleepy town of Pasadena, Barby, Richard, and the members of the Suicide Squad had a clear view of the stars from their backyards. Since the Great Depression, the number of businesses was shrinking, down 52 percent in the decade since 1929. One benefit of the sluggish economy was that there was less light pollution in the night sky, leaving a velvety-black canvas for their starry-eyed schemes. As the friends discussed airplanes, Barby found the conversation infectious. She was full of the naïveté of nineteen, and spaceflight seemed an attainable goal to her. They discussed everything, from fuel to fins.

The Suicide Squad men were dreamers, but they were also troublemakers. The previous year, they'd tried to move a cylinder of nitrogen dioxide from outside the chemistry building. The valve suddenly jammed, causing a fountain of toxic, liquefied gas. For weeks, the resulting brown patch of grass on the lawn irritated the university's gardeners but made Barby smile as she passed it on the way to work. Unfortunately the next experiment wasn't as funny.

The group were attempting to test an unusual mixture — nitrogen dioxide and wood alcohol — to see how the combination might power a rocket motor. Barby was appalled. Thanks to her proficiency in high school chemistry, she knew how dangerous nitrogen dioxide was. Inhaling the gas can kill you. To mix it with a cheap alcohol and then set it on fire was a death wish. Barby shook her head; the men were certainly earning their reputation.

They took the dangerous mixture and poured it into a small rocket motor. They then attached a fifty-foot rope with the rocket motor swinging off the end and hung the pendulum in a stairwell from the top floor of the Guggenheim Aeronautical Laboratory, all the way to the basement, like a giant rope swing. How hard the pendulum swung translated into how high a rocket might one day fly. But it didn't go so well. The first time they tried their experiment, the engine misfired and a cloud of toxic gas saturated the building. It caused every metal exterior it touched to rust and tarnished every polished surface. The building housed an expensive new wind tunnel, the largest in the world, and its once-shiny metal was soon covered in spots of orange and brown. It looked like the wind tunnel had a case of measles. The accident earned the men the moniker the Suicide Squad, a nickname that didn't bode well.

The group worried that their future at Caltech was as ruined as the rusted wind tunnel. Although Ed and Jack were not students, their future in rocketry was inextricably linked to the university. So it was a pleasant surprise when they learned that they could continue their experiments; they just had to move them outside. Using a metal platform attached to the side of the building, they hauled up their rocket-motor pendulum and carefully hung it over the side of the platform. When Barby looked up at the explosion that March afternoon, she was watching the platform carrying all the equipment smash into bits. It could have been worse — Frank could have been killed. At the last minute, he had been called away from the experiment to deliver a typewriter to his adviser's home, while Ed and Jack carried on alone. Returning to campus, he found a piece of the pressure gauge buried in the wooden beam right where his head would have been.

This accident, in full view of the student body, brought renown to the Suicide Squad, though it wasn't a desirable notoriety. Barby and Richard teased the group mercilessly. As easy as it was to joke about the accident, Richard was seriously grateful Barby had been nowhere near the platform when it fell.

Richard and Barby loved each other in the passionate fashion of newlyweds, the years not yet smoothing the sharp edges of their union. They fought and made up, the tears and laughter running together. They had eloped, celebrating their tender young marriage by moving from Ohio to Southern California. Richard was twenty-one. Barby was two years younger and turning heads at the all-male Caltech campus. With her dark hair curling at her shoulders, dark brown eyes, and petite, feminine frame, she was the very picture of a wholesome midwestern girl. She had just the kind of job one would expect. She worked as a typist, spending her days clicking away at the keys, while fitting in classes at Occidental College, in Los Angeles. She was incredibly bright; in high school she took advanced math and chemistry classes, often the only girl in the rigorous courses. As she toiled in school she had no sense that the coursework would ever influence her future. She took the classes simply because she enjoyed them and spoke of mathematics lovingly. Despite her teenage fascination, she was snarled in the limits of being born a woman. None of the options before her — schoolteacher, nurse, secretary — felt quite right. Yet whichever career she chose could hold only a transient charm. Now that she was married, her days of working would last only as long as she and Richard remained childless. Motherhood, the career she was formed for, loomed large.

Richard, like Barby, was also discontented with work. To make ends meet, he drove a truck for a delivery company while attending graduate school at Caltech. Unlike Barby, he could see opportunity on the horizon. He wanted to be an engineer and knew that if he worked hard enough, he could get there. What Barby and Richard didn't realize was that while they joked around with the Suicide Squad, their fates would end up tied to the wild group. In less than a year, Frank would approach them with a tantalizing job offer.

■ ■ ■ ■

In 1939, the National Academy of Sciences awarded a grant to the Suicide Squad, now more formally known as the GALCIT (Guggenheim Aeronautical Laboratory at the California Institute of Technology) Rocket Research Project. It came just in time. Without a way to fund their rockets, the group had been on the verge of disbanding. Jack and Ed had taken part-time jobs with the Halifax Powder Company while Frank began research for the Soil Conservation Society. That first award, $1,000, rescued the group, bringing them back together. When they were awarded a second grant the next year for ten times as much, it was life-changing. It was the U.S. government's first investment in rocket research. In deference to the Army Air Corps, which had proposed the funding, they changed their name to the Air Corps Jet Propulsion Research Project. Their goal was clear: develop a rocket plane. The risky project was the beginning of what would become the Jet Propulsion Laboratory.

The influx of money meant that the group could finally hire some help. Knowing they would need skilled mathematicians, Frank approached the Canrights. Barby knew the job would be far from a sure thing. She wondered if she could depend on the longevity of the reckless group. She and Richard would be leaving good jobs to work for men who were not known for their reliability. Yet the offer was tempting.

If she accepted, Barby would once again be the only woman in a group of men. It was a job she hadn't expected, yet one she was eminently qualified for. Math was a comfortable second skin. She would always feel more at home with a pencil in her hand than at a typewriter. In addition, the position held prestige, allowed her to work alongside her husband, and paid twice what she made as a typist. More than the money, it offered her the opportunity to use her neglected math skills.

It wasn't just the rocket research group that Barby was becoming a member of. She was joining an exclusive group whose contributions spanned centuries. Before Apple, before IBM, and before our modern definition of a central processing unit partnered with memory, the word *computer* referred simply to a person who computes. Using only paper, a pencil, and their minds, these computers tackled complex mathematical equations.

Early astronomers needed computers in the 1700s to predict the return of Halley's Comet. During World War I, groups of men and women worked as "ballistic computers," calculating the range of rifles, machine guns, and mortars on the battlefield. During the Depression era, 450 people worked for the U.S. government as computers, 76 of them women. These computers, meagerly paid as part of the Works Progress Administration, created something special. They filled twenty-eight volumes with rows and rows of numbers, eventually published by the Columbia University Press as the plainly named *Mathematical Tables Project* series. What they couldn't know was that these books, filled to the brim with logarithms, exponential functions, and trigonometry, would one day be critical to our first steps into space.

The dream of space exploration was what initially tugged at the Suicide Squad. They worked on engines during the day, but at night they talked about the limits of the universe. Even before they received federal funding, their group attracted new members. In 1936, Caltech graduate students A.M.O. Smith and Hsue-Shen Tsien joined the Suicide Squad. The lure of being part of the audacious gang was so great that Weld

Arnold, an assistant in the astrophysics department at Caltech, bribed his way in by offering Frank their first (unofficial) funding, $1,000, in exchange for his role as photographer. The first installment, $100, was paid in a wrinkled wad of one- and five-dollar bills, delivered by Weld on a bicycle. No one questioned where he got the money; they were only too happy to have some.

The group made fun of the alien spaceships they saw in the movies, laughing at their implausible designs, while simultaneously relishing a screenplay Frank had outlined in which rocket scientists were, of course, the heroes. Wrapped up in their fantasies, the team talked endlessly about their version of a spaceship: a rocket plane.

But before they could build a plane they had to find a new place to work. The Suicide Squad's amplified destruction had gotten them kicked off the Caltech campus. They drove up into the deserted hills, choosing for their own a dusty canyon called the Arroyo Seco. Although only a few miles outside Pasadena, it felt like a world apart. They were far from prying eyes, the walls of the canyon screening their experiments from the outside world. The canyon itself was seen as some kind of monster by the town below. Although Southern California seemed to offer a constant supply of sunshine, occasionally the clouds gathered and the rain came down hard. When it poured, the watershed of the Arroyo Seco filled, funneling down to the homes and businesses below and causing flash floods. The residents of Pasadena cursed the canyon and decided to find a way to control the rages of nature. In 1935 the WPA began building a maze of concrete channels, transferring the power of the untamed tributaries to human hands. The once-wild Los Angeles River, now lined in concrete, was cut down to a trickle, dripping down the valley.

The streams and riverbeds became nothing more than dusty indentations in the land (in Spanish *arroyo seco* means "dry streambed"). While the Arroyo Seco felt remote, far from any residential area, it was still a relatively quick drive from Caltech, where the Suicide Squad kept their equipment. The downside was that its dry, rocky landscape dotted with scrubby brush made it particularly susceptible to wildfires. Of course, concern over sparking fire would hardly deter the Suicide Squad from lighting up the night sky.

They began to carve out a home in the isolated canyon and adapted their experiments to match. The group was lean, with

Theodore von Kármán, Frank's graduate-school adviser, acting as director, and Frank as chief engineer. The Canrights joined the group along with a few new engineers and found that the dry stream made a perfect bed for firing rockets. They dug test pits and built a few small buildings to house equipment. Despite the developments, the area was still the wilderness to Barby. The dust covered her shoes and got in her hair. The grit found its way into everything — her car, her purse, even her lipstick. Grime notwithstanding, the team was content. The remote canyon concealed their loud, often-dangerous experiments, yet their isolation heightened their eccentric reputation. Hidden in the hills, tinkering with explosives, they were often perceived as mad scientists.

Rockets were considered fringe science, and the people who worked on them weren't taken seriously. When Frank asked one of his professors at Caltech, Fritz Zwicky, for his help on a problem, the teacher told him, "You're a bloody fool. You're trying to do something impossible. Rockets can't work in space." In fact, the word *rocket* was in such bad repute that the group purposely omitted it when they formed their institute, the Jet Propulsion Laboratory. Some scientists at the sister Guggenheim Aeronautical

Laboratory at the Massachusetts Institute of Technology snickered at them, while Vannevar Bush, an engineering professor at MIT, derisively said, "I don't understand how a serious scientist or engineer can play around with rockets."

The idea of strapping rockets to a plane was pure science fiction, as likely as the UFOs the Suicide Squad ridiculed. Planes were dependent on piston engines spinning propellers. Yet this design had a built-in speed limitation because propellers lose efficiency as they approach the speed of sound, 760 miles per hour. At high speed, shock waves occur around the propeller, creating drag and slowing the plane. A few scientists had an audacious scheme to skirt the limitation: they would get rid of the piston engine and propeller altogether, developing a jet engine capable of creating enough thrust to keep the plane aloft. Critics scoffed at such an idea. It was clearly impossible, since any engine powerful enough to perform such a feat would itself be too heavy to fly through the air.

Jet engines propel planes much like an inflated balloon whose opening is held tightly closed and then suddenly opened. As the air rushes out the narrow opening, it makes the balloon fly. This is because the crammed air molecules rush from the high pressure inside the taut balloon to the low pressure outside. With the size of the exit restricted, the molecules racing out create enough thrust to propel an object forward.

Before World War II, the idea existed only in laboratories, notably those of Hans von Ohain in Germany and Frank Whittle in England. With jet engines for airplanes still in the experimental stages, the idea of a rocket-powered plane seemed overwhelmingly naïve to experienced aeronautical engineers. A rocket engine would be even more complex than a jet engine because, although it worked on the same principle, the rocket engine didn't use oxygen from the air to combust its fuel. Instead, it carried its own oxidizer, making the mechanism intricate and heavy.

Despite the outlandishness of their ideas, Frank and his team pursued their rocket plane in earnest. Frank detailed his hopes for the plane when writing home to his mother, describing with precision the technological hurdles they'd have to overcome. His mother, a piano teacher who instilled in him a love of music, could hardly keep up with the science but marveled at the audacity of his work.

Frank's mother might not understand why

he wanted to build a rocket plane, but she was proud of him. Although she was born in the United States, her family, like Frank's father, was from Czechoslovakia. Frank's parents met while playing in the Houston Symphony Orchestra and hoped to raise a family as devoted to music as they were. When Frank was seven, they moved back to Czechoslovakia, spending five years in Moravia. Between music lessons, Frank sketched balloons and airplanes, his dreams of flight punctuated by the compositions of Verdi. Under his pencil, science and art were intimately joined, forming a basis that would influence him his whole life.

When Frank was twelve, his family moved back to the United States, and he found himself in Brenham, in east-central Texas, surrounded by corn and cotton. Life in the small town could be trying for an adolescent. Frank was teased for almost everything he inherited from his dad, from his complexion to his last name. When he received his degree in mechanical engineering from Texas A&M, his mother knew he'd leave Texas and never come back. He soon proved her right, departing to pursue his PhD at Caltech. It wasn't the musical career that his parents had wanted for him, but his upbringing had planted within him the seeds of artistry, patiently sitting dormant until they were ready to bloom.

Barby felt a kinship with Frank. They had both left their families behind. Neither wanted to move back home, yet they both missed their mother terribly. Every week, they wrote long letters home. Frank's letters were almost like a diary. He recounted with scientific precision his feelings, thoughts, and actions. Barby's letters, on the other hand, were filled with the feminine details she knew her mom loved.

In addition to dances and dinners, Barby was excited to share with her mom news of the government funding streaming into the newly formed institute. But not everyone was delighted with JPL's new military backing. Jerome Hunsaker, who headed the aeronautics department at MIT, was dismissive. "Von Kármán can take the Buck Rogers job," he said. Hunsaker's group was working on deicing plane windshields, a far more respected assignment in aeronautical engineering, albeit less flashy than what JPL was about to try.

The "Buck Rogers job" Hunsaker ridiculed was that of developing the long-dreamed-of rocket plane. But the army didn't want rockets to explore the limits of Earth's atmosphere. Instead, they needed them to propel heavy bombers into the air from the short runways on aircraft carriers. The bombers didn't have enough thrust to achieve such a feat on their own. Thus, the audacious project could be summed up with one question: Could Frank and his team strap rockets onto a plane?

Barby was sitting at a lunch counter when she first heard the term "JATO." Frank explained to her that it stood for "jet-assisted takeoff." The name made her smile. It seemed people would go to any lengths not to use the word *rocket*. Barby's husband used the more casual moniker of strap-on rockets. No matter what they called them, it was time to transition from firing rockets in the dry riverbed to firing rockets attached to a plane chained to the ground. August 1941 was a long string of early mornings for Barby.

Waking up at 5 a.m., she dressed carefully in dresses or skirts, heels, and stockings. The men she worked with didn't bother with formalities and didn't worry about what they looked like, donning shirts without jackets or ties and pulling on comfortable boots. Barby, on the other hand, faithfully did her makeup each morning and smoothed the waves of her hair. Unless she preserved her curls by knotting a head scarf under her chin, they would soon be blown out on the gusty airfield. Whether wind or dust, it seemed she couldn't escape the elements.

Before she and Richard left in the morning, they'd drink coffee in their rose-colored kitchen. As they talked about their work that day and their plans for the evening, Barby prepared herself mentally for the tasks ahead, knowing that emotions could be raw on the airfield. She let music calm her frazzled nerves, sometimes singing "Every Day's a Holiday" by Glenn Miller or "Boogie Woogie Bugle Boy" by the Andrews Sisters on her way to work.

Dawn broke bold behind the foothills as she and Richard drove to March Field, a small airfield an hour east of Pasadena. The air was still, perfect for their experiments. By afternoon, the wind would pick up, whipping Barby's dresses around her knees and casting doubt on the success of their strap-on rockets.

The early tests were riddled by failure. The same winds that caused Barby's hair to whip around her face also rattled the plane on the runway. They had set up a small airplane, broken off its propeller, and tethered it to the ground with chains. The engineers hoped these would steady the

42

craft and limit accidents. The chains were there for safety because their rockets weren't yet ready to take the plane into flight.

The plane they had tied down was an Ercoupe, a small single-seater with a low fixed wing covered in shiny aluminum. It weighed only 838 pounds and, after the war, had the distinction of being sold in the men's department at Macy's. The team secured the rocket engines, starting out with two on each side, directly onto the fuselage of the plane, ripping a ten-inch-wide hole in the skin underneath the wings to bolt it on. In the cockpit was Lieutenant Homer Boushey, a former student of von Kármán's, now an army pilot. It was up to him to ignite the engines filled with explosive-packed powder.

The first time they ran the experiment, the rocket engine misfired. No one knew why. The second experiment was much worse. Four jet units were attached to the airplane, and one of them failed immediately. Its exhaust nozzle bounced down the runway, eventually striking the fuselage of the plane and tearing a large hole in its skin before shearing off one of the combustion chambers. That combustion chamber was thrown clear of the airplane, about a hundred feet. In a lab notebook, they wrote, "The blow was rather violent causing the rear attachment of the angle irons to pull loose and the dural wing covering immediately above the exhaust nozzle position to stretch, pulling loose 4–5 rivets." The group were shaken up by the accident. They had managed to rip apart what Ercoupe's advertisements proclaimed to be the "world's safest plane." At least no one was hurt.

In addition to her notes on the experiments, notes similar to those every engineer recorded in a slim, brown lab notebook, Barby made long charts of numbers. She calculated the thrust produced by each rocket engine and how it corresponded to the flight results. She was looking for clues in the performance of the rocket engine — hidden data that might reveal how to get the plane to fly.

With the airplane in pieces, the team worried that Boushey, the test pilot, would decide to leave. They weren't sure if they could find anyone else willing to fly for them. Luckily, Boushey decided to give it another go. Jack Parsons later noted: "The pilot deserves credit for his willingness to continue flight test as soon as the airplane was repaired."

Over the next week, they repaired the plane and built a secure holster for the cylindrical bottle-shaped rockets. They even added two more rockets, bringing the count up to six. When the pilot got back into the cockpit, everyone was more than a little anxious. They pasted posters to the nose of the plane, demanding BE ALERT! DON'T GET HURT! The signs served as a reminder of their close call. Barby held her breath as the plane hovered in the air, pulling against its chains. That flight, only a few feet off the ground, was the first hint that the rocket plane they had once dreamed of might actually work.

Four days later, on August 12, 1941, they took off the chains. The airfield was quiet. Barby spoke hardly a word. It seemed that all their hard work had been building toward this one experiment. Happily, the results matched their high expectations. The rockets were able to reduce by half the distance the plane needed to take off. As Boushey got out of the cockpit, he was grinning. It was exactly what the army needed, and it demonstrated that JPL could deliver. On that sunny day in August, the team took a photograph alongside the plane with its rockets strapped on. The petite aircraft would soon change the future of JPL.

Standing on the airfield, Barby felt the cool touch of the metal plane on her warm skin. Even in the hottest part of the day the shell reflected heat back to the sky. Similar to the patchwork of parts that formed the rocket plane, the pieces of Barby's life had also come together in the past few months. The science classes she had taken, the risk in moving from Ohio, and even her unfulfilling work as a typist at Caltech had all culminated in this one accomplishment.

Like Barby, the rocket plane was just beginning to show what it could do. Now that they had strapped six rockets onto it and watched it take off, it was time to push the limits. Although they were no longer called the Suicide Squad and their ranks had expanded slightly, they hadn't stopped taking risks. The next step was to attach twelve JATO units to see if the rockets alone could power a launch. When the small plane went airborne without the aid of a single propeller, it made the first American rocket-powered airplane flight. The timing could hardly have been better. Four months later, a rocket-powered plane would be urgently needed.

The Canrights were enjoying a quiet Sunday afternoon on December 7, 1941. Barby was in the kitchen, cooking and listening to the radio, when the announcer interrupted the program with breaking news. The Japanese had attacked Pearl Harbor. Barby fell to the kitchen floor, tears streaming down her cheeks. The war had hit home. Hawaii suddenly seemed very close to California. Barby and Richard were glued to the radio for the rest of the evening. In their dark hour, Barby heard the first lady's potent voice on the broadcast. When Eleanor Roosevelt said, "We know what we have to face, and we know that we are ready to face it," Barby knew that their work would now take on a new importance. Going in to the lab the next day, they might have been talking about Pearl Harbor, but they were thinking about the rocket plane.

But achieving a short runway launch with a trim Ercoupe was a relatively minor accomplishment. The army needed to lift a fourteen-thousand-pound bomber into the air. In one month, Barby filled more than twenty notebooks with rows of neatly printed numbers. Each column represented a value from the experiment, plugged into lines of exquisitely complex equations. One of the key computations Barby was responsible for was the thrust-to-weight ratio, an equation that allowed the group to compare the performance of the engines under different conditions. She repeated the calculation many times, sliding the numbers into the equation with the ease of slipping on a pair of shoes. It was all building to one singular achievement.

It took just a year for the JPL rockets to boost the Douglas A-20A bomber into the air. They experimentally fired the JATO units on the heavy bomber forty-four times, the rockets needing only minor fixes. The project was a success. For the second time, Barby Canright's face beamed with pride as she stood next to the bomber. It was time to take the work out of the lab and bring the technology into production. Frank and von Kármán set up a company, Aerojet, to manufacture rockets while they continued their research in the Arroyo Seco.

Money and success brought support for the ragtag group, and they made the California canyon their permanent home. All JPL needed now was more employees. Barby was excited when Frank told her he was hiring two more computers, a man and a woman, Freeman Kincaid and Melba Nead. Until then, Barby and Frank's secretary had been the only two women at the institute. Barby, who didn't spend much time with the secretary, had felt the lack of female companionship.

Melba, on the other hand, was overwhelmed. Attending her first party at Jack and Helen Parsons' house, she felt shy among the group of people she barely knew. Perhaps sensing her reticence, an older gentleman came up to her. "I'm von Kármán," he said pleasantly, extending a hand. Melba took it, awed to meet the director of the lab. The intimate feel of the gathering soon swayed her. She mixed among the engineers and her fellow computers and began to feel at ease.

One of those computers was leaving. Barby's husband was promoted to engineer. It was what Richard had always hoped for. Although Barby's experience was similar to his, she was not promoted and hadn't expected to be. It was simply one of the limits of being female. Although she loved her work, with Richard's promotion and subsequent added income, she was thinking about starting a family.

While they considered having children, Richard was launching something new at the lab. He was going to look at the performance of their rockets underwater. In preparation, the group dug a channel into the dirt near the test pits and filled it with water. The engineers sank their engines into the ditch, the water creeping into the engine and up the fuel line. The motor was only

49

nine inches deep, yet it still looked hope-
lessly submerged to Barby. JPL was trying
to develop what they called a hydrobomb.
While it was essentially a torpedo, they
didn't dare call it that. Only the navy was
allowed to develop torpedoes. Richard and
his team fired the engines, expecting them
to sputter and die. Instead they worked just
fine underwater. In no time at all Richard
was leaving the channel behind and moving
to a nearby lake where the motors could be
submerged six feet deep. He'd bring back
the data to his wife, excited for her analysis.

Not long after Richard's promotion, JPL
hired two more women, Virginia Prettyman
and Macie Roberts, rounding out the computer room to a team of five: four women
and one man. The new recruits didn't seem
promising at first. Virginia and Macie, or
Ginny and Bobby, as they soon became
known, had never heard of a computer
before. They answered the want ad with
little idea of what they were getting themselves into. Despite the newcomers' naïveté,
the computers immediately became good
friends. They spent every day working
together, sweating over their calculations,
observing experiments in the test pits, and
chatting with the engineers. And since their
houses were practically next door to one

another in Pasadena, they often ate dinner and relaxed together in the evenings.

Most of the employees drove to the lab, occasionally carpooling. Freeman and Melba preferred the streetcar. They got off at Ventura Street, a stop that looked like a desolate canyon with a road running through it, then walked across a rickety bridge over the dry streambed to get to the office. At the site, there were only a few structures: an old barn, two small laboratories, a shop for liquid propellant, two hydraulic presses to shape the metal, and Building 11. Building 11 was the engineering building, and it sat right next to the test pits, which made up Buildings 5 through 7 and 10, although they were little more than shacks covering the pits in the ground where the rockets were fired.

Building 11 was small but brand-new, with a conference room, a darkroom, and freshly painted offices for the engineers and computers. One side of the computer room was framed in windows, filling the space with California sunshine. Each of the computers had her or his own wooden desk, and when the sun hit them, they turned a golden hue.

The room was never quiet. Between their large electric calculator, slide rules, and the general hum of conversation, the five computers made a lot of noise. But nothing was as loud as the noise from the test pits. It was so shocking that it often caused them to jump. Things only got worse when the field team decided to add a warning sound. For this, one of the mechanics pulled the cable of a Ford truck horn. The horn went "Aruugah!," making employees jump almost as high as when they heard the explosions themselves. Neither noise was popular with residents whose newly built homes were within earshot.

For a little quiet, Melba sometimes walked down the hall. She would chat pleasantly with Frank's secretary, Dorothy Lewis, and then proceed into his small office to discuss data. Frank, all of twenty-nine years old, had just taken over the role as acting director of JPL.

Von Kármán left the lab in 1944 to launch the air force's Scientific Advisory Group. His decision to leave set off a scuffle over the JPL directorship. Clark Millikan, professor of aeronautics at Caltech, was aching to take the reins of the fledgling institute. Despite Millikan's years of experience, von Kármán preferred to turn over the lab to his former student, who, although relatively untried, made up for it with his zeal for research.

It must have been strange for Barby to watch Frank grow up in front of her eyes, moving from student to professor in a short period. By necessity he had to be serious now, at least most of the time. He still pulled pranks around the lab, but mostly late at night, when he had the grounds to himself. It was a rocky transition from carefree member of the Suicide Squad to leader of a major research institute. One day, Barby and the other computers at JPL watched with disbelief as Frank harshly disciplined one of the engineers.

Whiling away time between JATO tests in Muroc, California, today Edwards Air Force base, Walter Powell was playing with a toy airplane. Frank was curt with him: "Put away the toy, Walt. It's not a playground." Walter was furious. For the first few years their work had always had an element of play. Now things were changing. When Frank went back to his office, Walter couldn't stop thinking about his rebuke. If Frank didn't take him seriously, he would make him listen. He grabbed a hatchet and stood outside Frank's office, holding it over his head. Letting out a yell, he brought the blade against the closed door. Once, twice, three times.

Through the shredded wood of his office door, Frank could make out Walter's face, red with anger, and began to scream for help. A few men came running. They tried talking to Walter, but he was shaking with anger. One of the engineers was holding a pair of scissors and had an idea. He walked over to Walter and cut off his necktie. The hallway fell silent. Then laughter began to percolate through the group. Soon even Frank was laughing. Walter didn't laugh, but he dropped the hatchet. He was incredibly embarrassed. For a month, it was all anyone at the institute could talk about. Barby and Melba would act out the final dramatic scene, Barby playfully chasing Melba with a pair of scissors. It was a long time before Walter would wear a necktie to work again.

To avoid future hatchet jobs, Frank personally did all the hiring. He was careful to build a dedicated staff as the institution expanded. After establishing the lab in the desolate canyon, he wanted to make sure the small group worked well together. Given their long hours, they had to be more than just co-workers to each other — they needed to resemble a family.

The computer room worked as seamlessly

as a machine, notebooks passed from desk to desk as the five colleagues spent their days transforming raw numbers into meaningful data. Their prize possession was a single Friden calculator. It looked nothing like the modern, sleek devices we're used to today that can perform hundreds of functions and sit in the palm of our hand. Instead, the calculator was the size of a bread box and heavy. When they first received the Friden, Barby was excited to be in command of a machine that so few people knew how to use. It was the latest technology and much faster than a slide rule, though it could only add, subtract, multiply, and divide. It was a dull gray and looked like a typewriter, but instead of letters, the keyboard held rows of repeating numbers, from 0 to 9. Advertisements for the calculator boasted that with a "flick of the key" the Friden could "automatically transfer products from dials to keyboard." Only once the numbers were typed into each individual column could the "fully automatic" calculations begin.

The calculator dispensed a small piece of paper showing the equation and its solution at the top of the machine, like a sheet of paper in a typewriter. Looking at the complex contraption now, it's hard to believe

Advertisement for Friden calculators

that it was able to perform only simple functions. Of course these simple functions were just the tip of the iceberg — Barby and the other computers had to do everything else

56

by hand. Their fingers became rough with calluses from gripping a pencil eight hours a day.

Barby was no longer calculating how many rockets were needed to lift a bomber into the sky. With that project completed, the group turned back to trying to pierce the edges of space. They had to find a way to propel a rocket to an altitude higher than that achieved by a simple helium-filled balloon. To devise the perfect motor, the engineers and computers had to solve four equations describing the relationship between the motor's physical properties and their rates of change. As the group worked together, it became clear from their calculations that they would need to focus on propellants.

Melba, Macie, Virginia, Freeman, and Barby were responsible for calculating the potential of rocket propellants. Macie, perhaps because she was twenty years older than her fellow computers and obsessed with using precise terminology, would get annoyed if someone mistakenly called a rocket propellant "fuel." She had come to engineering late in life, after working as an auditor for the Internal Revenue Service, and so had taken her lessons in rocket science to heart. In her strict and proper way she would gently remind the transgressor that a propellant is not composed of fuel alone. It also includes an oxidizer, an element such as oxygen that is able to accept an electron, thus setting in motion a powerful oxidation-reduction reaction, often called a redox reaction. These reactions, in which electrons are transferred, create energy whether they occur in a rocket engine or in a cell in the human body.

Fuels can't burn without an oxidizer like oxygen. Oxygen's powerful pull on electrons, those tiny particles with a negative charge, is needed for the fuel to combust. This is important, because if rockets were eventually to travel to space, where there is no oxygen, they would have to carry their own oxidizer.

Virginia and Barby sat outside eating their lunch one day. Virginia was complimenting Barby's new hairstyle: "The short bangs are so cute. You look just like Bette Davis." Barby thanked her, running a finger through her new stylish bangs and carefully patting the tapered hair curling in at the nape of her neck. That day she was feeling especially pretty in a bright white shirtdress cinched tight at the waist and white pumps. They were taking a picture of everyone who worked at the lab, and she wanted to look her best. The white was a mild act of defiance for Barby, her stand against the dust that whipped around the canyon.

As they talked about hairstyles, Barby brought the conversation back to the propellants they discussed in the computer room.

"I hear Jack has an idea for a new one," she said, recalling her conversation with Richard the night before. "You're not going to believe what it's made of — asphalt."

Virginia shook her head. "That sounds like Jack," she said.

As crazy as it sounded to use the heavy asphalt that paved roads, no one knew what would best make rockets fly, so everything was fair game. At JPL, the team tested a wide range of solid, liquid, and gas options. They loaded the fuel and oxidizers into rocket motors that were housed in the test pits in a dirt field. These were directly adjacent to a handful of permanent buildings and the row of tar-paper shacks that made up the lab. Then they fired them.

Gauges on the motors measured how fast the exhaust gas left the rocket motor and how the mass of the propellant changed over the course of the test. Technicians took pictures of the gauges after every test and brought the film to the darkroom in Building 11. In the darkroom, Barby, Melba, Macie, Virginia, and Freeman hovered over the photos of the gauges in the dim light and carefully recorded the data on blue graph paper. They'd bring their notebooks back to the computer room and begin work.

By measuring how quickly the exhaust left the rocket engine, the computers could analyze how much force was generated from each experiment. From the raw data, they calculated by hand the thrust (the force propelling the rocket forward), the rate of combustion, and the velocity (the combined speed and direction). After noting these values in their brown notebooks, they plugged them into the Friden calculator and triple-checked them with a slide rule. Melba preferred the simple, straightforward nature of the slide rule. It looked like a ruler, but by placing the pointer at one number and sliding the middle section of the ruler into the proper position, they could use it for multiplication, division, square roots, and even trigonometry. It took Melba years to feel as comfortable with the Friden as she did with her slide rule.

The calculation the engineers and computers were most interested in was the specific impulse, the change in force that accumulates as a rocket uses fuel. Specific impulse indicates roughly how much momentum builds up as the propellant is being thrown out the back of the rocket. The faster the propellant is thrown, the faster the rocket can travel. Having a high specific impulse means less fuel is needed to go farther. This calculation is the simplest way to compare the effectiveness of different propellants. It took four different equations for the computers to get to the specific-impulse equation. They had to compute thrust and velocity first. They would then plug these numbers into a formula that calculated the thrust per unit mass flow of each propellant.

These calculations could not be done quickly, since they were all done by hand. It took only seconds for a rocket engine to be fired, but analyzing that one experiment could take a week or more for the human computers. Notebooks quickly accumulated, often six to eight of them for each experiment. Barby liked to stack them on her desk, forming a wall of paper. As the notebooks piled up, so did her feeling of accomplishment. Then, at the end of the experiment, after the final report was written up, she'd clear the notebooks off her desk.

On a mild autumn morning, Barby and Macie were eager to begin analyzing the first experiments using asphalt as a base in the rocket fuel. The computers had been whispering about it for months. Only part of the gossip was about the fuel itself. No one had ever tested asphalt before, it was true, but the engineer who thought it up was also a curiosity.

Barby had been friends with Jack and his wife, Helen, from the early days of the Suicide Squad. Jack was brilliant, but also eccentric. It wasn't until he met Frank that his genius began to shine. He was always coming up with quirky solutions to their engineering challenges.

His engineering designs weren't the only unusual thing about him. Jack and Helen were often gossiped about at work. Jack talked about science fiction stories as if they were real, and he had separated from Helen after joining a bizarre, cultlike religion. Although Jack was by far JPL's most peculiar employee, they were thankful to have his rocket-fuel genius.

The new propellant that Barby and Macie were excited about was a unique mixture of liquefied asphalt with a potassium perchlorate oxidizer. The computers still had to figure out what proportions of fuel and oxidizer were needed to work in a rocket. The best mixture, they calculated, was 70 percent Texaco No. 18 asphalt combined with 30 percent Union Oil lubricating oil. The technicians liquefied the asphalt-oil combination by heating it to 275 degrees Fahrenheit and then added crushed potassium perchlorate. The propellant was mixed and allowed to cool, becoming a solid round block, a cake of rocket-blasting power. They called it Jack's cake.

The technicians and engineers packed the black powder cake tightly inside the combustion chamber of an engine lying at the bottom of one of the test pits. The engine looked like a dirty, rolled-up newspaper. A clay nozzle lay at one end, connecting the propellant with the igniter. On the other end of the engine lay the charge, which emitted a smoke trail, so they could follow the exhaust as it flew down the test pit. The engine, anchored in the test pit, was under intense pressure, and when it was ignited, the ground shook. Seconds later the exhaust hit the hillside, and huge clouds of white smoke made of potassium chloride, a by-product of the propellant, rose from the pit.

The computers collected their data from the gauges on the engine and then began to calculate. Their goal was a lofty one: they were trying to find a propellant that could deliver a thrust of 1,000 pounds over the course of ten to thirty seconds. No powder rocket had ever accomplished such a feat. At JPL they weren't sure it was even possible. Most of the tests of black-powder propellant ended in explosions. The seals of the engine failed or the charges cracked and the whole thing burst into flames. Jack's cake, however, was different.

The computers found that Jack's unusual propellant had a specific impulse of 186 and an exhaust velocity of 5,900 feet per second. It delivered a formidable 200 pounds of thrust. It was exactly the kind of fuel the military needed, because it was powerful yet used common (and cheap) ingredients that could be stored at a wide range of temperatures. Almost immediately Barby saw her work finding its way into rockets owned by the U.S. Navy.

The work was secret, the reports classified. It was still wartime, and rocket research concentrated on military applications, not scientific exploration. For some, the war felt like an interruption. In the words of Suicide Squad member Ed Forman, "Our dreams of designing rockets for scientific research at high altitudes and for space flight had to be deferred for several years." On the other hand, without the war effort, JPL might never have existed at all. Started with pocket money that was quickly used up, it survived solely because of military funding.

For Barby's part, she was proud to be part of the war effort. Frank shared her feelings, writing home, "Some of the gadgets we helped to develop saved several lives in the Pacific recently." California's location — uncomfortably close to Pearl Harbor — stirred fear in its residents. Newspapers discussed the probability that Japan would attack California, and Japanese Americans were being rounded up and sent to internment camps. The need for military might was clear. In this atmosphere, the human computers at JPL lost their only male member, Freeman Kincaid, who joined the Merchant Marine, an auxiliary group to the navy during wartime. His departure, and the small pool of male candidates who might replace him, made the group distinctly female.

Whether they worked for the military or for themselves, JPL was unwaveringly pursuing rockets, still the subject of many jokes in the outside world, and ready to move beyond the strap-on rockets used to lift bombers. The group wanted to design missiles, but there was still the problem of propellants. They might have created an exceptional military solid propellant, but it was unknown whether liquid propellants could provide more thrust. The group divided in two: the solid and liquid propellant sections. The computers crossed borders, working with engineers in both sections. In weekly lab meetings, they all came together to apply their expertise and share their results.

In the hunt for new weapons, they would need a lot more computers. As the lab expanded, Frank decided to promote Macie to supervisor of the group. He didn't take the promotion lightly; he was also trusting Macie to interview and hire the new computers, in addition to assuming a manager's responsibilities. Macie was a natural for the job. She was the mother hen, and was interested in building not just a team, but a family. Because of her, the computing section at JPL would be entirely composed of women.

As Macie was rising in the ranks of JPL, Barby saw her future at the institute faltering. She was pregnant. It was getting harder and harder to conceal her growing belly at work, and she knew that soon she'd have to quit. There was no such thing as maternity leave. She was thrilled to be having a baby but sad to say good-bye to the group she'd been a part of since its birth.

■ ■ ■

The computers stood in the crowd at the
Tournament of Roses Parade on a clear
New Year's Day, 1943. In 1942 the event
had moved, for the only time in its history,
to North Carolina, in a preemptive effort to
spare it from possible attacks on the West
Coast. Now the parade was back in Pasadena, where it belonged. As girls in pastel
crinoline dresses slowly waved from their
floats, Macie recognized one of the prin-
cesses: a mathematics student at Pasadena
Junior College. The girl hadn't planned to
be in the parade, but tryouts for the Tournament of Roses Royal Court were mandatory for every girl older than seventeen
enrolled in women's physical education
classes, a requirement. Even if they had no
interest in participating, each was required
to walk up a flight of stairs and across a
stage while a panel of judges appraised her
figure, beauty, and grace. Macie smiled at
the sight of this young girl, gifted in math,
riding atop a float. She wondered what opportunities awaited her.

With Macie to lead them, a group of
young women were about to leave the lives
expected of them. Each would go from be-

ing an oddity in school, one of only a few girls who flourished in calculus and chemistry classes, to joining a unique group of women at JPL. The careers they were about to launch would be unlike any other.

CHAPTER 2
HEADED WEST

Helen Yee Ling Chow heard the droning of planes overhead and the thud of bombs dropping. The sounds vibrated through her very bones. She could feel her brother's heartbeat pulse through his body, closely pressed to hers. Their arms were wrapped around each other. Tears ran down Helen's cheeks and pooled in the crevices of her older brother's neck. Terrified of making a noise, they felt a fear that was intensified by the silence imposed on them. In their dark hiding place, the only thing the children could hear was the war closing in all around. Hong Kong was falling.

Nearly six thousand miles away, the bombs dropped on Pearl Harbor. On the same fateful day in December 1941, Japan attacked both the United States and British Hong Kong. Just as the military bases lining Pearl Harbor found themselves unprepared for the sudden, violent attack, Hong Kong was woefully ill equipped. The colony's military defenses, a combination of British, Canadian, Indian, and Chinese forces, were outnumbered four to one.

A year earlier, before the war changed everything, Helen and Edwin had held hands reluctantly. Their mother had pleaded with them to stay still as the family took a picture together. Standing in the sunshine of Manila, the Philippines, far from the violence in China, Helen grasped her brother's hand for only seconds before dropping his sweaty palm in disgust. She couldn't be persuaded to pose again. Instead, she and Edwin and their two sisters ran in circles, teasing their parents and resisting every threat or bribe their mother offered. To touch each other, even for a brief moment, was loathsome. Now, huddled in a dark closet in their house, they couldn't get close enough. In addition to every other paralyzing fear, Helen realized she didn't know where their mother was.

While the United States was thrown into World War II in one devastating attack, China had been fighting since Japan invaded it in 1937. In a world descending into the chaos of war, Helen's mother had stood as the family's constant. By the 1940s, the Japanese held the fringes of China and were closing in. The family moved again and again, within and beyond China, trying to escape the escalating carnage. Helen's father, a general in Mao Tse-tung's Red Air Force, calculated his family's relocations based on military intelligence, but even those forewarnings couldn't keep them safe from the mounting destruction. When he moved the family to Hong Kong, his nerves calmed. The city was a safe haven under the protection of the powerful British Empire. The empire had never surrendered a colony; surely they would never submit to Japan.

These hopes shattered as the bombs rained down on the Pearl of the Orient. Helen's mother was at a neighbor's house. Trapped inside, she felt helpless to protect her children. When the thundering quieted, she raced home, shouting their names. She found Edwin and Helen clutching each other in the closet while her other two daughters crept out of their nearby hiding spot and hugged her close. Helen whispered softly, her voice faltering, "We thought you were gone."

The family slipped out of Hong Kong right before Black Christmas. On December 25, the British surrendered Hong Kong to Japan, and inhabitants were subjected to widespread rape and murder. Helen's father led the family back into mainland China, where they searched for safety in the countryside.

Few mothers could look beyond survival at such a harrowing time. Helen's mother was different. She valued education highly. It seemed they were already losing everything to the war: their home, their safety. She didn't want to sacrifice her children's schooling as well. Wherever they moved, she made private schools a necessary part of their plan. She hounded her daughters and son about their homework and began to talk seriously to Helen about college. It was apparent from an early age that she was especially talented in mathematics. Helen grew up valuing education above all.

At sixteen, Helen could see her country crumbling at her feet. It was 1944. Late one night she heard her father tell her mother that the invasion was worsening. The Japanese were launching a major attack. This time, there was nowhere safe to run. She heard her father talk about the Americans. They were covertly funding the war effort in China, funneling tens of millions of dollars into Chiang Kai-shek's army. At the same time, President Roosevelt approved a volunteer group of a hundred civilians to fly fighter aircraft in China. The men, known as the Flying Tigers, were the first Americans to fight alongside the Chinese. They wore a mix of Chinese and American insignia as they battled in the Pacific, the noses of their planes painted with the bold faces of sharks, teeth gleaming.

As Helen lay awake that night, thinking about her father's words, she wasn't thinking about survival. She was hoping she wouldn't have to leave school. She adored her teachers and thought about college often, wondering what it would be like to leave her family, to leave China. She loved to sit with her mother and indulge in these fantasies, the war receding into the background, if only for a little while.

In these reveries she imagined America: brick buildings dotting college campuses as in the pictures her teachers had shown her; classrooms filled with happy students, far from the terrors of invasion and death. In these daydreams she wasn't sure what she would be studying in these flawless classrooms or what career she would be preparing for. She only knew that she wanted to be anywhere other than where she was.

Her dreams swelled as the war ended in Allied victory. Edwin made his way to the States for college, but for Helen, it wasn't to be. Instead, she stayed in China and enrolled in Canton College. For two years she worked hard at school. However, like all teenagers, she didn't have her attention focused exclusively on her coursework.

She met a boy. Arthur Ling's education had been derailed by the war. He'd completed four years of school before World War II. Now he was told he'd have to start all over again, since the enrollment records lay in ruins. Arthur was well liked and the student body president of Canton College, where he and Helen first met. Despite his delay in getting his degree, he seemed to have everything going for him. Yet losing so many years of education left him adrift. He wasn't sure what he wanted to do with his life. While Helen was entranced by this young man she barely knew, Arthur formed no commitments, to either his coursework or his admirers.

Her crush on him, arising in the wake of her turbulent teenage years, wasn't enough to keep her in China. In 1946, her perfect grades, earned in the face of hardships her American classmates could little imagine, secured her a full-ride scholarship to the University of Notre Dame.

Helen moved to Indiana filled with the fear and excitement that most eighteen-year-olds experience. Though she found herself sometimes thinking of Arthur, her home felt very far away. Her English, which she had always prided herself on, seemed shaky in the presence of so many native speakers. Even though this opportunity was what she had so desperately wanted, at night she cried for her mother.

Her American education didn't settle the question of what she wanted to do with her life. She majored in art and hoped to create the window displays of big department stores. She loved looking at them, each one a snapshot of a beautiful, pristine life at once desired and completely unattainable. Even if you bought everything in them, you could never re-create the view they promised.

Helen minored in math, a subject that seemed as impractical as a Bloomingdale's store window. She couldn't think of a single career possible for a woman with such a degree. However, this knowledge didn't stop her from devouring the math curriculum at Notre Dame. The only girl in a class of men, she didn't feel intimidated. Instead she felt invisible.

Barbara Lewis knew what it was like to feel invisible, but you wouldn't think it to look at her. She not only shared a name with the first female computer at JPL, Barby Canright, but also her home state: Ohio. In high school she was loud, vivacious, and popular. She quieted down only in her math classes. Like Helen, she was the only girl in the room. Before class the boys would huddle around their desks in small groups, discussing their homework and the girls they liked. Unlike her approach in her other classes, Barbara rarely raised her hand to ask questions, instead toiling over the assignments alone. Yet she didn't feel discouraged. She liked her teachers, and she took every math class her Columbus, Ohio, school offered, from trigonometry to geometry to calculus.

Although she was surrounded by boys in class, there weren't many other men in her life. Barbara's father died when she was just fourteen. He had worked long hours, every day except Sunday, pulling in forty-five dollars a week. As a bookkeeper for a produce company, he was used to keeping numbers in his head even as he delivered fruits and vegetables to the local markets. Sitting in his truck, Barbara would watch him with awe as he calculated numbers at tremendous speed, tearing sheets off his white notepad, one per grocer.

When he died of a heart attack, he left his wife, three daughters, and son heartbroken and without an income. Barbara's mother didn't seem to have much to recommend herself to the workforce. She was from a small mining town in Pennsylvania and had made it only through the eighth grade. But what she lacked in formal education she made up for in determination and savvy. She got a job as a secretary for the IRS and saved enough to buy a new, six-room, two-story house. She had always been a disciplinarian, but now as a single parent she was especially strict. Her children had to come directly home after school and begin their homework. She felt her lack of education keenly, and this pushed her to encourage her children, especially her three daughters, to attend college. Barbara's older sister was the first in the family to do so, heading off to Ohio State.

By the time Barbara finished high school, her older sisters had graduated from college and moved to California. Barbara was desperate to join them there. California seemed a magical place, full of movie stars, warm weather, and exclusive colleges that she dreamed of attending. She pictured herself at the University of California at Los Angeles or the University of Southern California, surrounded by palm trees and near the sparkling Pacific Ocean. Many of her classmates had similar dreams of going to California, though their fantasies centered on being discovered and becoming a movie star like the sultry Lauren Bacall, whom they watched on Saturday nights at the Westmont Theatre. Unlike her friends', Barbara's dreams were not woven of glitz and glamour.

Barbara was a pretty girl with thick brown hair and bright brown eyes. She was nineteen and a late bloomer. With her girlfriends she had confidence and ease, but boys made her nervous, and with them she became silent and dull. In her California daydreams, boys were but a blur in the background.

With her elder daughters begging her to join them and her youngest daughter desperate to go, Barbara's mother gave in, packing up their home in Ohio and driving out west. Barbara, her little brother, and mother rented a small cottage in Altadena, a town fourteen miles northeast of Los Angeles.

Life in California was not as Barbara had imagined. Her mother came home every night exhausted from fighting traffic. The schools she had dreamed of seemed as out of reach in Altadena as they had in Ohio, at least for a girl without a car of her own. Instead she enrolled in the local junior college and immersed herself in math classes.

Her sisters lived in Pasadena, the town next door. They were both secretaries, a job that Barbara secretly frowned on for herself. It didn't fit the ambitions she had for her life. The problem was, she didn't see many alternatives. When she spoke with a teacher about her career options, the choices were simple: secretary, teacher, nurse. There seemed to be no science in her future.

As she lamented her prospects, her eldest sister, Betty, sympathized. Then she had an idea. She worked at a place called the Jet Propulsion Laboratory, and although her job didn't put her directly in contact with the computers, she had noticed them, making calculations in their room. Peeking in, she had seen one woman banging away on some odd machine. She decided to mention it to her sister. "There's this girl," Betty began. "She enjoys her work and there's this big thing on her desk which seems kind of interesting."

Barbara looked at her curiously. "What is it?"

"Well, I don't know. I've never seen one like it before. But I think she's pretty good at math."

This was all Barbara needed to hear. The next day she went with Betty to her office.

They left the paved streets of Pasadena and took to the dirt roads to arrive at JPL. The buildings were set deep in the canyon. It seemed they were miles from civilization.

It was Barbara's first job interview. She was nervous as her heels clacked down the flights of stairs and long hallway. She couldn't believe how much the job paid: ninety cents an hour. Minimum wage was only forty cents an hour. When she walked into the interview room, her anxiety faded. She had assumed her interviewer, who she knew might be her future supervisor, would be a man. Seeing Macie Roberts, with her gray hair and sweet smile, was a surprise. Barbara shook her hand warmly. She felt suddenly at ease.

Susan Greene was five years old and living on the West Coast on December 7, 1941. After that dark day, she and her classmates readied themselves for Japanese attacks at school by hiding under the desks. It seemed inevitable that the war would wash up on their shore.

Sue was born in Los Angeles. You could tell just by looking at her that she was a California girl. With her thick blond hair and bright blue eyes, she always attracted attention. Sue was only nine when her father died. He collapsed from his second heart attack, and just like that, the family was left without their compass. He was a strong, well-liked man who always cared for his family. Sue was proud of his degree from Harvard Business School and his career in corporate insurance. With his death, the Greenes were set adrift. A housewife, Sue's mother seemed unsure how to proceed with her life now that her husband was gone. Sue was frustrated and couldn't understand why her mother didn't find work right away, especially as the year dragged on. *It's not what I would do,* a nine-year-old Sue thought, torn between anger and grief.

A quiet girl, Sue was slow to make friends. She loved books, although her reading was excruciatingly slow. Writing was worst of all. She despised putting words on a page and went to any lengths to avoid it. The most natural way to avoid writing prose was to immerse herself in numbers instead. There were no embarrassing letters for her to unconsciously invert. Instead she reveled in the clear simplicity of numerals on a page.

Although she was accomplished in math and science, it wasn't where Sue envisioned her career. Grown into a stunning young woman, she began to model part-time. She walked up and down platforms in small department-store fashion shows, a smile plastered on her face as she showed off in dresses, skirts, and swimsuits.

However, Sue didn't aspire to be a model either. She enrolled at Scripps, a small women's college tucked into the San Gabriel Valley, outside Los Angeles. Her chosen major was art, a subject whose chief attraction was that it promised little writing, and she dreamed of becoming an architect. Her major seemed to be fighting against her. She simply didn't have artistic talent. What Sue didn't struggle with was math. In fact, the math offered at Scripps was too basic for her. Instead, she decided to register for classes at Claremont, the men's college next door. When she discovered that the first-semester calculus class was full, she signed up for second-semester calculus. How hard could it be?

It turned out to be pretty hard. She had to learn both the differential equations she was being taught in class and the integral equations she had missed in the first semester. It was a giant leap in understanding. She was used to the tidy answers of algebra. Now she had to get used to producing an equation as the solution to a math problem. It was like answering a question with another question. The differential equations would cut the equations into small pieces while the integral equations sewed them back together. There was a reason they were taught separately; it was a lot to take in at once. She struggled, especially as she didn't like studying and had never been a great student.

Because of this, she wasn't surprised when she got a C, but it didn't stop her from signing up for more classes. Her professor was impressed with her moxie and soon came to realize that Sue was more than a pretty face in his otherwise all-male classroom. As her aptitude for math became clear, he hired her to grade his graduate-student papers and perform statistics in research projects. When Sue confided how unhappy she was with her art classes and her inability, due to her grades, to transfer to UCLA to study architecture, he sympathized and encouraged her to consider math and engineering. But Sue was losing her appetite for school. After three years, she dropped out.

Aerospace was booming in Southern California. What had begun in 1933 as 1,000 workers had exploded into a commercial enterprise of over 300,000 by 1943. By the end of World War II, American aircraft manufacture constituted the largest single industry in the world. Jobs were everywhere. Directionless, Sue applied to be a typist at Convair, an aeronautics company in Pomona, California. She had little enthusiasm for the work when she dropped off her application, but she hoped for a steady income.

The next day, Sue returned to Convair, and the recruiter took her aside. The company needed computers and was willing to train their recruits. "Do you like numbers?" he asked.

"I love numbers," Sue replied brightly, silently adding to herself, "Much more than letters."

Sue was hired as a computer, a position she had never heard of. Each morning she signed in at the security gate and then punched in with her time card. She found herself spending her days with one other woman, surrounded by equations. They were given the raw data from the company's rocket tests as well as the equations the engineers needed solved. From this the two computers would write out each step of the solution by hand. Sue would cram pages of large tablet notebooks with her calculations in blue ink. It was far more than simple arithmetic; it required all of Sue's training in geometry and calculus.

The lines of text and numbers formed an

intricate pattern of commands. The computers plotted how each command would lead
to the next, trying to keep the complicated
system as simple as possible. To a casual
observer it looked like a jumble of numbers
and letters with no meaning at all. Yet there
was an inherent elegance in the clean series
of commands, each one building on the
next, bringing the solution closer. A circle
around a number brought the solution from
one equation into the command line of the
next. It took skill to keep the equations
clean. A less skillful computer would clutter
her notebook with unnecessary equations,
oblivious to the beauty and utility of keeping the commands tidy. They were building
something, and the architect in Sue loved
the feeling of construction. She was completely engrossed in the work, never looking
up at the clock.

Although she couldn't know it yet, Sue
was programming. The lines of commands
that she built were the forerunners of the
first computer programs. They would one
day easily translate into lines of code, and
Sue would find herself putting the same
craftsmanship into clean, streamlined programs built with a digital computer that she
had into her work with paper and pencil.

While she wrote equations in neat lines,

her love life was frequently messy. There were simply too many boys to choose from. She met Pete Finley at a bridge club when they were students, he at the all-male Caltech and she at Scripps College. At first she didn't think much of him. He was two years older and studying chemistry. He'd been very sick with valley fever the previous year — the fungal infection had invaded his body, causing him unbearable muscle and joint pain. The illness had made him serious and aloof. Sue at first dismissed him as an overly reserved man but slowly grew to love his thoughtful, softhearted personality. Yet when he asked her to marry him she shook her head; she figured there had to be someone even better out there.

Unfortunately, Sue found the world of men outside college to be lacking. Although she was surrounded by men at Convair, among her colleagues there was nobody she wanted to go out with, much less marry. Two months after turning down Pete's proposal, she met him at a friend's wedding in Northern California. The months of bad dates cast him in a more flattering light. Suddenly, Sue realized she'd made a mistake. As they sat together talking, Sue blurted out, "OK, I'll marry you." Pete looked at her, surprised; he hadn't repeated his proposal since she had first said no. When he looked in her eyes, he realized she was dead serious. They laughed together, and Pete took her hand, leading her to the dance floor. They were back together.

They married on a sunny California day in 1957 at the Church of the Good Shepherd in Arcadia. Sue told her mother after the wedding that she didn't want kids right away. Nodding with a superior smile, Sue's mother didn't say a word. She wouldn't put any pressure on her daughter yet, since she knew that the fierce independence of a twenty-year-old girl often softened with time into the desire for motherhood.

In spite of her plans, as these things are wont to happen, Sue became pregnant soon after the wedding. Her mother hugged her and was so happy she cried. As Sue's belly grew, her commute down the 10 Freeway from Pasadena to Convair seemed to balloon as well. The traffic was terrible. Sue hated sitting in her car on the backed-up freeway. She wanted a job closer to home, but she knew that, as a pregnant woman, she wouldn't get hired. Realistically, she wouldn't even be able to keep her current job once her employer found out she was going to have a baby. She knew what was expected of her, but she hated the idea of leaving the work she loved. Looking over the flyers at a bulletin board at Caltech, she came across a job posting for computers at JPL, just a short drive from campus. *Wouldn't that be convenient?* Sue thought dreamily. *I could do that job.*

But soon all thoughts of work were gone. As her due date neared and her pregnancy became obvious, she had to leave Convair. At home, she got the baby's room ready and started picturing her life as a housewife and mother. The small kicks within, growing stronger each day, made her mindful of the future. She was getting excited. At night, Pete would marvel at her belly, wondering if they were going to have a boy or a girl.

A week before her due date, Sue started feeling contractions. It was finally time. She woke up Pete and called her mother to meet her at the hospital before they hurried into the car. Sue was whisked off into labor and delivery while Pete was confined to the waiting room with the other fathers, the sounds of women having babies emanating faintly through the open door.

Labor was agonizing and stretched into a second day. The pain racked her body and sapped her strength. Finally the moment was at hand; the doctor encouraged her to push. After one last effort Sue's child entered the world. "What is it? What is it?" she called out, eager to learn if she had a son or a daughter. "It's a boy!" the doctor announced. Trembling from her exertions, Sue let the words sink in. She was the mother of a little boy. She was so happy. Yet the room was too quiet. There were no cries from the infant. Across the room Sue could see the bluish tone to his skin. As they wheeled the baby out of the room, the nurse told Sue something was wrong. "Your baby needs help. He's not breathing," she said hurriedly. "We'll know more soon."

Sue and Pete named their little angel Stephen and hoped for the best. Heavy with postpartum hormones and easily alarmed, Sue could do nothing but wait and pray that her son would pull through.

Two days later, when the doctor came in, she could tell from the look on his face that the news wasn't good. "I'm sorry," he began. "There was nothing we could do." A guttural, savage cry escaped Sue before her body succumbed to heaving sobs. She clung to Pete before falling off the hospital bed onto the floor and dragging him down with her. She couldn't feel anything, couldn't hear the nurses rushing to her, helping to get her back into bed. She tore at her hair, mindless of the pain. Her mother and husband talked to her, but there was nothing anyone could say. She was overcome with guilt. She had said she didn't want a family. Was this punishment for those thoughtless words? What she wouldn't give to take them back.

Before she left the hospital she held her tiny lifeless newborn in her arms. Stephen was swaddled in receiving blankets and looked impossibly small. *Wake up,* Sue shouted silently, *wake up.* She touched her fingers to the small heart-shaped face. The skin was still warm. His lips formed a perfect pink pout. Sue held her son for only a few minutes and then let him go. There would never be an explanation. Her baby boy was lost forever.

Sue was drowning in her grief. At the grocery store she would look with bewilderment at the people surrounding her. It seemed incredible that in the midst of her crumbling existence, the world kept spinning and people went on with their daily lives. She stared at the women ahead of her in the checkout line, wondering how it was possible for them to have no inkling of her devastation.

Although Sue wasn't religious, she decided to go to church to have them say a blessing for her baby. While she didn't believe that because he had died before he was baptized he was headed for an eternity in limbo, she thought a few kind words from a minister would help ease her own troubled mind. She stood at the door of the church nervously before pulling on the door handle. It didn't budge; it was locked. As she turned away, she felt the stinging pain of loss and wondered if the torment within her would ever fade.

Graduating from Notre Dame, Helen was anxious to leave Indiana and live with her brother, Edwin, in Pasadena, and to join her parents, who had also moved there. She got her first glimpse of the valley town in 1953. It seemed small, dusty, and crowded with palm trees. Despite these dreary first impressions, the town would become her home for the next sixty years.

Helen had thought she'd find work decorating department-store windows, but the industry on the West Coast wasn't what she expected. She found her job applications continually passed over, usually for someone who had a connection to the employer through a family member or a friend. Discouraged, Helen wasn't sure what kind of work to do. She'd graduated from a top college with excellent grades, but no one wanted to hire her. As her feelings of self-worth plummeted, her dependence on her family intensified.

Edwin had moved to Pasadena to work as a structural engineer at JPL. One evening, he came home enthused about a job he had seen posted. It was for a computer. He knew immediately it would be perfect for his sister, the math genius. Helen was enthusiastic too. Perhaps all those classes she took in college wouldn't be for naught. Her nerves and excitement mounting, she tried to shake off feelings of inadequacy. She worried over her qualifications and even her accent, hoping she'd be good enough for the job. She once thought mathematics was an impractical whimsy and could scarcely believe that it was now a viable career option.

■ ■ ■ ■

Part II
1950s

■ ■ ■ ■

Barbara Lewis (later Paulson)

Janez Lawson

Helen Yee Chow (later Ling)

Susan Finley

CHAPTER 3
ROCKETS RISING

It had taken Barbara Lewis years to get to this point. She lovingly touched the stark white paint on the giant missile before adding her loopy signature on the blank canvas of its skin. It was April 1955, and a small crowd had gathered, saying their good-byes to the thirty-nine-foot-tall structure that had dominated their lives for the past ten years. Dismembered and loaded onto a convoy of trucks, it was headed for its ultimate test, the White Sands Proving Ground in southern New Mexico, just sixty miles north of the border with Mexico. As they bid the missile farewell, the group at JPL thought their struggles with the troublesome rocket were finally over. They were wrong.

It all started in the late 1940s with a program called the Corporal: a guided-missile system unlike anything JPL had attempted. The army wanted a new weapon, a long-range jet-propelled missile that could

The Corporal missile containing Barbara and her colleagues' signatures, 1955 Courtesy NASA/JPL-Caltech

carry a thousand-pound warhead for a hundred miles at a speed capable of eluding an enemy fighter aircraft. It was Barbara's first project at JPL and seemed headed for quick success. Their early prototype had flown forty miles into the atmosphere in October 1945 at White Sands. The rocket just touched the edges of space — the highest a rocket had ever flown — before crashing back down to Earth. That model was known as the WAC Corporal, WAC standing for "Without Altitude Control," since it had no guidance system, and also for "Women's Army Corps," since it was smaller than other missiles given military-sounding names. The group referred to it as the little sister. It was a stepping-stone before they tackled the larger, more technologically advanced Corporal, designed to stand nearly twice as tall.

Translating the little sister's success into a missile capable of carrying a warhead was not as simple as they had hoped. JPL was still assessing the use of liquid fuel in rockets. Liquid propellants held the promise of packing the maximum possible heat into the smallest number of molecules. They could ignite quickly and burn rapidly. Yet the same capabilities that indicated such promise also made these propellants inher-

Frank Malina (middle) weighing the WAC Corporal at White Sands in 1945 **Courtesy NASA/JPL-Caltech**

ently dangerous, as those who had been at JPL for some time were only too aware.

Tests of the liquid propellants had been explosive. Only a few years before Barbara started, the group at JPL had set the hillside behind the test pits on fire, incinerating not just the dry brush but also much of their equipment. The problem lay in an unexplained phenomenon. The liquid propellants had the habit of making the engines throb. The pulsing would start slowly and then build, until the motor couldn't take any more and exploded into bits. To make matters worse, the throbbing was sporadic, making the explosions unpredictable.

Barbara knew little about the danger. With her plump cheeks and soft skin, she looked even younger than her nineteen years. Underneath her schoolgirl façade was a woman determined to fit into the rocket culture of JPL. It wasn't easy; she found the shock of explosions caused by experimental mixtures of liquid hydrogen, oxygen, and nitrogen jolting. The people were loud too; the boisterous conversations around the lab were both exciting and a little overwhelming. Mostly, though, it was the warning sound of the old Ford truck horn that still made her jump.

But each boom represented new data for Barbara. She calculated the thrust produced by a mixture of aniline and red fuming nitric acid, a violent mixture that caused a red glare to blaze out of the rocket's engine. From the tedium of their daily work, Barbara and the other computers were unknowingly computing something earth-shattering; the same qualities they were helping refine in the liquid propellant would one day put the first humans on the moon. They were helping to develop a hypergolic propellant, a combination of fuel and oxidant that would ignite on contact. Separately, the components were stable, but once mixed in the rocket combustion chamber they would catch fire. Two decades later, hypergolic propellant would fill the tanks of the Project Apollo launch vehicles.

Barbara used her calculations of the test data to determine how missiles would fly. It took an entire day to calculate a single trajectory. When she was done, her notebook held a prized piece of work: her hand-drawn picture of the path the Corporal would take as it flew through the air. Barbara's notebooks, and those of the other computers, would be covered with trajectories as they sought out the ideal mix of engineering components on the missile.

In 1948, at the same time as they were working on the Corporal, they were also modifying its little sister, the WAC Corporal. Barbara found the calculations for the little sister especially intriguing since they were now launching it as a two-stage rocket. The slim American rocket would sit atop the Nazi V-2, a ballistic missile best known for bringing Paris and London to their knees. When the war ended, the enemy rocket, as well as the Nazi scientists who developed it, had been captured and brought to the States. Its potential was chilling: it could target a city from two hundred miles away.

The idea of combining the power of the V-2 with the high-flying WAC Corporal was ingenious. The engineers dreamed that by uniting the two they could burst through into outer space. The V-2 would pack a powerful punch and then detach, firing the WAC Corporal as the V-2 fell back to Earth. The WAC Corporal could then fly higher than ever before. The engineers at JPL called this combination the Bumper WAC.

To predict how high the Bumper WAC could go, Barbara calculated the amount of thrust produced by each rocket engine and used the weight and height of the rockets to determine their launch velocity. She also had to account for the effects of gravity and drag. Her calculus now came in handy as she tracked each variable as a function of time. The work was hard on her hands. Her right index finger was lined with thick red and white calluses, the result of clutching a pencil for hours a day. Her grip on the pencil often made her hand perspire, leaving pucker marks across the graph paper.

Barbara used a slide rule and a Friden calculator to check all her work. She was still shaky with both devices, since she'd never used either before coming to JPL. She loved the Friden, but even such advanced technology couldn't do everything she needed. For one thing, it couldn't calculate logarithms, which tell us how many of one number we multiply to get another number; if $2 \times 2 \times 2 = 8$, that means we need three 2s to get 8, or, in mathematical notation, $\text{Log}_2 8 = 3$.

So Barbara had to turn to a set of frayed brown-covered books in the computer room. This was the *Mathematical Tables Project* series, whose volumes were oversized, awkward to hold or carry, but filled with data precious to Barbara and her colleagues. To calculate the Bumper WAC's trajectory, she turned to the tables of atmospheric density as a function of altitude. The air thins as elevation increases, and the computers needed the WPA books, as they were known around the lab, to get the exact value.

Barbara deftly drew two peaks. She predicted the modest rise and fall of the V-2 rocket as it ignited and then plummeted back to Earth, making way for the little sister to soar higher. She computed that the two-stage rocket had the capability of making history, of flying farther into space than any man-made object ever had. Barbara and the team of engineers and computers didn't just calculate how high the rocket could fly, but also how far from the launch point. The group expected to find the burnt remnants 64 miles away. Under the engineers' direction, the computers calculated that reentering the atmosphere would likely destroy the rocket. It was a pioneering analysis of how the barrier of Earth's atmosphere might impact a fast-moving projectile. This way of thinking was more aligned with planning a space mission than weapon design. Years later, the engineers' foresight at calculating the heat caused by reentry would come in handy.

While they worked out the kinks of the little sister, the Corporal took to the air on May 22, 1947. It was the first test of the large missile, considered all-American, since it had the only large-thrust motor to be exclusively developed and built in the States. It was foolhardy to expect success right off the bat. JPL was used to hard-won success born from repeated failure. Everyone was surprised when the mammoth soared to a height of 129,000 feet before reaching its target 60 miles away. Martin Summerfield, one of JPL's engineers, stood dumbfounded as the numbers came across the radio. When he related the news of the missile's success to Macie Roberts, she shook her head in disbelief. It seemed almost too easy.

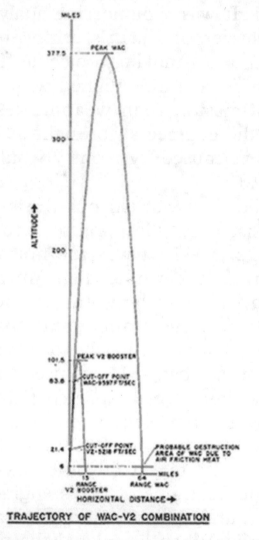

Trajectory of the Bumper WAC drawn by computers at JPL in 1948
Courtesy NASA/JPL-Caltech

The hard work was over. All they had to do now was make more Corporals and test them to bring the missile to the pinnacle of its ability, and then pass it on to a private contractor for production. When Barbara signed her name on one of these Corporals, bound for testing on the missile range, she was giddy with the notion of the product of her work flying high above the earth. She could picture her name rising into the sky above White Sands.

For Barbara, although it was only a day's drive away, White Sands seemed like the Wild West. The missile range there was only a few years old, but it was already the site of exquisite success and painful failure. The sand dunes were made of gypsum, which colored the stark, desert landscape a bright white and made the sand as soft and pliable as chalk. At the bottom of the Tularosa Basin, in an area walled off from the world by the surrounding mountains, the army had discovered a perfect hiding spot for secret military experiments. Since the early 1940s, engineers from JPL had been traveling to the Mojave, where they tested missiles too big for their own California canyon. In those early days in the desert, the engineers huddled in tents whose canvas walls were barely able to keep out the fine sand.

However, after Pearl Harbor, the need for the secluded testing site became pressing, so much so that the army expanded its presence in the basin, taking 1.25 million acres of the isolated land for its own and building more facilities. A large concrete pad was constructed as the firing area, with an adjacent blockhouse, the control center, protected by ten-foot-thick concrete walls and topped by a steel-reinforced roof that rose like a pyramid. The remote facility attracted plenty of army research, and treks to the desert soon paid off. In just one year, 1945, it had been the site of the Trinity explosion — the first nuclear detonation — and the launch of the highest-flying rocket known to man. Now, with the war over, the amenities at the missile range improved. The engineers would take the train out to White Sands, where, instead of tents or even hastily constructed barracks, spacious houses and a swimming pool greeted them.

The engineers at JPL were wild to go there. Far from the eyes and ears of their families and friends, the missile range gave them free rein in both their experiments and their appetites. It was where men roamed unfettered, working all hours, then playing poker and drinking late into the night. They often crossed the border, partying and finding female companionship in nearby Juarez, Mexico. Computers rarely went to White Sands. Barbara couldn't say she had much desire to go. While seeing a launch made possible by her calculations would be an undeniable thrill, she witnessed enough male rowdiness in Pasadena. White Sands wasn't the place for a nineteen-year-old girl who was looking to be taken seriously.

The raucousness wasn't confined to White Sands. The work environment at JPL was casual, exceptionally so for an army institute. It was a by-product of the earliest days, when the empty canyon played host to wild experiments and general scientific mischief. This history, together with the lab's native California attitude, imbued JPL with a happy, spontaneous spirit that no military affiliation could counter.

The dress code reflected their laid-back approach. At first, Barbara was surprised to see professional men spurn neckties and sport short sleeves. They might be relaxed and comfortable this way, but Barbara wouldn't consider coming to work looking so informal. Every morning she carefully selected dresses and skirts, wore high heels, and always, no matter how hot the day was, put on stockings. Barbara was playful with her clothing, but not at work. She wasn't interested in attracting anyone at JPL. Not that there wasn't ample opportunity. The other girls were eager to fix Barbara up. "Oh, give him a chance," they would implore her when a handsome young engineer looked her way. But Barbara would shake her head and say, "No, thank you." She clung to her schoolgirl wariness of men; she couldn't be comfortable around them, no matter how attractive they might be.

Some men at JPL were downright repulsive. One engineer in particular seemed to embody all that was treacherous for young women not on their guard. Macie Roberts was careful when he said he needed to work with a computer. "You will not go to his office," she would say. "He only comes to our room to work. Don't meet him anywhere else." Barbara was curious; why couldn't they go to his office? She asked another girl, who laughed and then quietly said, "I'll show you later." At the end of the day, the pair sneaked over to his office. They waited until they were sure he was gone and then peeked into the small room. Barbara was stunned. Every inch of the man's walls was covered in pictures of beautiful women, all in different states of undress. She had never seen girlie pictures before and immediately broke out in laughter. Giggling, the two hurried off, not wanting to be caught. The experience didn't do much to calm Barbara's anxiety over men, but it certainly convinced her to heed Macie's warnings.

In general, though, the women got along famously with the engineers. This was important, since they worked long hours together. As a team, they bounced ideas off one another and spent hours discussing how their designs influenced the velocity of their rockets, from the shape and size of the Corporal's tail fins to the inner workings of its engine.

In Barbara's mind, an engineer was a man. There wasn't a single female engineer at JPL, yet she never thought of her job as women's work. It was a respected position, one that men eagerly applied for. It just so happened that their applications were all turned down. A man's name was all Macie needed to see to reject a promising computer applicant. Macie saw men as a potential disruption to her group. She couldn't imagine that a man would listen to her. Men, she believed, were likely to see themselves as bosses and women as employees — not the other way around.

There was another reason Macie spurned male applicants. She labored to find a group of women who all got along, who were friends as well as colleagues. The room sparkled with happy conversation, and the work shone as a result of their fruitful collaboration. Barbara was happy with how things were; she loved the girls she worked with too well to wish it any other way.

Macie was an enigma to her computer girls. She was fifty years old, ancient in the eyes of the roomful of twenty-somethings. She'd begun work at JPL late in life, and the girls couldn't understand why she'd entered the field at all. Her husband had a good job as an accountant with the IRS; she certainly didn't need to work. Furthermore, the girls often puzzled over her strained relationship with one of the computers: Virginia Prettyman. Virginia had briefly been married to Macie's son, a man the computers didn't much care for. Their relationship had barely lasted a year. Tensions occasionally flared between the two women, especially when Virginia started dating an engineer at the lab. Despite these provocations, Macie acted with strict propriety and never betrayed her feelings. Barbara would watch her from the corner of her eye, wondering what emotions were swirling below the surface.

Macie came to work early in the morning. Any girl running late would give her a wary glance as she dropped her purse on her desk, breathlessly mumbling a hasty excuse or apology. With a wave of her hand, Macie would dismiss the need for explanation, yet there was something about her strict demeanor that put the computers on their guard. Her silence was often her most effective method of discipline.

Macie was strong with her girls, but inside she sometimes felt weak. As she weaved in and out between their desks, looking over their shoulders, she found she couldn't always keep up with their equations. The math was undeniably demanding and often above her skill level. When Barbara needed help, she wouldn't turn to her boss but instead asked the other girls. Together they would go over the equations methodically, searching the compact rows of numbers and symbols. They would laugh over foolish mistakes, tease each other over arithmetic slipups, and bond when they experienced the deep satisfaction of solving a particularly challenging problem. It didn't feel like a job; it was more like being part of a secret society.

Riding the trolley on her way to the lab, Melba Nead looked just like any other woman starting her workday. No one would suspect what she really did all day. As the computers chatted comfortably during a lunch break one day, one of them said they were "just like a sorority," that being a part of the close-knit group of women made her feel like she'd never really left college. When Macie overheard her, she wasn't amused. "You're professional women," she reminded them.

It never snows in Southern California. It rarely even rains. That's what Barbara was thinking as she looked out the window of her home in Pasadena one cold day in January 1949. She had seen plenty of snow in Ohio, but like everyone else, she wasn't prepared to see the dry California landscape covered in a blanket of white. She had given away her winter coat years ago and had no idea how she would keep warm in the chilly weather. She bundled up as best she could and drove carefully to the lab. JPL, nestled in the foothills, had gotten the worst of the storm; it was under a foot of snow. Barbara was cautious walking over the small footbridge employees used to cross from the parking lot to the lab. The arched bridge had become hazardous, with people slipping every which way. Chilled to the bone and with wet feet, Barbara made her way to the computer room, in Building 11.

She had spent so much time there during the past year that the building had become her second home. It wasn't a very comfortable home. There was no heat, for one thing, a fact that made all the girls unhappy on this particular Tuesday morning. It was simply a small wood-frame building with concrete floors that was sweltering in the summer and cold in the winter. The location was convenient, though. Across the street, practically built into the hillside, were the outbuildings that housed the experiments. Barbara and the other girls would simply walk across the street to get the data, copying the raw numbers into large twelve-by-eighteen-inch tablets, and then walk back to their desks to analyze the experiments.

On a winter day like today no one wanted to go outside for work. Outside, the lab was quiet, muffled by the snow. There were no blasts or truck horns blaring to make Barbara jump out of her seat. But the computer room was abuzz with talk; no one had ever seen weather like this in Pasadena. Macie told her team to quiet down. Her voice was soft, but her strict manner brought instant respect from the girls. Yet even Macie knew today would be different. The women were acting like giddy schoolchildren, excited to see their first snowfall. No one wanted to sit still at the desks. Instead they stood at the large windows, rubbing their hands to keep warm, mesmerized by the rare sight of snow in California.

It had been a hard winter for the lab. The Corporal project was supposed to be an easy success. Instead, the first test had been a lucky fluke, and the lab watched their lovingly crafted creations crash into the desert, flames lapping up their sides. They held their breath as the missiles were loaded onto the trucks, unsure what to expect. With hope fading, the Corporal missile earned the nickname the rabbit killer. It seemed unlikely it would ever fly high enough to kill anything else.

The Bumper WAC was also struggling at White Sands. The last round of testing was especially disappointing. The pipes that pumped the alcohol into the combustion chamber had split, causing the entire tail of the rocket to tear off and the rocket to collapse in on itself. The long string of failed launches made for gloomy holidays at the lab. The staff grumbled their way through the Christmas party without the typical enthusiasm of the season.

In the meantime, the army was looking for a new place to test rockets. White Sands, beloved by the engineers for its wild nights and camaraderie, had become untenable. A stray V-2 rocket had flown over El Paso, Texas, before crashing in Juarez, leaving behind an enormous crater, fifty feet wide and thirty feet deep. Luckily no one was hurt, but the danger was clear. White Sands was too close to too many people. Rockets needed to fly over the ocean, not over the desert.

The War Department was researching several sites. The team at JPL were pulling for the front-runner, which happened to be in their backyard outside San Diego, a convenient three-hour drive down the coast. When the War Department selected the California location, everyone was excited — everyone except Mexico's president. With the wounds of the Juarez incident still fresh, the Mexican government wouldn't consent to having missiles buzzing over Baja beaches before heading out to the Pacific Ocean. The War Department had to settle for its second choice: Cocoa Beach, Florida.

The sleepy Florida town was isolated, yet the weather was sunny and clear. One drawback was that rockets would have to fly over the Bahamas on their way to the open ocean. Luckily, the British government had no objections. The site had an advantage

119

that would become important years later when the range became part of the Space Coast. Because the town was close to the equator, rockets got a boost from the rotational speed of Earth, which is more powerful at the equator than anywhere else. This meant that launches required less engine thrust than was necessary elsewhere.

Rural Brevard County, Florida, was a maze of low-lying, one-lane bridges connecting an extensive network of citrus orchards, famous for producing Indian River oranges and grapefruit. Dark clouds of mosquitoes swarmed the wet, marshy land, making the area all but uninhabitable until the advent of DDT in the mid-1940s. Armed with a new weapon against the pests, fishermen and farmers were moving in. The reaction to the new missile range was mixed. On the one hand, it would bring jobs and a new economy, but it would also bring outsiders and dangerous missiles. Some dreamed of selling off their land and homes to the government for a pretty penny while others feared their homes would be forcibly taken away, bulldozed to make room for a launchpad.

Back in California, the mood at JPL was dark, with botched rocket launches piling up and now the news that future launches would take place clear across the country. Barbara felt the disappointment keenly; it was difficult to have her work mired in failure. The frustration seeped into her home life, making her more serious and withdrawn. Her mother always good-naturedly asked how her day was, but Barbara felt unable to convey the challenges she and the others were facing. Their work was classified, but even if it hadn't been, its technical details were formidable, serving to further insulate her from life outside the lab's gates. On the other hand, the shared experience bonded her more deeply to the women she worked with at JPL.

Barbara sometimes felt smothered by her mother's expectations. She was single and in no hurry to settle down. Her family hoped she would find a husband soon, yet none was in sight. As Barbara came home at the end of the workday, her feet dragged on the walk that led to the front door. Once she was inside, her mother chided her before Barbara even hung up her hat: how did she expect to get married if she worked such long hours? Her sisters constantly tried to match her up. Even at church she couldn't avoid the well-meaning comments and inevitable, awkward fix-ups. It seemed everyone had a son who would be perfect for her. Only at JPL was she free from this crushing weight. No one expected her to date at the lab; in fact, it was frowned upon. There was freedom in the work, as her success was measured in her calculations instead of in the number of marriage proposals accrued. And yet sometimes, lying in bed at night, all the fear of a lonely future rushed in on her. *Should I be worried?* she thought. *Will I ever have a family of my own?*

Barbara felt little trepidation on that snowy January day as the computers, unable to stay inside, finally went out to make snow angels, build snowmen, and lob snowballs through the frosty air. The release was just what they needed, a welcome respite from plotting trajectories and from workdays that were lengthening, despite the waning light of winter, as they approached the next launch date.

Over the next few days, as the snow melted, dotting the lab with muddy puddles, it also left clarity behind. Discussing the recent problems on the Bumper WAC with the engineers, computer Coralie Pearson recognized a discrepancy in their tests. The rocket trajectories they had spent a day calculating had assumed a full tank of propellant, but the launches were being performed with only a partial tank. A full tank gave an extra thirteen seconds of burning time. The engineers had initially dismissed the difference as unimportant, a mere matter of seconds, yet it was certainly affecting their calculations. Willing to try anything, the engineers agreed that the next round would have a full tank. Other changes were afoot. The nozzle of the Bumper WAC was covered with a shallow dish to keep air pressure constant while the rocket gained altitude.

The staff at JPL were down to the last few launches scheduled for White Sands, and the pressure was on. At 1:15 a.m. Mountain time on February 24, 1949, the engineers and technicians began preparations. The technicians connected circuits and detonators, examined the O-rings, checked the weather, and began radio silence. At 7:15 a.m. the engineers were ready to fire the rocket. But the weather wasn't cooperating. Clouds moved in. After being up all night, the group had to wait another seven hours for the skies to clear. The day was breezy, more so than they liked, but they decided to try anyway. At 3:14 p.m. the commander began the countdown: "Three, two, one, *fire!* Missile away!" The rocket rose steadily. Thirty seconds later the V-2 rocket detached. The little sister slipped away, its three jet-black fins exposed. With the extra boost, it raced faster, now reaching 5,150 miles per hour. The rocket left the atmosphere and speeded into space. It reached 242 miles above Earth. It was the greatest velocity and highest altitude any man-made object had ever achieved. The news was relayed to the group at JPL, which immediately erupted in cheers. Everyone hugged Coralie, who turned as red as a rocket's nose cone at all the attention. Finally, Barbara thought, it feels like spring.

As the rockets grew more successful, the team had to confront the reality of their ultimate use. While those at JPL were focused on piercing the limits of space and breaking barriers, the rockets they had just designed were destined to be loaded down with warheads. Their goal was not exploration but military might. Cocooned in their cozy academic setting, they could easily deny this basic fact. With the success of the Bumper WAC, Barbara realized for the first time what all this might mean. The realization made her anxious.

Outside the lab, Barbara was careful not to talk about her work to anyone. The lab used a color-coding system to differentiate which employees had access to sensitive information. A red stripe running down an employee's JPL badge meant their work was classified. Some employees, such as Barbara, also had a blue stripe across their badges. This meant their work was classified and secret. Barbara was careful to keep the file cabinets, holding the computers' clandestine calculations, locked up at night.

Given these restrictions, Barbara kept her professional and home lives separate. She didn't discuss her work with her mom and sisters, and at church or out with friends, careers were rarely a topic of discussion among the women. Their importance was seen as marginal in comparison to their social lives. It was only among her fellow computers that she spoke freely.

A red shadow had fallen across the United States, and fear of Communists infiltrating American institutions was rampant. As of 1949, when the USSR detonated First Lightning, its first atomic bomb, at a remote site in Kazakhstan, the United States no longer stood alone in nuclear technology. America was shocked at the speed with which the Soviets had been able to produce atomic weapons. Like most of her countrymen's, Barbara's blood ran cold at the news that American scientists with secret Communist ties had leaked information to the USSR.

The hysteria grew. Stories of spies concealed in America's laboratories dominated the headlines. JPL held meetings on the growing Soviet menace while the FBI pried into everyone's past. Until then, Barbara hadn't paid much attention to the news. She loved music on the radio but didn't listen to newscasts. She liked going to the movies but rarely watched the newsreels. She almost never read the paper. Twenty-year-old girls weren't expected to discuss politics or be knowledgeable concerning world events. Now, however, tensions on the world stage would directly affect her.

The Red Scare was no longer simply a headline; it was destroying the lives of those she worked with. At JPL everyone knew one another, and they all knew Hsue-Shen Tsien, a founding member of the lab. He was an expert in V-2 rockets, his knowledge acquired during World War II. Originally from China, he came to America in 1935 to study at MIT. Like Frank Malina, JPL's acting director, he'd received his PhD at Caltech, and almost immediately was attracted to the Suicide Squad. Though he was a quiet man, something about the audacious group drew him in. He'd been involved with JPL since its inception, playing a key role in its success before serving in the U.S. Army.

It was in the army, while serving as an honorary colonel, that Tsien consulted for Operation Paperclip, which aimed to capture key Nazi scientists after the war before Russia could get hold of them. The United States was desperate to get their hands on Nazi rocket technology, whose sophistication far outstripped that of the Allies'. Tsien, an accomplished, well-respected rocket scientist, was a natural choice to interview the enemy scientists. When Wernher von Braun and Rudolf Hermann, both notorious for their expertise in rocketry, were captured, Tsien was one of the first to talk to them. Both Tsien and Frank had long been chasing the technology contained within the Nazi V-2 rocket. To finally learn its secrets was intoxicating. They couldn't wait to bring both the technology and the Nazi scientists to America. Tsien dreamed of what JPL could do with such a rocket.

Ironically, just when the promise of the V-2 rocket in America was starting to pay off and the two-stage Bumper WAC that Barbara and the team at JPL built was starting to fly, things began to fall apart for Tsien.

In the clutches of McCarthyism, the FBI accused him of going to secret Communist meetings disguised as Caltech graduate-school parties. They found Communists among the shy young man's friends. His Chinese origins intensified the government's fears, especially since he had recently returned to the Caltech campus and was visiting JPL more frequently. Finally, in 1950, the government revoked his security clearance. He was banned from the very lab he had helped build.

To many employees at JPL, the accusations were absurd, and yet, with new indictments popping up in labs across the nation, it seemed that spies lurked everywhere. Still, the majority of those at JPL believed Tsien was innocent. The subject was too sad to incite much gossip. Tsien was brilliant and well liked; the charges against him seemed impossible.

For five years, Tsien and his family were held under house arrest before being deported to China. While he was forcibly ejected and labeled a traitor, the Nazi war criminals he helped bring to the States were being given more freedom and resources than ever before. In 1950, the same year that Tsien began house arrest, von Braun and his team of German scientists were arriving at the Redstone Arsenal, in Huntsville, Alabama, their importance in rocketry development recognized and encouraged.

Back in his home country, Tsien's contributions to China's space program would earn him the title Father of Chinese Rocketry. It's tempting to imagine what innovations he might have brought to the U.S. space program had he stayed. While government reports, made as late as 1999, have continued to denounce Tsien as a spy, these accusations have never been substantiated.

Frank, the director and founder of the lab, was another casualty of the Red Scare. Unlike Tsien, he had openly attended Communist meetings in the late 1930s before renouncing the party in 1939. He wasn't a Communist, but his politics weren't easily defined. His liberal leanings bristled against the current political climate. The growing tide of paranoia about Communist scientists and his own moral uncertainty about developing weaponry led him to leave both JPL and rocketry forever. It was hard for the computers to watch Frank, the heart and soul of the lab, depart. Yet they knew that his sensitive nature made him too fragile to stay. Retreating from rocketry, he would embrace his artistic nature, creating kinetic paintings that interwove his dual passions of science and art.

On a spring afternoon in 1955, the same year that Tsien was deported to China and Frank was opening a show of kinetic art at a gallery in Paris, Barbara and her friends signed their names on the white-painted metal of the hundredth Corporal built at JPL. It was a momentous occasion, celebrating the decade the team at JPL had spent optimizing the weaponry, the result of a painfully long string of failures. They relaxed as they watched the missile, emblazoned with their signatures, dismembered and loaded onto a convoy of trucks. The Corporal needed a vast amount of support equipment: a massive air compressor, air supply, platform, and launcher. The cranes swayed as they lifted the cumbersome equipment. The erector, designed to raise the missile into position, was still painted a cheery red color, a reminder of its previous life at an apple orchard. Two separate tankers filled with highly explosive liquid fuel, their formula the result of years of research, followed. The missile itself was packed into a giant shipping container. Altogether, the convoy stretched sixteen miles. It looked like a battalion headed to war.

The sun was low in the sky, casting long shadows that danced across the lawn. Some of the women waved as they watched the trucks leave the gate and head for the desert. Sadness rose up in Barbara; it felt like a child was leaving home. The engineers and computers sat on chairs and drank champagne until the sky turned pink. The celebration was gay but hushed. They confidently expected success, but past disasters had taught them to not celebrate too soon.

One week later a dozen technicians and engineers eased the rocket covered in their signatures onto the launchpad at White Sands and began the countdown. Then, with a single press of a button and the command "Missile away!" they fired. The rocket rose slowly at first, and then suddenly took a nosedive into the desert brush before exploding. Flames consumed it while giant black clouds of smoke filled the air. When they put out the fire they found only unrecognizable fragments. Despite its being the hundredth Corporal built, the engineers had no idea what had gone wrong. For now, their signatures were scattered across the New Mexico desert.

It seemed JPL was fated to wrestle with its weaponry even as those at the lab began to envision a future without it. They would embark on this journey without their founder. Much to his dismay, Frank would

The Corporal missile depicted earlier containing Barbara and her colleagues' signatures, now smashed across the White Sands landscape, 1955 **Courtesy**

NASA/JPL-Caltech

have to watch from afar as JPL's dream of exploring space slowly came true. He would never get to experience the thrill of adapting his technology to probe the limits of the universe. But Barbara Lewis would. First, however, she would become a beauty queen.

CHAPTER 4
MISS GUIDED MISSILE

Barbara Lewis carefully unfurled the curlers from her thick, dark hair. The big night was finally here. Tonight she would laugh, dance, and perhaps even take the crown at JPL's Miss Guided Missile contest. She delicately ran her fingers through the curls to loosen them before pulling back the strands closest to her face and securing them with a black velvet ribbon. She felt optimistic about her chances at the beauty contest tonight, but not because she thought herself prettier than the other girls competing. The Miss Guided Missile contest was barely a beauty contest in her eyes. The winner was chosen based on her popularity more than her trim figure and crinkly crinoline dress. Every spring, a girl from each department would sign up for consideration, with voting open to all. Mindful of this, Barbara had used her wiles to sway her colleagues. She wasn't particularly handy in the kitchen, but she baked three batches of chocolate chip cookies, filling a small basket with the treats. Armed with her cookies, Barbara walked around the lab, handing them out with a smile, openly calling them a bribe and cheerfully declaring, "Vote for Barbara!"

Before the voting commenced, however, Barbara's co-workers hoisted her atop a convertible and drove around the lab. With the wind blowing through her hair, she smiled and waved. She felt a little silly and laughed nervously. Barbara might not be the prettiest girl in the lab, but she was sociable and easy to work with. All the computers were rooting for her. She imagined the director of the institute crowning her at the summer dance. Yet she didn't dwell on her possible victory, since it was merely a lighthearted affair. No one took it too seriously. Barbara, representing the computing section, was competing against Lois Labee, a chemist, and Margaret Anderson, who worked in the research design division. They were all young, beautiful, and very good at their demanding jobs. As odd as it seems by today's standards, the beauty contest was a result of JPL's progressive hiring practices. As the bouquets were handed out and an attractive woman crowned the winner, the competition was unintentionally highlighting the presence of educated young women working at JPL. After all, other laboratories would have found it impossible to hold such a contest in the 1950s; they simply didn't hire enough women.

Barbara put on a modest shirtdress, the hem skimming her calves. It was black with tiny white polka dots, and she'd purchased it especially for the occasion. She buttoned the collar down conservatively but then, as a nod to her femininity, cinched the belt at her waist, showing off her slim figure. She pulled on her stockings and gave her new shoes an admiring glance before slipping them on. The black satin peep-toe heels were the latest fashion. A little dark red lipstick and she was ready to go. She twirled happily in front of the mirror before going downstairs to show off to her mother and sisters.

The computer room was starting to burst at the seams with new girls coming in. JPL had a new army contract, and Macie Roberts had been searching for as many qualified young women as she could. Between 1950 and 1953, JPL's annual budget had doubled, from roughly $5 million to $11 million. The work was doubling too, and yet management was hesitant about expanding.

The lab had always enjoyed an intimate feel; they didn't want to destroy the culture they had built. With this in mind, Macie was careful to recruit only women she thought would work well with her team.

When Janez Lawson applied, she was obviously a perfect fit. She was graduating from the prestigious University of California at Los Angeles with a degree in chemical engineering. Janez, born and raised in Los Angeles, came from an affluent family. Her mother and father tried to give her and her younger sister the riches they had only dreamed of growing up. But her parents' success didn't stop Janez from working hard at school. She loved chemistry and math. Although she was usually the only girl in her classes, she pursued science with a single-minded determination. Not that she was just a bookworm. With her good looks and bubbly personality, Janez was destined to always be the most popular girl in her class.

At UCLA she joined the Delta Sigma Theta sorority, which recognized her achievements by awarding her a scholarship. The group provided the perfect counterpoint to the long hours she spent studying. Janez sometimes slipped away from the library to relax at the beach with her friends or help plan the annual White Christmas formal. With her sorority sisters she was fun and silly, while in the classroom she turned serious. Her senior year marked the culmination of her happy student years. Her sorority sisters elected her president of Delta Sigma Theta, and she was about to graduate with honors. As her college years came to a close, she started researching her job options, but she had no expectation that she'd ever be able to re-create the joyful mix of camaraderie and science.

One day, Janez stood in front of the job board at UCLA and examined her choices. Although she was an engineering major, she barely glanced at a job posting from Douglas Aircraft Company calling for engineers. She already knew that she was excluded from their elite, almost exclusively male ranks. Sandwiched between appeals for sheet metal men and stenographers, an advertisement from Caltech caught her attention. COMPUTERS URGENTLY NEEDED it said in large block letters across the top of the page. In smaller type below, the job description read: *Computers do not need advanced experience or degrees but should have an aptitude and interest in mathematics and computing machines.* In a sea of available jobs, this one stood out. It was distinct in offering a professional job in mathematics at a premier academic institute. The fact that the job didn't require a degree was code, signaling to Janez that it was open to women. For a woman wanting to become an engineer, taking a job as a computer was like entering the field through a secret back door.

And so, on a spring morning in March 1952, Janez confidently shook Macie's hand. "I'm Janez Lawson," she said, smiling warmly.

"Mrs. Roberts, supervisor of computing," Macie said in her usual curt style. Instead of exchanging niceties, she dove right into her questions. "I see you're graduating from UCLA?"

"That's right. I'm receiving my bachelor's degree in chemical engineering. As part of the program I've taken every advanced mathematics course offered."

"Have you used a Friden calculator before?"

"I've seen one, but we haven't used them in class." Janez hesitated before adding, "But I learn quickly."

"Do you enjoy working with other women?"

"Well," began Janez as she adjusted her words diplomatically, "there have been

138

hardly any women in my classes at UCLA. I do love working with women, though. As president of my sorority I've organized many events with the girls in our house. Our winter balls are always highly regarded. Of course I've had my mother as a role model. She's very active socially."

Macie was impressed. Janez exuded confidence. The young woman had an air of maturity and competence. Macie was sure she would be an invaluable addition to their team. There was only one obstacle preventing her from hiring her on the spot: Janez was African-American.

For all its liberal attitudes and laid-back manner, California was undeniably segregated. Schools, neighborhoods, and workplaces were all delineated by race. With the postwar boom, African Americans were moving to Southern California, especially to Los Angeles, in increasing numbers. The city's population rose from 75,000 in 1940 to roughly 250,000 in 1950. From all over the country, people were flocking to Southern California with visions of sunshine, beaches, and futures as movie stars. It was a land of dreamers. To accommodate the influx, developers bulldozed orange groves and replaced the lines of green and orange with rows of tract homes. Yet these new neighborhoods offered little diversity; African Americans were confined mostly to a few areas in the growing city. The Lawson family was part of a burgeoning community in Santa Monica.

The decision by JPL to hire Janez Lawson was not made lightly. She would be the first African American hired for a professional position at the institute. She was continuing a family legacy. Her father, Hillard Lawson, was the first African-American city council member in Santa Monica. Questions were raised, chief among them: How would the staff react to her? Macie was quick to answer for her girls, certain they would accept Janez as one of their own. The engineers, she was sure, could be similarly persuaded. Janez was hired.

As the group took their first steps toward racial integration, the pressures of the Cold War were also mounting. The design of the Corporal missile, at least in concept, was set, and thus JPL's work on the project diminished. Now it was time to make the missile reliable. To do this, they turned over the project to a private contractor who would manufacture and test the rockets in consultation with JPL. The winning bidder was Firestone Tire and Rubber Company. While the company had yet to work on missiles, they offered the advantage of proximity, since their factory was based in Los Angeles. Yet from the beginning, the relationship between research institute and contractor was tense. Drawings delivered from JPL to Firestone were often frustratingly incomplete, while JPL lamented Firestone's inconsistent quality and workmanship. The chaos wasn't good for missile development. Sometimes the missile's guidance system worked perfectly; other times it sent the giant rocket careening into the bushes. The engineers brought the kinks in the system to the computers, and they worked together to fix them.

Part of the problem was that the guidance system was merely a patchwork of existing technology left over from World War II. Although the engineers at JPL recognized that an all-inertial system — one in which the missile can correct its own course — was ideal, they had no time to build it. Their contract with the army meant they couldn't waste time tinkering. Instead, the missile used a radio-command guidance system, an approach the Germans had experimented with during the war. Using radar and Doppler, they tracked the position and velocity of the missile and then kept it on course with a radio transmitter.

The hastily-thrown-together guidance system frequently failed. The computers joked that a light breeze was all it took to knock it over. Corporals were now rolling off the assembly line at Firestone, but the missile no longer felt like their baby. The lack of consistency in manufacturing brought frustration and disappointment. There was a growing desire at JPL to build their designs in-house, where they could control every aspect of development, but this wish wasn't practical with weaponry. While they could build a handful of rockets themselves, they didn't have the means to mass-produce them in the quantities needed for war.

While JPL struggled with their relationship with private contractors, they had also begun work on a new project: the Sergeant. The weapons system would have a more sophisticated guidance system, as well as improved accuracy and range, and because it would use compact cakes of solid fuel that fit inside the missile, it wouldn't take a sixteen-mile convoy to get the rocket off the ground. It would be the most advanced missile system the world had ever seen. But the project was still a twinkle in JPL's eye; it hadn't yet been approved by the army. With American troops on the ground in Korea, however, it seemed inevitable that a powerful yet nimble weapon would be needed. The solution seemed to rest in a forgotten World War II engineering marvel.

In the 1930s, a group of scientists in Great Britain were getting desperate. War with Germany was imminent, and they needed to develop an anti-aircraft weapon, but they had limited materials to work with and almost no money. They designed a slim and simple two-inch rocket to launch at enemy aircraft, using the only materials available to them: thin steel pipes. The problem was that the flimsy outer casings of the rocket would melt away when exposed to the explosive combustion of the rocket engine. They needed a way to insulate the delicate casing from the core of the motor.

Harold James Pool, a chemist with the reaction group at the British Woolwich Royal Arsenal, came up with an elegant solution. He invented a structure hidden within the rocket: a beautiful five-pointed star. From the outside it looked like any missile, but the solid propellant inside had a star shape carved lengthwise out of its center. The space between the propellant and the outer casing was filled with an insulating seal. The star protected the outer casing from the high heat of the motor but had other important advantages. Because combustion was contained within the star, it kept the rate at which the fuel burned constant. The rocket was thrust into the air with a more powerful and consistent acceleration than ever before. But problems arose. The scientists' rudimentary fuel, the only one available, leaked into the seal, causing their rockets to deteriorate from the inside out. With no feasible solution, Pool and his team abandoned the burning star.

Although it was no longer practical, Pool could not let go of his brainchild, convinced it was the ideal design for rockets. He drew it from all angles, trying three-, eight-, ten-, and twelve-pointed stars. He believed the star would give the rocket a consistent burn, which could yield a steady thrust and lend the rocket exceptional power. But it was all numbers on a page. With the pressures of war on Great Britain, the government had no funds to experiment with the design. As World War II came to a close, Pool's ideas made their way to the United States. An appendix attached to a memorandum sent to JPL in late 1945 described the star shape and contained a few equations. Intrigued, the group at JPL began playing with the design in the late 1940s.

The computers and engineers worked

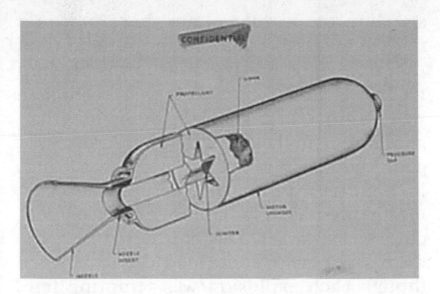

Rocket motor showing the internal star propellant
Courtesy NASA/JPL-Caltech

together to fix the technical problems. Not inhibited by the limited resources of wartime, the team found the solution casily. The difficulty seemed to be rooted in the leaky materials. To solve this they could simply bond the star propellant directly to the case and use a different propellant material not likely to be as troublesome. The designs, on paper at least, were flawless.

But once the numbers came off the page, things started to fall apart. The first time the Sergeant rocket engine exploded, the boom rumbled through the computer room, startling the women. Late that afternoon the engineers brought in the remnants of the full-scale motor, now only twisted tendrils of steel, for the women to see. There was no trace of a star left. Something had gone wrong in their calculations. And it kept going wrong. For twelve successive firings in 1950, the star split open and the rocket motor prematurely exploded, not coming close to its target. Despite the danger, the team stubbornly continued the tests, even though each explosion was tempting fate, opening the door to potential accidents.

The engineers and computers were closing in on a solution, however. Part of the problem lay with the star itself: its points were too sharp, causing the entire structure to crack under pressure. The women's calculations showed that by rounding the points of the star and using a thicker casing, they could make the rocket fly farther before it exploded. However, the overwhelming number of failures had made Louis Dunn, director of the lab, worry over safety. He shut down the project, much to everyone's disappointment.

The fate of the burning star was still uncertain when Marie Crowley started at JPL in 1951. She came to the lab after working briefly in the data reduction group at Aerojet. The company manufactured rockets and missiles and had also been founded by the Suicide Squad — Frank Malina, Jack Parsons, Ed Forman, along with Martin Summerfield, and their adviser, Theodore von Kármán — in 1942. Aerojet's connection with JPL meant it was straightforward for Marie to obtain an interview at the lab, which she hoped would be for a more interesting job. She liked the engineers she worked with but found data reduction dull. She was plugging numbers into equations blindly, with no view into the bigger picture of what the calculations meant. The days became an endless stretch of square roots, logarithms, and polynomials. She wanted something more.

Lost in the drudgery of everyday calculations was the beauty that first drew her to math. There was splendor in how numbers could describe nature so perfectly. The Fibonacci numbers, first introduced to Europe in 1202 by an Italian mathematician to describe the expanding nature of rabbit breeding, appear in every part of our world. The sequence of numbers — 1, 1, 2, 3, 5, 8, 13, 21, 34, 55, 89, 144 . . . — forms a pattern in which, after the first one, each successive number is the sum of the previous two. The power of this sequence is such that it is echoed in the number of petals in flowers: sunflowers have precisely 55, 89, or 144 petals. It defines the spiraling way leaves wind around a plant, the prickly scales of pinecones and pineapples, and the shape of seashells. The numbers are reflected in a starfish's five arms, the number of bones in our fingers, and even the way living cells divide.

Marie developed an appreciation for the Fibonacci sequence at Immaculate Heart College, in Los Angeles, where she had recently finished her double major in chemistry and mathematics. She was the first person in her family to graduate from college. Her father, hiding his pride, warned her, "You'd better make money." Like Depression-era babies everywhere, Marie above all wanted to find a good, steady job. But she was crushed when she learned there were no positions in chemistry available at JPL. The department already had three women, which the manager, a man, had determined was the ideal number. Unlike Macie, he saw the fairer sex as unstable employees, liable to leave as soon as they were enticed by marriage or children. Perhaps he was letting his personal life color his view of women in the workforce — both his mother and wife had stayed home to raise children

— despite the fact that the women in his department had been there for years and had no plans to leave.

Although Marie couldn't work in chemistry, there was an available computer position, and she decided to apply. She was nervous as Macie interviewed her. Macie was a small woman, and to Marie she looked like a mother-in-law, not a boss. One of the first questions surprised her: "Do you mind working with colored people?" No one had ever asked Marie that before. She answered, "No."

After she started work, she understood why Macie had asked her that unusual question. She would be sharing a large wooden desk with Janez Lawson. By this time, the computers had moved from their cramped, drafty quarters in Building 11 to the bright, new two-story Building 122. Wedged next to the engineers, the women were in an ideal spot for conversation between the groups. The computer room had large windows to let in the sunshine. Sometimes it was a little too sunny — there was no air-conditioning, and in the heat of the day, drops of sweat lined the computers' brows and moistened their palms as they scribbled away in their notebooks. By now, there was an abundance of Friden calculators, one for every desk, but only one of them was capable of square roots, so they still had to take turns on it.

In their shared space, Janez and Marie became close friends, working on projects together and spending time at each other's homes when the workday ended. Janez confided to Marie that she loved working with scientists. "Scientists are less prejudiced," she said. "They're caught up in all these things that the average person isn't even interested in." Marie laughed; she couldn't agree more.

Marie was impressed with Janez's proficiency in mathematics. It was obvious to her that Macie thought the world of her as well. Janez was one of only two computers whom JPL sent to the IBM training school. The training would come in handy with the arrival of its first computer not made of flesh and blood. The IBM 701 was the company's first commercial scientific computer, and they called it the defense calculator. While the term "computer" had been used to describe a person who computes since the 1600s, it had been used for machines as early as the late 1800s. Although still more often used for people, the word became increasingly common in describing electronic machines in the 1940s.

The IBM 701 was a delicate dance of tubes and memory. It was filled with tens of thousands of germanium diode tubes, each one roughly the size of a thumb, which acted similarly to lightbulbs, able to amplify electrical signals. The tubes routed the data, called binary digits, or "bits," from input to output. The computer also featured an advanced electronic memory system, using black magnetic tape as wide as a sheet of letter paper wound around reels. The technology of using magnetic tape to store audio recordings had been around since World War II. While appalled at the heinous consequences of the Nazi regime, American GIs couldn't help but admire the quality of their audio recordings. You could listen to a song in your bunk in the wee hours of the morning, and it sounded as if the orchestra were playing live to an audience, without the hissing pops and needle scratches that were part of the playback of 78 rpm records. Little did anyone expect how the technology would be modified.

IBM was one of the first to adapt it for computer memory instead of audio recordings. Just like its audio cousin, the Magnetophon, the IBM 701 used tape whose surface was coated with rust particles. The machine would write information onto the tape using magnets. The magnets created a current that in turn magnetized the rust particles. Each magnetized particle was a stored piece of data. Each reel of tape could hold two million digits, and the computer had four reels.

It took a room with the same square footage as most of the computers' houses to contain the IBM 701. It wasn't just one big box but eleven separate components that, together, weighed a whopping 20,516 pounds. Notwithstanding its size, the 701 moved IBM into the computer business. At first the company didn't think it would have many customers for the machine. At a stockholder meeting, IBM's president, Thomas Watson Jr., explained that they were expecting to sell only five of them, but "we came home with orders for eighteen." One of those orders was for JPL.

Despite a monthly rental price starting at $11,900, the 701 came with no instruction manual. To use the machine one had to learn an obscure numerical code. Even the simplest of operations, such as obtaining a square root, involved an incredible amount of programming. Even worse, the giant was prone to overheating. Although IBM boasted that the computer could perform sixteen thousand addition or subtraction operations a second, the system was constantly failing. A single burnt-out tube torpedoed the entire thing, making the computers and engineers suspect its accuracy and reliability. With her special training at IBM, Janez was one of the first to do any computer programming at JPL.

Marie was a newlywed, married to her collge sweetheart. Their life together was delayed when Paul was drafted to serve in the Korean War. Between his basic training and deployment, they saw little of each other. It was heartbreaking to be young and in love with a man who was never home. Marie felt lonely in the empty house; it seemed she was waiting for her life to begin. She escaped her feelings of isolation at work. While her husband fought the Cold War as a soldier in Korea, she was doing her part designing weapons at home.

Although she didn't carry a gun like her husband, her life was still sometimes at risk. When Marie was at Aerojet she heard a boom break the silence of a quiet Thursday afternoon, and the ground trembled underneath her feet. It was the loudest sound she had ever heard. She had become somewhat used to the explosions triggered by the large motor tests, but this was something different. As she looked around at the other computers and engineers she shared a workroom with, they heard shouting through the open windows.

Minutes later one of the engineers came into the room, his face covered in sweat. "There's been an accident," he explained. "It's the solid propellant." He looked around gravely at the roomful of employees. The engineer explained that they had been mixing the new solid propellant when it exploded. No one quite knew why. "Was anyone hurt?" Marie asked, but before he could get the words out, she saw the answer on his face. He nodded. The room fell silent again, and they could hear the faraway sound of an emergency vehicle on its way.

Eleven men were dead or dying in the test pits merely two hundred yards away from where Marie sat. She had become inured to the frequent explosions and even the minor injuries surrounding them. Death, however, shook her out of her complacency. These were her friends. Marie and the engineers she worked with considered the equations they'd calculated, agonizing over whether their math had killed their co-workers. The Cold War, and with it their army contracts, were creating pressure, driving them to hurry. The urgency weighed on them daily. Not long after their pencils left the page, their notebooks were run down to the test pits. Their work was rarely even double-checked. No safety precautions were in place, and there were no inspections.

Transferring to JPL, Marie found little to admire in the safety standards. They were equivalent to Aerojet's rushed approach. While there was little opportunity to check their work, at least at JPL there was a large group of computers all looking over one another's shoulders. Marie also found the work far more exciting. She felt she was finally in on the action, able to understand what her math was accomplishing and playing a key role in development. The hours, however, weren't any better. The computers often sat at their desks for twelve hours a day, five days a week. They were exhausted, yet they needed to be more vigilant than ever about their math.

The intensity of their work eroded their social lives outside the lab. Marie could feel her old friends slip away as she begged off dinner invitations and lunch dates. Conversely, within the gates of JPL their relationships were strengthening. The long days they spent together weren't enough — the women were constantly planning evening parties where they would chat about their lives and JPL. They met regularly, Marie holding a spaghetti dinner at her home, Virginia Swanson (Ginny to her friends), inviting everyone over for a cold-cut smorgasbord. Janez would put off her long drive home to Los Angeles and linger among her friends in Pasadena. One night in Marie's house in Alhambra they all gathered for a potluck. Barbara sat next to Patsy Nyeholt, the two of them chatting happily while Janez laughed with Ginny. Ginny and Marie held hands as they toasted the evening, all the girls raising a glass. Marie playfully brought a spoonful of food up to Ginny's mouth, and they both laughed as their friends took a picture of them looking silly. The computers couldn't seem to get enough of one another.

Most days the computers and engineers ate their lunch outside at long tables rather than in the cramped commissary. Sitting at a table, surrounded by her colleagues, Marie felt the warm sunshine on her back as she listened to the conversation around her. She let the mundane details of her daily computations slip away while her co-workers discussed their latest designs. Contemplating the big picture and discussing the limits of their rockets were her favorite parts of the day.

Although the lab was growing, it was still

small enough to have a family feel. The JPL staff trusted and depended on one another, not just with their work, but also, given the nature of their experiments, with their lives. Unfortunately, accidents at the lab were bringing them closer together. At her first accident, at Aerojet, Marie had been merely a witness; now she would be the cause.

Marie was working on the size of the nozzle opening for the Sergeant. It was a simple cylinder positioned at the exit of the rocket, but its size and shape were surprisingly critical. The nozzle accelerates the burning-hot exhaust as it leaves the shell. The faster the nozzle can get the exhaust to leave, the more thrust is generated to propel the missile upward. Marie was trying various nozzle sizes, calculating how fast they pumped the exhaust of nitric oxide and kerosene. She would open the nozzle wide in one calculation and then collapse it to almost nothing in the next. She wanted to try every combination she could.

But time was running out, and she needed to get the data to the engineers for the round of tests that afternoon. She ran the formula quickly and sent it over. Sitting at her desk, she was mulling over the equations in her head when her reverie was broken by the wail of a siren. The buzzing whine meant that the experiment was about to run. Deep in the gravel pits, they were about to fire the engine based on her calculations. Suddenly her blood ran cold. She had forgotten to take the square root before sending over the calculations. Panicked, she ran to the phone, dialing the number as she heard a big boom sound over the hill. The phone emitted nothing but dead silence; the lines were always cut in preparation for an imminent test. In her mind she could picture the disaster, a giant explosion, a fire, and even perhaps some of her colleagues killed. She put the receiver back in its cradle and waited anxiously. All was quiet.

Luckily, there was no death or dismemberment to haunt Marie. Instead an engineer appeared at the door looking slightly annoyed. "Well . . . ," he said, letting the word hang in the air. "I know," Marie replied. "I'm sorry." Despite the fact that her mistake had been the cause of an errant rocket engine, JPL called for no discipline or review. Instead Marie's punishment lay in the anguish she had felt in those moments of waiting. The memory of that crushing feeling would stay with her, reminding her that with the numbers and formulas she scribbled in her notebook, she had the power to affect the lives of her colleagues.

■ ■ ■ ■

The team had designed the Sergeant to be the pinnacle of technologically advanced missile systems. It was the culmination of JPL's expertise in rocketry and a beneficiary of what they had learned from their many mistakes. The rocket would be as big as the Nazis' V-2 but able to carry a warhead nine times as heavy and with a guidance system so sophisticated it could reach its target from eighty-four miles away. Unlike the Corporal, which took nine hours to ready for launch, the Sergeant needed only ninety minutes.

Marie was entranced by the instrumentation that would be incorporated in the Sergeant, which was truly cutting-edge. The focus in their group was widening from jet propulsion to electronics. The new director of JPL, William Pickering, was behind the changes. Unlike his predecessors, he wasn't a rocket man — his research interest was in electronics, and the Sergeant's command system was a technological leap. The Corporal missile had used a command guidance system, in which signals are sent from a ground station via radio waves to the missile. The system had drawbacks, namely problems with accuracy, the need for a large ground crew, and, more worrisome, its vulnerability. The enemy could detect the Corporal's radio signal and possibly jam it or even take it over.

To avert this, JPL was developing an inertial guidance system. This new system used accelerometers and gyroscopes placed within the missile to track its speed and position. The rotor spun while the gimbals swung around in varying directions. "It's like a spinning top," the engineers explained to Marie. The gyroscope seemed to defy gravity, at once spinning around an axis and stubbornly maintaining direction. The strength of its inertia gave the rocket stability. Large gyroscopes had found a place in rockets for years, but the new small ones powered by tiny electric motors were special. The ones JPL was testing in their rockets were covered in aluminum and steel and entwined in electrical wiring. The devices did not look particularly advanced, but within their casings was a delicate balance of movement.

The gyroscopes were not only graceful but also had the potential to significantly improve the accuracy of missiles. Mounted onto a stable platform along the main axis of the missile, a gyroscope maintained its position in space, fighting against the movement of the rocket. As the rocket gained speed and altitude, the gyroscope had to work harder. With cables connecting the gyroscope to the fins of the rocket, the more it resisted, the more strongly it shifted the fins back and forth, correcting the rocket's position.

Now JPL needed no external reference points from a ground station to control the rocket. The computers calculated the effects of Earth's gravitational force on the missile using the velocity and orientation data the new instruments offered. They played with hybrids of radio and inertial guidance. Labs all over the world were experimenting with gyroscopes to guide rockets, but no one had proved an all-inertial guidance system was possible. This made the army hesitant to approve JPL's designs. Before the U.S. government could fund such a radical new technique, JPL had to prove it was feasible. The computers were unsure whether they could ever get the new approach to look pretty, even on paper.

One morning one of the girls came into the computer room, giggling over a book she held pressed to her chest. Jean O'Neill's nephew had lent her the book excitedly, wondering how much of the fantastic story it contained was true. The cover showed a rocket flying to the moon, a robot falling from the stars. The book was *Moon Ahead,* by Leslie Greener, and Jean had read all of its 256 pages in two nights. Much of the science fiction in the book had made her laugh, but what surprised her were the technical descriptions of rockets blasting off into space, grappling with gravity and overcoming it thanks to a modern marvel: gyroscopes. As silly as the fantastical story was, there was a kernel of real science in its pages. The girls gathered around, laughing as Jean read passages aloud and admiring the illustrations of the rocket flying in space.

Americans were fascinated with rockets and space, although not to the extent of those working at JPL. Everywhere the computers went they saw rocket toys and outer space–themed Tupperware parties and heard radio programs featuring spacemen. Perhaps it was this national obsession that drew Janez Lawson to JPL's work on theoretical projects. Just as when she was an honor student in college, something about the "what-ifs" entranced her. She spent her days grappling with the most sophisticated missile system in the world, the Sergeant, while she spent her evenings planning her wedding.

Janez was marrying the love of her life: Theodore Bordeaux. Theodore wasn't from a well-to-do family and didn't have a professional job. He was a junior at Los Angeles State College, a far cry in prestige from Janez's alma mater, UCLA. But Janez didn't care; she thought he was brilliant. They shared an ardent love for math and for each other.

In contrast to the other girls, Janez didn't live in Pasadena; few African Americans resided in the conservative, predominantly white suburb. Although her social standing in Los Angeles was high, in Pasadena things were different. Her grandmother worked as a cook for Pasadena's prominent Jowitt family, so Janez knew all too well the importance of social hierarchy in the town. Peeking from the kitchen door as a child, she had witnessed the Jowitts' garden parties: ladies dressed in bold print A-line dresses with crisp collars, whispering about one another. By 1950 these same women were heating up school board meetings, strongly opposing desegregation and pushing out the school superintendent who promoted it. Despite the racism that surrounded them, the Jowitts adored Janez's grandmother. They bought her a house and a car and even sent her on vacations. It was in this house that Janez often spent the night, especially after working long days in the lab.

Most of the time, however, she commuted from her mother's home in Santa Monica. It was twenty miles down partially constructed freeways and roads twisting through the canyon. The horrendous traffic made the trek — often more than an hour each way — feel much farther. Her mother fretted over her driving that distance every day, even suggesting she find a job closer to home, but Janez wouldn't hear of it. She had found a special group of women to work with at JPL and knew this kind of professional position wouldn't be easy to find elsewhere. Still, she must have sometimes been lonely on that long drive. She was the only African American in the group, and her commute was symbolic of how much further she had come than many of her colleagues.

Sometimes during her drive she wondered what married life would be like. Fantasies about moving into a house all her own with her husband crept into her thoughts. She was twenty-four years old, an old maid in the eyes of many friends who had married straight out of college, and she was ready to settle down. She dreamed of becoming a mother and raising a family. She hated the idea of giving up her work, but how would Theodore react to her long commute? It worried her.

Their August wedding was an elaborate affair. The young couple said their vows in a church in Santa Monica before heading to their reception at the Wilfandel Club, the oldest African-American women's club in Los Angeles. Sandwiched between Janez's friends and family were her close friends from JPL. Marie Crowley's eyes filled with tears as she watched Janez walk down the aisle in a white lace gown with folds of tulle peeking out from the bottom of the skirt. The wedding party danced in the garden in the moonlight, the smell of orchids all around them. Pearl Bailey, the famous actress and singer, sang "Takes Two to Tango," and the dance floor filled with couples. As Marie watched the couple drive off for their honeymoon, she was happy for Janez, yet she wondered what would become of her now.

For most American women, marriage meant being a housewife, but many of the computers had found a way to reconcile the two, managing their home and work lives with the poise of a surfer riding a cresting wave. The working wives kept their balance the best they could, unafraid of sometimes getting wet. Janez was a rare talent; the computers couldn't imagine that such a brilliant woman would simply leave science behind. It would be a sad loss for the team.

As Janez's life was changing, the Sergeant project was coming to fruition. By 1956 the computers were completing their calculations at JPL and watching from afar as the missile underwent testing at White Sands. In contrast to the many accidents and delays of the Corporal, the Sergeant testing went relatively smoothly. Before they knew it, they were watching newsreels of the Sergeant flying over White Sands. It was the finest missile they had ever seen, and it would be the last weapon the girls would ever work on.

JPL's contributions to weaponry would only ever have limited success. Bureaucratic interruptions delayed the missiles from entering production, meaning that they became obsolete not long after they were operational. By the time the girls saw pictures of the Sergeant strapped to an army jeep in Korea, they had moved on, rarely giving thought to the missiles they once helped develop. Instead, they would find that their calculations were needed for a new kind of exploration.

The Miss Guided Missile contest was coming to a close. The music was slowing down, and the lights dimmed. Barbara smiled as she posed for pictures. She was second runner-up. She smiled brightly next to the winner, the pretty Lee Ploughe, the lab's nurse. Lee towered over her by nearly four inches, but Barbara's spirits were soaring. Few women would be as happy coming in third as Barbara. Being singled out in the contest made her feel like a vital part of the lab. The beauty title held a deeper meaning for her. Her responsibilities at work were increasing, and her popularity in the contest cemented her role among the computers, where she was functioning more and more as a supervisor. Barbara held one of a dwindling number of Miss Guided Missile titles. The beauty contests wouldn't end yet, but their name was about to change, reflecting a deeper transformation afoot.

Barbara and Macie were the first of the computers to have a hint as to where their calculations were about to take them. Sitting in the cafeteria one day was a man whose work had long inspired both admiration and repulsion in the lab. They knew that this man, a Nazi war criminal, was about to take them on the ride of their lives.

CHAPTER 5
HOLDING BACK

The inky-black night seemed to seep out of the sky and bleed into the ocean. Barbara Lewis stood overlooking the beach in Santa Monica, watching the dark waves crest and fall. The breeze was cool, causing little shivers to run up her back despite the warmth of the June night. Barbara's date, a man named Harry Paulson, gestured to the thin cotton wrap covering her shoulders and asked if she was cold. Barbara smiled and shook her head. The majestic coastline distracted her from the chilly air. Above, stars glimmered in the dusk while the surf and sand turned an indistinguishable gray in the dim light. She watched the beach stretch to the north, the lights of Malibu twinkling in the distance. "It's so different at night," Barbara remarked to Harry as his hand grazed her elbow.

She had met him at the Pasadena Presbyterian Church, and although she was shy about accepting dates, she found him irresistible. He was tall, not quite handsome, but with a kind face and a calm demeanor. He made her laugh, and when she spoke, Barbara could tell he was completely present, listening to her words eagerly. She turned her head to take in the Santa Monica Pier ahead of them and watched the flashing lights of the Ferris wheel paint the ocean pink and red. After dinner they had strolled downtown, wandering aimlessly along the paved sidewalks until they reached the eroding sandstone bluffs. Now Barbara stood between the two worlds, one heel planted firmly on concrete while the other sank into the soft, sandy earth of the weathered ocean cliff. Her work at JPL was similarly shifting: she was standing on the solid ground of missile development while her toes dipped into the world of space exploration. She could see where they were going as clearly as she could see the waves ahead.

The first sign that their dreams of space were nearing fruition came in the JPL lunchroom. Barbara sat with Macie Roberts and watched as a tall, handsome man with wavy brown hair and blue eyes took a seat in the crowded commissary. Wernher von Braun was a legend, a superstar, and a former Nazi war criminal. Despite his notoriety, Barbara couldn't help feeling sorry for him.

Amid the camaraderie and noise of the lunchroom, von Braun looked lonely eating his lunch. He was one of the world's preeminent rocket scientists. His articles and books on the intricate science of outer space, in which he imagined the first space station — complete with living quarters and a rocket-powered elevator — were so entertaining that Walt Disney used him as a consultant and later a star for his "Man in Space" films. As a photographer snapped his picture beside the creator of Mickey Mouse, it was hard to believe von Braun had once been America's enemy.

The computer girls passed back and forth a worn copy of *Collier's* magazine, a page dog-eared over von Braun's byline and the headline MAN WILL CONQUER SPACE SOON. Underlined was the sentence "Within the next 10 or 15 years, the earth will have a new companion in the skies, a man-made satellite that could be either the greatest force for peace ever devised, or one of the most terrible weapons of war — depending on who makes and controls it." They relished his words. It all sounded fantastic and improbable, and yet here they were working on the satellite. His enthusiasm perfectly matched their own.

Von Braun's fame, in a field where Barbara was just beginning her career, demanded admiration; however, seeing him in person made her uneasy. His unlined face brought her back to a moment in her adolescence when a voice on the radio had described London as a collapsed heap of wood, brick, and cement, brought to its knees by the world's first ballistic missile. While thousands of Londoners suffered shock, von Braun had sipped champagne. Yet a decade had changed so many things. The Vergeltungswaffe Zwei ("Vengeance Weapon Two") rocket, better known as the V-2, was now a mere plaything at JPL. The man behind that weapon was now casually eating lunch across from her.

Macie shuddered to remember the early whispers about von Braun. "He's bloodthirsty and arrogant," engineers told her when he was first captured and brought to the United States. "He's nothing but a murderer." But the whispers wouldn't last long. The former SS officer, with his affable, easy manner, was quick to make friends. He had a knack for discussing rocketry in all its complexity with the engineers in the offices after horsing around with the mechanics in the pits. He could explain the science so neatly that even a layperson could understand the basics. Despite his terrible past, he was becoming an integral part of America's future in space. Strikingly, the first U.S. Army collaboration culminating in a project not involving weaponry would rely heavily on Wernher von Braun.

Just as Macie knew his past, so she knew why he was at JPL: Project Orbiter. Ever since Macie had started at the lab, in 1949, plans for the first satellite had been in the works. They had long dreamed of shooting a spacecraft so high that it would reach a perfect balance between the tug of Earth's gravitational pull and its own inertia. With the forces equalized, the satellite could orbit Earth. Just as the moon carves a gravitational path around our planet, their satellite would need no external power to encircle the globe. The idea of a satellite ceaselessly orbiting Earth had been around since Isaac Newton's time. The power to achieve it, however, was new.

In 1947 William Pickering shared this idea in a paper in which he recommended that "extensive cosmic ray studies be deferred until a satellite rocket can be produced." Even then he had the project, both its scope and its ultimate scientific goal, clear in his mind. The U.S. government, however, wasn't interested in funding projects without a clear military purpose. The proposal languished until a symposium in 1954 at which Pickering, now JPL's director, strongly advocated for an earth satellite as the U.S. contribution to the International Geophysical Year.

Conceived of four years earlier at the suggestion of physicist Lloyd Berkner, the IGY would be a worldwide science project, the largest cooperative study of Earth ever conducted. Held from July 1957 through December 1958, the year would take advantage of the extraordinary solar activity predicted for that time period. Countries from around the globe would devise new ways to study Earth, including the use of cosmic rays, gravity, ionosphere physics, oceanography, and meteorology. JPL was abuzz with talk of the IGY. In the computer room they wondered excitedly what experiments were afoot.

"The International Geophysical Year is special because of solar cycle nineteen," an engineer explained to Barbara. "The sun will be intensely active. We'll see the greatest number of sunspots in recorded history."

As Barbara spread the news to the women, she saw that one of the new hires was staring at her blankly. She knew that one wouldn't last long. The problem was becoming common. As the need for more computers grew, they took more chances, hiring girls with limited experience in the hope that Macie's team could train them to become proficient in math and science. It didn't always pan out. Being a computer wasn't a job just anyone could do. Barbara and Macie found themselves lamenting when their applicants lacked competence in math or science.

When Macie first read Helen Chow's application, she was encouraged to see she had graduated from the University of Notre Dame with a minor in mathematics. This was exactly the kind of girl she wanted to hire. Meanwhile, Helen fretted that her degree wouldn't be enough to get her a spot at JPL. She was desperate for the job and hoped Macie would give her a chance. Even if math hadn't been her major, it was the subject she had always been best at.

Edwin dropped her off at the personnel department one morning before going on through the gates to his office. "Good luck," he called back over his shoulder. He wasn't worried. He knew his baby sister was smart and would almost certainly be hired. Helen didn't share his confidence. She had received many rejections, for jobs far simpler than this one. She filled out her application and then took a seat in the small waiting room, where she nervously tapped her fingers on her knees.

It was a long wait. By the time she was called into the interview room, she had worked herself into a froth of nervousness and could barely speak. Helen's first impression of Macie was of a strict old lady. Despite her cumbersome accent, Helen answered Macie's questions about her education and experience with math. She tried to remain calm as Macie inquired about her background and education. Recovering from her fit of anxiety, Helen explained that she had chosen art as her major, hoping it would lead to a career. She spoke of her math classes, on the other hand, the way some girls described going to the movies. They were pure entertainment for her; she never dreamed she would be able to get a job using those skills. It was exactly what Macie wanted to hear.

Helen next interviewed with Barbara. In some ways Barbara was the opposite of her supervisor. She was young, very friendly, and eager to welcome new women to the group. Although she wasn't officially the supervisor, Barbara trained the new girls and oversaw their progress. Her engaging personality won Helen over immediately. It felt as though they were destined to become fast friends.

Before Helen left the lab, Macie offered her the job, something she rarely did on the spot. She was so confident in Helen's skills that she wanted to get her started right away. Helen was stunned; she couldn't believe someone had finally taken a chance and hired her.

Barbara was somewhat fatigued with the new hires. They were bringing on an average of two women a month. Each new girl took an extraordinary effort to train, and the brunt of this work automatically fell on her. Still, she believed Helen would last instead of fizzling out on the job as so many had before her. JPL was in the middle of a race, and they needed as many competent computers as possible.

The IGY was a time to begin anew the scientific exchange between east and west, so long interrupted by war. With the death of Stalin, in 1953, the opportunity for worldwide cooperation was open. Yet the race to develop the first satellite brought intense competition instead of collaboration. America wanted to beat the Soviets badly. A secret race was also unfolding within America's borders. The army, navy, and air force were each preparing competing designs for satellites, and none of them knew what their rivals were proposing. A special government committee appointed by the Department of Defense would decide the winner.

The competition made everyone at JPL tense. To distract Barbara from the strain of her job, Harry took her on a date to the Hollywood Palladium, on Sunset Boulevard. Harry and Barbara joined the crowd on the enormous ten-thousand-square-foot dance floor. Despite the venue's size, the big band with its horns and drums had no trouble filling it with music. The floor was packed with couples, and there was barely room to dance, much less breathe.

Barbara felt overwhelmed. Her mother had just died of a heart attack, the same ailment that had taken her father's life, leaving her and her siblings without parents. It was hard for Barbara to accept that her mother, who had always been so strong, was gone. She was only fifty-seven years old. The anonymity of the ballroom was comforting, and Barbara lost herself in the music. Harry held her close as the band started up her favorite song, "It Had to Be You." She looked up. The twinkling bulbs on the ceiling looked like the stars. Her mind wandered back to space.

No rocket in existence packed enough punch to deliver a satellite into space. Project Orbiter was intent on changing this, and JPL engineers began to design the spacecraft they hoped to boost into the beyond. The computers and engineers worked together to develop the satellite's shell and antenna. It had to be sprightly enough to career into space but also strong enough to protect the delicate scientific equipment from the effects of the atmosphere and beyond.

Although the vacuum of space has no temperature, objects flying through it do. The range of these temperatures is formidable: over 120 degrees Celsius in the sun, and in the shade lower than minus 100 degrees Celsius. The challenge facing JPL was like that of designing a ship that could sail in both the freezing seas of Antarctica and boiling water. The engineers chose fiberglass for the shell and antennas and then played with the design as they attempted to find the perfect balance between strength and speed. The final satellite, the computers estimated, would weigh in at around five pounds.

As light as the satellite was, they needed enough thrust to fight the massive pull of Earth's gravity and then move through the atmosphere and into orbit. The gas molecules of the atmosphere collide with the skin of the rocket, slowing it down. A smooth, waxy skin on the rocket lessens this friction, just as it's easier to skate on smooth ice than bumpy. This atmospheric resistance requires a massive amount of energy to overcome. In fact, the energy cost to get from Earth to the moon is nothing compared with the cost of simply escaping Earth's atmosphere. Because of gravity and atmospheric drag, if you don't give a rocket enough thrust, it will simply be hurled back to the ground. From this perspective, the giant leap for mankind was in leaving Earth's atmosphere, not in a single step on the moon. There was only one way to accomplish this: multiple rockets set to fire in stages.

"Why do we need so many rockets?" Marie asked Barbara. "Why can't we just use one big rocket?" Listening to the conversation was Margaret Behrens, affectionately known as Margie. Margie was eighteen and had been at JPL only a month. A pretty girl with soft blond hair and shrewd eyes, she had been hired straight out of high school and was remarkably bright. Yet behind her sweet manner was a personality formed by growing up in her father's house. She bristled against authority, a consequence of struggling against his strictness. Macie, with her kind, motherly demeanor, acted as an antidote. Her fellow computers soothed Margie's insecurities and incited her curiosity. She didn't want to just crunch numbers; she wanted to understand what her calculations meant. In this case, they were solving the riddle of multistage rocketry.

"To get into orbit we have to launch a satellite at seventeen thousand five hundred miles per hour," explained Barbara. "That's five times as fast as the V-2. There's no rocket in existence that can go that fast. And even if we could build a rocket capable of going that fast, it would shake all the instruments until they were jelly." Marie laughed and nodded as Barbara continued. "So we make our rockets ride piggyback on each other. By doing a staged system we drop off the fuel tanks as we go. Once those fuel tanks run out of fuel they're nothing but dead weight, and if we get rid of them, that's less work for the upper-stage rockets to lift, so the satellite can fly higher." Marie and Margie nodded together, picturing the rockets giving each other a push. Instead of using one forceful rocket moving so fast that it would shake their instrumentation to its doom, they would employ a series of rockets capable of maintaining speed. The sequence of rockets was similar to the way the women at JPL helped each other out, the group steadily building momentum.

As part of the rocket sequence, the computers were working with small rockets known around the lab as Baby Sergeants. A scaled-down version of the larger Sergeant missile, they were only 4 feet long rather than 34 feet, and so slender that their diameter was a mere six inches. The small missile was like a toy to the women; it packed no military might. On its own it could do little but inform their calculations for bigger missiles, but the engineers and computers determined that if the Baby Sergeants were clustered together, they could pack a wallop. By lacing together fifteen Baby Sergeants, the computers calculated they could potentially produce 1,600 pounds of thrust for five seconds. This amount of power was perfect for the upper stages. But the sleek power of the Baby Sergeant, made at JPL, would also have to be combined with the massive strength of the Redstone rocket, made by von Braun's team at the Redstone Arsenal.

Originally a chemical weapons–manufacturing facility, producing such toxic products as mustard gas, the Redstone army post in Huntsville, Alabama, became home to von Braun and 126 other German scientists in 1950. They were sent there from Fort Bliss, Texas, the former base of operations for Operation Paperclip, the program that brought Nazi scientists to the United States after the war. Nestled in the Tennessee Valley, the lab was fertile soil for rocket research. By 1956, von Braun's contributions were appreciated, and he was made director of the development operations program at the new Army Ballistic Missile Agency at Redstone. With his new position he was ready for collaboration with JPL.

The Redstone rocket was the spitting image of von Braun's V-2 missile. It was massive — an impressive 70 feet high and 6 feet wide — and could produce 75,000 pounds of thrust. The computers and engineers called it the workhorse. It was just the rocket needed to give their satellite its first push into space.

The team readied its proposal for Project Orbiter as the excitement grew at JPL. The computers and engineers strolled around the lab with wide smiles on their faces. Barbara could feel them leaving the shackles of making war machines behind. JPL, although a military institute, had been built on dreams of space exploration. Now it was really happening. For von Braun too, the project represented freedom. For the first time, he was working for the greater scientific good. Together with his team in Alabama, JPL planned to launch four scientific satellites, the first one going up as early as September 1956.

But on August 9, 1955, their confidence was shattered. The U.S. Department of Defense Committee on Special Capabilities, making the decision in preparation for the IGY, had chosen the navy's satellite, Project Vanguard, over theirs. Project Vanguard had a few advantages over Orbiter. Orbiter was designed to do the scientific minimum powered by a dependable and tested rocket system. Vanguard, on the other hand, was more scientifically ambitious but was powered by the Viking rocket, still in development. Vanguard's proposal included a glittery bevy of scientific studies to be done from space once the satellite was up, including investigating ultraviolet light emitted in the vastness of space (such as that from young, hot stars); measuring the intensity of Earth's gravitational force; and studying cosmic rays, the highly charged particles from outer space that surround our planet. In response, JPL promised to match Vanguard's scientific prowess, but it was too late. Vanguard was the winner. Only their design would be funded, and the other projects would be scrapped.

There were bitter protests from JPL. In addition to the design differences, the computers knew that one of the reasons Orbiter hadn't been chosen was that the government wanted to preserve the focus of the army — whose ranks JPL belonged to — on missiles. With pressures from the Soviets mounting, there was strong feeling that the army should perfect nuclear warhead missiles before heading into satellite research. Moreover, rumors swirled that von Braun's involvement had hindered the proposal. Although he was a central figure in U.S. rocket research, his Nazi past still incited resentment in Eisenhower's administration. It was a blow. Around the lunch table, the computers and engineers lamented what fools the government bureaucrats were, yet there wasn't anything anyone could do. Project Orbiter was dead.

While everyone gloomily shuffled around the lab, Barbara was practically skipping. "How can you be happy at a time like this?" one of the computers asked her. "It's Harry," Barbara replied, smiling shyly.

Barbara's co-workers thought she was a lost cause when it came to relationships. She'd worked for JPL for almost a decade without any serious romantic involvement. She wouldn't date anyone at the lab, despite having been asked out numerous times. Because she spent all her time at work, she had little opportunity to meet anyone anywhere else, and any man she did date she scrutinized and found wanting. At twenty-seven, she was seen as an old maid by the younger computers. Now as she sat at her desk, on a day when she should be reeling from the Project Orbiter news, she felt nothing but the thrill of being in love.

When she first met Harry, Barbara was pessimistic. She had been unimpressed by the men she'd dated from church up until then. Her active mind made it unbearable for her to spend time with someone without her intelligence and passion. And Harry hardly seemed like the man she had been waiting for. He was nine years older, as evidenced by the silver dusting the edges of his chestnut-brown hair. True to her nature, she wasn't thinking of romance when he came up to her and introduced himself. Yet the longer they talked, the more she was intrigued. Like her, he didn't act self-conscious or timid. He talked with a natural ease, like a man who was well liked and comfortable with himself. He was funny, and she found herself laughing.

"How do you keep yourself busy?" he asked good-naturedly. He was expecting to hear her say she worked as a typist or a teacher and so couldn't help raising his eyebrows when she said, "I'm a computer at JPL." This was always a delicate point in her conversations with men. One of her past dates, a physician who liked to boast, couldn't understand her lack of ego when he learned what her job entailed. She described the work modestly, but her enthusiasm shone through. Much to her surprise, Harry seemed to find her work as fascinating as she did. He could see her eyes sparkling with excitement as she described her days spent hunched over a notebook, calculating the capabilities of rocket engines. The look in her eyes was a challenge to him. He wanted to make her eyes twinkle like that.

Barbara had never experienced the kind of romance Harry offered. He picked her up for their dates and whisked her away to candlelit dinners in swanky restaurants all over Los Angeles. Harry worked in insurance and had a knack for striking up a conversation. He talked with the same zeal

Barbara did, and they found dinner naturally leading to dancing and then to long conversations late at night as they held hands, savoring the last moments of their date.

One Saturday evening he picked Barbara up early to go dancing, remarking how pretty she looked. She wore a dress Harry loved; it was black knit with a large white collar and clung to the curves of her body. They set off, driving on the Arroyo Seco Parkway through the stark brown hills of Pasadena. As they crested a rise in the San Gabriel Mountains, Los Angeles was spread out before them, the late-afternoon sun bouncing off houses and buildings. The city looked small nestled between the mountains and the ocean. "Where are we going so early?" Barbara asked. "You'll find out" was Harry's reply, a sly smile on his face.

Harry was feeling an intense need to embrace life. He'd just finished a round of tests with his doctor and been declared healthy. Only a few months earlier he'd had a scare when his doctors had mentioned the possibility that he had cancer. Not only was the disease frightening, but in the 1950s, such a diagnosis carried the sting of shame, since some believed that sufferers were paying for their sins, that cancer was the consequence of an unclean life. When Harry learned that he wasn't sick after all, he wanted to celebrate. It was Barbara he turned to.

When they pulled into the Hollywood-Lockheed air terminal in Burbank, Barbara was shocked. Harry delighted in seeing her eyes pop as she begged him to tell her where they were going. He shook his head and laughed as Barbara squeezed his arm. "No time to explain," he said. "We have a plane to catch." They flew to San Diego and then caught a cab to the famous Hotel Del Coronado. "It's just like I told you," Harry said teasingly. "I'm taking you to a dance. We'll fly back home tonight."

Barbara was breathless at the sight of the imposing white hotel sitting at the ocean's edge. American flags beat against the breeze from atop red-tiled turrets. It was a hotel where celebrities such as Joan Crawford and Donna Reed could be found relaxing on the weekends. On some evenings, a yet-undiscovered Liberace played piano while Lucille Ball and Desi Arnaz practiced their comedy act. Just walking in the doors rendered Barbara starstruck.

She and Harry stood on the deck, her arm in the crook of his, her head on his shoulder as the sun set over the ocean. *This is what it's like to be in love,* she thought. But she wasn't ready to tell him. She wasn't even sure she wanted to be in love and get married. The idea of pledging herself to another was terrifying. It was enough for her to savor these moments, to be loved this intensely, even if it proved fleeting. She watched the gold disk of the sun drop languidly into the ocean and turned to dance with Harry in the gleaming ballroom.

Barbara's future was muddled. Just as she wasn't sure where she was headed in her relationship with Harry, she wasn't sure where her work at JPL was going. When the team had been working on Project Orbiter the goal was evident: developing the first satellite. Now, with the project rejected, their objective was no longer clear. They were still going to strap the Baby Sergeants onto von Braun's Redstone rocket, but it was now called the Jupiter rocket and funded as a ballistic-missile program.

Barbara might have been glad to know that, with the parts sitting on the shelf and the design in front of them, JPL wasn't planning to stop building a satellite. They were going to ignore the chain of command and go ahead with their plans. With their collaborators, von Braun and the Redstone team, they began testing nose cones. They cleverly stated that their goal was to find a nose cone that could survive the destructive effects of reentry into Earth's atmosphere. The problem was that when the surface of the nose cone falls through the flammable gases of the atmosphere during reentry, the friction between them causes heat, igniting the gases and engulfing the nose cone in flames. But to test the nose cone, they would have to build the whole rocket and send it out of the atmosphere. This was the real point. Under the guise of the Jupiter ballistic-missile project, they strapped the Baby Sergeants onto the Redstone rocket, exactly as they had planned to do in Project Orbiter.

The new design was known as Jupiter-C, and the computers soon began to calculate how best to structure it. The rocket would be divided into four stages. The first would be the Redstone rocket, sitting at the base. The next stage would be a spinning tub of eleven Baby Sergeants, followed by a second tub of three Baby Sergeants. Finally, the fourth stage would contain the payload, the forbidden satellite itself, strapped onto the top of the nose cone while a lone Baby Sergeant gave it a final nudge into space. The unauthorized fourth stage would be restricted to designs on paper; they wouldn't be allowed to actually load the satellite onto the rocket.

Small electric motors rotated the tubs and started them spinning even before takeoff. The spinning tubs gave the rockets stability and ensured that small differences in thrust between the individual Baby Sergeants would not cause problems. As the rocket launched, the spinning increased slowly to stabilize the rocket, which was otherwise prone to bending from the uneven thrust of the Baby Sergeants. Helen Chow knew this calculation had to be precise; if the spinning didn't perfectly match the Redstone's movement through space, the entire system would vibrate and fly apart, leaving only pieces. To prevent this she had the tubs spinning at 550 rpm before the launch and then, 70 seconds after liftoff, gradually increasing to 650 rpm. Finally, after 155 seconds, she calculated the speed could slowly increase again to 750 rpm, where it would remain until the missile reached the peak of its trajectory. She rechecked her math repeatedly until she felt sure the design was correct. With the numbers coming back from their ground tests, she was growing confident in the unusual scheme.

The engineers marveled at Helen's ability.

She worked quickly and accurately. Her knowledge of mathematics was exceptional, and if she had been a man applying for the job, she would likely have been hired as an engineer. This was true for many of the computers, whose education, frequently consisting of a bachelor of science degree, was identical to that of the young men being hired in engineering. Helen quickly became a favorite with the engineers, a go-to girl for problems that seemed impossible.

Meanwhile, Marie and the engineers at JPL were plotting a new tracking system, called Microlock, built on research from the early guidance systems of the Corporal. Scribbling away in her notebook, Marie was calculating how a phase-locked loop, where the output signal is in step with the incoming signal, might work. Similar to the principle of how a kitchen wall clock slowly loses time and needs to be adjusted every once in a while using a more accurate clock, Marie and the engineers estimated that by adjusting the equipment, housed in a twenty-five-foot-long trailer, they could detect very tiny signals as small as a milliwatt from three thousand miles away. This was critical, since the signal from the satellite would be sent using a radio frequency, the low power of which made it little more than a will-o'-the-wisp floating through the cosmos. The phase-locked loop took the signal from the satellite and the surrounding noise (the kitchen clock in the analogy above) and compared its frequency to an artificial reference without noise (the more accurate clock). The filtered signal would now be sensitive enough to detect the satellite moving even a few centimeters through the sky. Microlock was developing into the ideal way to keep track of the satellite, if they ever got a chance to launch one.

"Well, we might not know where Jupiter-C is heading, but I know where Margie is going tonight," Barbara teased mercilessly at the commissary one afternoon. Margie blushed and tried to deny her Friday-night plans, but the women wouldn't let up. "That's every weekend this month now," Ginny said, laughing at Margie's pink cheeks. The computers poked fun at Margie regularly about her budding romance with one of the engineers. They watched as the pair made awkward conversation around the lab, studiously avoiding eye contact. Everyone in the lab could see how serious they were getting. Margie was the youngest of their group, inexperienced in the ways of dating. Her youth and beauty meant that she was constantly underestimated. She was one of the brightest girls in the group and had seemingly limitless potential.

They all wanted her to go to college, and course catalogs found their way onto her desk frequently. While the computers liked to tease her, they watched with real concern as her relationship with the engineer developed. "She's too smart for him," Barbara said. "It'll be a mistake if she marries him. They simply won't last."

While the group fretted over Margie, Helen was surprised to find an old acquaintance had tracked her down, all the way from China. The last time she had seen Arthur Ling, he had been a carefree young man who flitted from major to major at Canton College until finally settling on a degree in history. Delayed by World War II, he took twice as long as Helen to graduate from college. Arthur was at a party after having finished school when he started up a conversation with a friend who worked in immigration. "Would you like to go to America?" he asked unexpectedly. Arthur thought his friend was joking and was surprised when he turned up with the visa paperwork the next day. Before he knew it, he was on his way to Los Angeles. He soon got in touch with Helen, but when they met again, their roles were reversed. He was no longer the big man on campus. He had slipped into obscurity while Helen's star shone brighter than ever. He was transfixed by her energy and smarts, and they started dating.

At JPL, Helen had little time to reflect on her new love interest. She was busy working on Jupiter-C. With the Microlock system equipped and the stages of the rocket design set, they were ready for their first test. The computers worked late the evening of September 19, 1956. The first launch of Jupiter-C would take place at 10:45 that night. Helen was uneasy. She couldn't eat a bite of food, and the coffee she'd had a few hours earlier was churning away in her stomach. But her mind was three thousand miles away on Launchpad 5 in Cape Canaveral, Florida.

The launch was secret, known only to the U.S. government. At the Pentagon, officials wrung their hands with worry. They weren't fooled by JPL's subversive attempts to mask Jupiter-C as a simple nose-cone experiment. It seemed the launch might be a ruse, that instead of watching a rocket fly and evaluating a nose cone, they might actually be witnessing the world's first satellite launch. With Cold War tensions swelling, Eisenhower feared political fallout if the U.S. Army launched the first satellite. Along with this concern was the need to keep the missiles the army was developing covert. It wouldn't do to have the top-secret rockets front and center at a launch.

The Pentagon needn't have worried. In fact, to prevent Jupiter-C from launching the world's first satellite, steps had been taken. The fourth and final stage of the rocket contained no fuel. The Baby Sergeant sat empty at its peak. Most important, there was no satellite strapped into the nose cone atop the launch vehicle. Instead, there were heavy sandbags inside.

On schedule, Jupiter-C Missile RS-27 was fired at 1:45 a.m. Eastern time on September 20. The rocket lifted off slowly, the support arm falling back while white smoke began to spread across the launchpad. The tubs of Sergeant missiles spun at the top of the rocket, creating a flash of black and white as they gained speed. A fiery blaze came straight down from the nozzle of the rocket as it lifted off. It was soon out of sight, but back in the control room in Pasadena, Helen was watching the numbers. They never got to see the launch itself, despite their desire to watch the rockets they helped build leave Earth in all their glory.

Thanks to the Microlock system, no image was necessary — they could track the rocket's path through space by numbers alone.

Her fingers flying across her notebook, Helen noted when the first-stage Redstone fell off and the second stage of eleven Baby Sergeants fired for six seconds before falling back to Earth. Then the third stage of three Baby Sergeants fired, sending the delicate instruments even farther up through the atmosphere. The third stage fell away, and the final stage, despite being filled with sand instead of a satellite, was speeding farther than any man-made object had ever gone. Helen's eyes popped when she calculated that it had achieved a Mach 18 velocity and climbed 3,335 miles into the air, setting a new record for altitude. With the numbers confirmed, JPL erupted in excitement, while in Alabama von Braun literally danced with joy. The launch was more successful than they had dreamed possible. Helen gleefully slipped into Chinese exclamations as both elation and weariness washed over her. They had done it, even though there was no satellite.

As the celebration died down, Helen sank into a chair. She was awash with feelings, happy at their success but frustrated with thoughts of what might have been. *If only there had been a satellite in the fourth stage instead of sandbags,* she thought, *we'd be celebrating the first man-made object in orbit.* There was no doubt in her mind, or anyone else's, that if they had gone ahead with their design and put a satellite at the helm and fuel in that final rocket, their creation would be circling the globe at this very moment. The sense of loss hit Helen hard while the lack of food and sleep preyed on her emotions. Her eyes filled with tears. She felt cheated. She took it personally. But there was still hope. *Now they'll have to give us a chance,* she thought.

CHAPTER 6
NINETY DAYS AND NINETY MINUTES

It was a cool, clear night in Washington, D.C., on October 4, 1957. Bill Pickering, JPL's director, was in town for a weeklong meeting of the International Geophysical Year participants. On Monday the Soviet delegate, Anatoly Blagonravov, had made a progress report. After he spoke, his English translator interpreted, "We're pretty close to launching a satellite." The man next to Pickering leaned over and whispered in his ear, "He didn't say that. In Russian, he said the launching was *imminent.*" Pickering nodded, unconcerned. Only a few months earlier, in June, President Eisenhower had made a similar statement when speaking of the American contribution to the IGY. Satellites were coming, but there was no telling when.

Now it was Friday night, and Pickering stepped into the eye-popping, gold-lined grand hall of the Soviet embassy. Gold veneer lined the railings of the winding staircase in wide strips, making the light bounce over the marble columns and crystal chandeliers. The cocktail party was packed with scientists, politicians, and journalists celebrating the end of the proceedings. Despite the warning he'd had on Monday, Pickering wasn't prepared for where the evening would take him.

It had been a challenging year at JPL. After the record-shattering test of Jupiter-C in September, they watched it stumble in May due to a guidance malfunction. The rocket flew an erratic arc before plunging into the ocean. When they recovered the payload, they found it ripped apart by sharks.

The third launch, on August 8, was flawless. Each stage uncoupled from the next with ease, sending the Jupiter-C higher. The rocket included fuel in the fourth stage, but at its helm was no satellite, only a sandbag. The supposed goal of the project, testing nose cones, was a success. The nose cone recovered after the launch was intact despite the extreme conditions of reentering the atmosphere. In calculating the effects of reentry, the computers had found their experience working on the Corporal project useful. Extreme heat and friction are capable of completely disintegrating objects entering our atmosphere. Even large rocks, such as meteors, turn a glowing red when they encounter the flammable gases that make all life on Earth possible. They become as hot as 3,000 degrees Fahrenheit before being burnt to a crisp. Roughly a hundred tons of meteor dust rain down on our planet's surface daily. Thanks to the atmosphere, it is just dust, not massive rocks.

To survive reentry, a new generation of nose cones had been designed. Instead of the sleek needles that reduced drag and helped ease rockets through the air after takeoff, these nose cones bulged obtrusively. Engineers across the country were finding that the thin models provided little protection from the extreme conditions while blunt shapes cushioned the nose cone in a thick shock wave of gas, sparing it from the atmosphere. First described in theory by H. Julian Allen at the Ames Research Center, in California, the successful nose cones might look clunky but were a key piece of technology in the ongoing space race.

Armed with a nose cone able to withstand the assaults of the atmosphere, the new rocket was rechristened Juno. JPL hoped that the new name, unencumbered by military association, would convince Washington of its potential in peaceful endeavors. They had clearly shown they had the capabilities to launch a satellite, so how could the brass say no?

Meanwhile, the navy's Project Vanguard was limping along. Because the design depended on rockets that weren't fully developed, each rocket of the multistage project was being launched separately. The first stage took off on a rainy night in December 1956. It was a success but paled in comparison to Juno, reaching only a third of its height. While Juno had three launches under its belt and an operational four-stage rocket, Vanguard had yet to test its second stage.

So it was a surprise to the computers when they learned Juno was being shut down. Helen Chow sighed as she got the notebooks ready for storage. Everything they needed to launch a satellite was written down on pages destined for a dark closet. It was heartbreaking to have their work boxed up when they had been so close. In response, the lab turned melancholy. Even the lunch table, usually a place of merriment, descended into crabby conversation.

Marie Crowley felt the change keenly. She'd left the computer lab the year before to join the chemistry department. Chemistry had always been where she wanted to be. Of the thirty-five people in the department, she was one of only three women. She enjoyed moving around the lab instead of sitting at a desk all day. She was comfortable among the chemicals and graduated cylinders, carefully setting up her experiments. One of her favorite parts was blowing glass. While laboratories bought some pieces of standard glassware, they needed to be able to make custom-designed pieces as well as repair the equipment they had. Every chemistry student learned the delicate art of bending and blowing glass. Marie held the glass over the Bunsen burner and watched the orange flames lap over the sides. Slowly, the solid glass turned loose while she spun it rapidly to form a cylinder before putting her lips up to the tube and blowing. In her hands the glass ballooned outward, forming a flask. There was beauty in watching the glass melt; it looked like water flowing in midair.

However, Marie missed the girls, and so at lunchtime she gravitated back toward her friends. At the outdoor tables, the computers' and engineers' conversations turned theoretical. They discussed satellites, space stations, and sending men into space. But now that Juno was shut down, they wondered if they would ever have a chance to launch a satellite.

Marie was testing liquid propellants that could be worn in tanks on a soldier's back. The idea was that the liquid might give bullets more zip than standard gunpowder could. It was a dangerous project, and Marie worried about designing explosive chemicals for a man to wear on his back. She was experimenting with nitric acid, which packed an explosive punch but was also highly corrosive. One day, while pouring the colorless liquid into a beaker, she suddenly felt a searing pain, as though the skin of her arm were ripping off. She looked down to see angry red streaks. She washed her arm immediately, crying not only from the pain but also from the knowledge that the scars would stay with her forever. She couldn't believe how foolish she'd been.

The accident unearthed new emotions. For the first time, Marie considered leaving science. While most of the time she loved working in the lab, she wanted a family. In the evenings, she and her husband giggled over names and dreamed of what a baby would bring into their lives. After years of Marie's working long hours while Paul fought abroad, he was home at last and they were finally ready. Marie couldn't wait to be a mother.

As excited as she was about getting pregnant, she worried about the chemicals she worked with on a daily basis — especially the radioactive ones. Could they harm an unborn child? She and her fellow chemists wore little to no protective gear, and there were few safety protocols to follow. Her accident with nitric acid showed her how dangerous the lab could be. Though it wasn't easy to leave a job she loved and colleagues who had become like family, Marie, filled with the anxieties of impending motherhood, reluctantly decided to quit.

Janez was leaving JPL as well. Like Marie, she was pregnant. In a time before maternity leave, she had few options. She had to quit. However, two kids later, she would find work in private industry as a chemical engineer at the Ramo-Wooldridge Corporation, in Los Angeles. JPL had given her the ideal experience needed to get a job in the aeronautical engineering section. As happy as she was to join the company, she'd miss her friends at JPL. She'd never belong to such a tight-knit group of female colleagues again.

Juno was also slipping away, but Pickering at JPL and Wernher von Braun at the Army Ballistic Missile Agency, in Alabama, wouldn't allow their plans for a satellite to be stalled. They believed that eventually the government would give them the thumbs-up to make a satellite. When that happened, they should at least have all the parts they needed. They kept everything in storage and continued to plead their case.

The stakes were about to get higher. Now, while socializing in the opulent USSR embassy on this October night in 1957, Pickering noticed Walter Sullivan, a science reporter for the *New York Times,* making his way through the crowd. Sullivan approached him and asked, "What have they said about the satellite? Radio Moscow says they have got a satellite in orbit." It was the first Pickering had heard about the satellite the world would soon know as Sputnik. He was stunned. As the news spread across the cocktail party, the vodka began flowing. Everyone toasted the success of the Soviet satellite. Overhead it was sending out a series of beeps, a song of triumph, as it passed over their heads every ninety-six minutes.

That night in Alabama, in response to Sputnik, von Braun pleaded with the new secretary of defense, Neil McElroy, fresh from his first tour of the Redstone Arsenal that afternoon. "Vanguard will never make it. We have the hardware on the shelf. For God's sake, turn us loose and let us do something," he implored him. "We can put up a satellite in sixty days, Mr. McElroy! Just give us a green light and sixty days." Von Braun's commander, Major General John Medaris, corrected him: "No, Wernher. Ninety days," he said. But McElroy wasn't moved. Instead he returned to Washington without committing himself.

Helen's heart dropped when she heard about Sputnik on the radio. It was maddening to think how easily they could have been first. Her thoughts turned toward the unsanctioned, top-secret satellite they had designed at JPL. It was currently hidden in a cabinet. An elongated cylinder, it was very different from the shiny, sphere-shaped Sputnik that was flying overhead. She was sure it would come out of hiding now.

To her surprise, the lab's satellite stayed where it was. Despite the anxiety Sputnik was inducing across the country, Eisenhower would not give JPL and von Braun the go-ahead. Although recognizing that the army could have launched a satellite the year before, the administration stubbornly clung to the idea that it should be kept separate from the army. Officials knew that if they were to launch satellites into space, they had to show that it was in the spirit of exploration, not military might. If they ignored this nuance, the politicians worried, the space race might turn into the space war.

They would wait for Project Vanguard. In Pasadena, the computers were beside themselves. Barbara Lewis seethed with irritation while everyone complained about the president. Chief among their frustrations was the fact that Sputnik wasn't scientifically savvy. The Soviet satellite did little besides measure temperature and atmospheric pressure. JPL could have easily launched something similar the previous year. Now it wasn't enough to match the Russians; the Americans had to show they were superior. With this in mind, JPL began calculations for Project Red Socks.

When Helen first learned of the plan, she thought it seemed utterly preposterous. The idea was to launch a rocket to the moon. They would beef up Juno, adding even more Baby Sergeants, and use the Microlock system to track the rocket. Barbara laughed when she saw the list of objectives: "1. Get pictures, 2. Refine space guidance techniques, 3. Impress the world." Fervently, the computers began calculating trajectories to the moon, but it felt more like a game of make-believe than actual work. It was hard to believe that after rejecting their sensible satellite proposal, the government would approve this fantastic journey. Sure enough, Project Red Socks didn't make it far. The Department of Defense, awash in fantastic proposals following Sputnik, couldn't take the nine rocket flights to the moon seriously. However, the computers didn't toss out their calculations. Instead they filed them away, hopeful they might prove useful in the future.

While the computers were plotting fanciful journeys, the Soviets launched Sputnik 2. The second Soviet satellite was more technologically advanced, equipped with Geiger counters and spectrometers to measure solar radiation and cosmic rays. More impressive, it carried the first living creature to be launched into space: an eleven-pound dog named Laika. Huddled together, several JPL engineers and computers stood outside the lab one evening and looked up into the night. The satellite looked like a floating star, zooming across the sky. They felt pangs of envy but at the same time marveled that the feat of engineering over their heads was real. Their calculations had taught them that it was an accomplishment not to be taken lightly, especially with an animal traveling inside — even though little Laika had passed away only hours after the launch. While the Soviets boasted of the health of their "four-legged astronaut," the dead dog, who had sadly succumbed to overheating, passed over their heads every 103 minutes.

In the five months since Eisenhower announced the United States would be launching a satellite soon, the Soviets had launched two. Americans couldn't be sure the Sputniks weren't some sort of weapon or spy machine. With their mysterious beeping, detectable by amateur ham-radio enthusiasts, and relentless passage across the sky, they brought feelings of uncertainty and fear. The American dominance established by atomic and hydrogen bombs had been supplanted by two swift metal spheres in space. Eisenhower's calm demeanor in the wake of defeat sparked anger. John F. Kennedy, then the Democratic senator from Massachusetts, accused the president of "complacent miscalculations, penny-pinching, budget cutbacks, incredibly confused mismanagement, and wasteful rivalries and jealousies." In the eyes of his critics, Ike had unforgivably let the Soviets win.

One month after Sputnik 2 blasted off, it was Project Vanguard's turn to launch a satellite. The television cameras were ready, broadcasting the event live to a nation eager to regain its reputation in science and engineering. "There's ignition. We can see the flames. Vanguard's engine is lit and it's burning," said Jay Barbree, reporting live on the radio on December 6, 1957. "But wait, wait a moment, there's, there's no liftoff! It appears to be crumbling in its own fire. It's burning on the pad! Vanguard has crumbled into flames. It failed, ladies and gentlemen. Vanguard has failed."

Those watching at home could clearly see that the rocket had lifted a few feet into the air before violently tipping over and crashing back down. Before it could even hit the ground it was engulfed in massive orange and red flames. The fuel tanks ruptured, causing explosions that rocked the launch-pad at Cape Canaveral. The clouds of fire and smoke grew bigger, overtaking the platform. Although likely caused by a fuel leak, the rocket's dramatic downfall would never be completely explained.

The headlines screamed FLOPSNIK, OOPS-NIK, KAPUTNIK, and STAYPUTNIK. The Soviets tendered their sympathies and, with a supercilious air, offered their technical assistance. The New York Stock Exchange shut down. Luckily, JPL was already hard at work.

A month earlier, amid intense pressure, the Eisenhower administration finally gave Pickering and von Braun the green light. Politicians were swiftly changing their minds about the laboratory, with Donald Quarles, deputy secretary of defense, testifying before the Senate Armed Services Preparedness Subcommittee in November that, in retrospect, the army should have been given the task of developing the satellite from the beginning. Rumblings of the need for a separate space agency began to echo through the halls of Congress.

As news of the authorization to pursue a satellite reached them, the computers jumped up and down with excitement. They got their notebooks out of locked drawers as the engineers opened up the cabinet concealing the forbidden shell they had secretly worked on. Everyone knew long days were ahead if they were going to get this satellite launched quickly. Luckily, thanks to Jupiter-C, much of the work was already done.

They called it Project Deal. The strategy was essentially unchanged from the rejected Project Orbiter, with modifications learned from Jupiter-C. The rocket would launch the satellite using a four-stage design. JPL's satellite skin would house instrumentation

213

developed by astrophysicist James Van Allen at the University of Iowa. Hedging his bets, Van Allen had cleverly made his equipment adaptable to either Project Vanguard or Orbiter.

The women spent their days and nights checking and rechecking trajectories while calculating the effects of temperature, speed, and pressure on the instrumentation. They worked with nervous energy, equal parts excited and anxious. They knew the stakes were high. There was no room for failure. Their home lives had to take a backseat as the work intensified and the January 29 launch date approached.

One day, Barbara came to work early, settling in at her desk. Ginny Anderson, formerly Swanson, looked her up and down, smiling. "What is it?" Barbara asked, running her fingers through her hair. She'd gotten ready in a rush, in the dark of the early-morning hours. Lately, she barely thought about what she wore day to day, instead just grabbing from the closet whatever clean dress was closest. "Look at your shoes," Ginny said. Barbara looked down. She was wearing one blue shoe and one black one. They both burst out laughing. Barbara spent the rest of the day pointing out her mismatched shoes to anyone who needed a laugh.

The big day finally arrived. But despite a clear January sky, the launch date was scrubbed, since winds were whipping around Cape Canaveral at 180 miles per hour. The next night the mission was canceled just an hour before the 10:30 p.m. launch time; the winds still hadn't died down. The engineers and computers were exasperated by the delay. After more than a year, waiting two more days seemed torturous.

In the midst of all this anticipation, Sue Finley entered the gates of JPL for the first time, on January 30. She didn't know what to make of the excitement in the lab. Everyone was running around busily. No one had time to talk to her, much less get her training started. Sue didn't care. She was still reeling from her loss. It had been only a year since she had lost her newborn son, and the experience had changed her in essential ways. She'd gone from wanting a career to desiring nothing but a baby. The idea of becoming a mother constantly occupied her thoughts. She wasn't sure she'd last long at this job at JPL; it was simply something to take her mind off her pain while she waited to get pregnant again. As she watched the computers whirl around the room, the sound of Friden calculators clicking furiously, she wondered if she could ever care about a job as much as they did.

On Friday, January 31, 1958, the wind died down. Barbara and Margie Behrens knew they were in for a long night. The night Sputnik had flown overhead, von Braun and Medaris had begged the secretary of defense to give them the OK to launch their own satellite, saying that it would take only ninety days. They were coming in right under the wire. It was just eighty-four days since Washington had authorized the mission. Tonight, full of anticipation, Barbara and Margie entered the "dark room," the mission control center built into the Pasadena foothills. Their eyes slowly adjusted to the dim light, which ensured that, as in a car at night, the backlit instrumentation could be seen clearly.

Their nerves remained on edge as they waited for the launch to begin. Margie played chess with Sol Galom, one of the engineers. He was a serious chess player, even penning a chess column for the *Los Angeles Times.* The two played calmly, as if they didn't have a care in the world. Barbara, meanwhile, was getting things ready. She set up her notebooks at the light table

216

and lined up mechanical pencils beside them. She took out graph paper, useful for measuring in both millimeters and inches, and chatted with another computer, Nancy Evans. They spoke casually but kept their eyes on the clock. As Barbara waited, she thought about Harry. She had seen him only a few hours earlier, when he told her how much he missed her and stole a kiss before leaving her to her work. They were supposed to have a date but, of course, Barbara was needed at JPL. Harry was beginning to realize what married life with her might be like.

No cameras were allowed near Launchpad 26A. The media wasn't informed that a second U.S. satellite attempt was scheduled, in case something went terribly wrong again. At 10:48 p.m. at Cape Canaveral, ignition started and the rocket fired. Once it was out of sight, Richard Hirsch, a member of the National Security Council, formally named the satellite Explorer. At the Pentagon, von Braun turned to Pickering and said, "It's yours now." The rocket was out of their hands, and they could only hope it would be a success. Success or failure would be ascertained by those at JPL. Back in Pasadena, data began to come across the Teletype. Barbara started her calculations, her pencil moving furiously across the paper.

Sitting at the light table, she could sense three very intimidating men towering over her: Richard Feynman, the famed physicist, now at Caltech; Feynman's former PhD student Al Hibbs, now director of Space Science at JPL; and Lee DuBridge, the president of Caltech. Feynman stood behind her and peeked over her shoulder as she calculated the satellite's velocity leaving Earth. He was unnaturally calm, a departure from his usually jumpy behavior.

The calculations thus far looked promising. The satellite was moving with the right speed to overcome Earth's gravitational pull and at the right angle to enter orbit. Yet they all knew that the real test would come after Explorer had made its first orbit around Earth and they could detect the signal again in California. If it wasn't moving with enough speed or in the right direction, the whole thing would come crashing back to Earth. They expected the wait to be about ninety minutes. On both coasts and in Alabama, men and women were quiet as they waited in the shadowy light of control rooms.

Notably absent from the JPL control room was their director, Bill Pickering. He, von

Braun, and Van Allen had all been shuttled off to Washington, much against their wishes. The government wanted to avoid the media disaster of Vanguard, but if the mission should prove to be a success, they wanted to have the three principal players available right away for a press conference. The men waited at the Pentagon for word, Pickering with an open phone line to JPL.

As they waited, General Medaris, the commander at Cape Canaveral, sent a message to JPL:

GEN MEDARIS SAID HAVE A CUP OF COFFEE — SMOKE A CIGARETT SWEAT IT OUT WITH US

The group took his advice literally, and the mission control room started to fill up with smoke as they waited with nervous energy. Barbara was not a smoker and was too nervous to drink any coffee. In response, JPL sent back a joking message characteristic of their laid-back California attitude:

WE ARE BEING NONCHALANT AND LIGHTING UP A MARAJUANA HA [sic]

The mood was anything but nonchalant. By 12:41 a.m. on the East Coast, Pickering had given up hope. They should have heard from the satellite by now. Obviously, the mission had failed. The trio at the Pentagon were despondent. Their wild claims of being able to put up a satellite in ninety days now seemed like a lot of nonsense.

Barbara, however, was holding on. She was tracking the satellite's movement by its shift in Doppler frequency. As Explorer flew through the air and into space, it sent electromagnetic waves back to a receiver on Earth. Similar to the way an ambulance's siren starts with a droning whine as it approaches an observer, reaches its full intensity as it loudly passes, and then changes in tone as it drives on by, the waves coming from the satellite changed in frequency depending on its relative velocity from Earth — diminishing the farther away it flew. By plotting the frequency of the waves against time, Barbara could chart the satellite's curving path into the heavens.

As the minutes passed, the quiet dissolved into rumbling and outbursts, the stress of the moment wearing on all of them. But finally the signal they had been waiting for came through. Barbara confirmed the position, repeating her calculations on paper several times before twisting around in her seat and saying, "She made it!" Behind her, the room erupted in cheers.

An engineer relayed the happy news to Pickering by phone at 12:49 a.m. Relief washed over him — the eight minutes they had been waiting to detect the satellite's signal had been the longest of his life. As he whooped with joy, von Braun remarked, "She is eight minutes late." At the Pentagon they called Eisenhower, who, away on a golfing trip, had been asleep. He responded with "Let's not make too much of a hullabaloo." It was too late for that; the celebration was already under way.

At 2 a.m. journalists were led into the great hall at the National Academy of Sciences, where von Braun, Pickering, and Van Allen awaited them. After making the startling announcement to the room that America had put its first satellite into space, the three of them held aloft a model of Explorer, wide smiles on their faces. At the same time, in Pasadena, Barbara leaned back in her chair. She was too exhausted to move. Her decade of work at JPL had culminated in a success so sweet she could do little but gleefully drink in the moment.

Margie, on the other hand, while delighting in the accomplishment, was still too young and new at the job to appreciate the magnitude of their history-making night. Yet the launch of Explorer 1 would shape her life in profound ways she couldn't yet imagine. Her life, both personally and professionally, was about to take off.

On Monday, Barbara and Margie could hear the cheering and applause before they even walked into the cafeteria. Everyone at JPL was celebrating. Spaceman costumes had been pieced together from lab equipment and a sign read MADE AT JPL BY HARD-BOILED EGGHEADS AND COFFEE-BREAKERS. Barbara laughed. The computers ate cake and enjoyed the celebration. Sue felt slightly uncomfortable to be celebrating when she had just started at the lab. At the same time, she was proud of her new workplace. Explorer's success belonged to America, and JPL, largely unknown to the public, was suddenly thrust into the spotlight.

A few days later, on February 5, the Vanguard rocket made another attempt. The computers were eager to see whether the navy-sponsored project would succeed with its second satellite. With the success of Explorer 1 they no longer felt the sting of competition. Vanguard rose high in the air before streaking back down to Earth. It had failed again.

Meanwhile, the engineers and computers at JPL were hoping to repeat their success as they readied themselves for the launch of Explorer 2. On March 5, they watched as the rocket blasted off. Each stage dropped off as expected until the fourth, a single Baby Sergeant, which didn't fire. Instead of going into orbit, the satellite crashed. It was a reminder of how fragile this all was, that there was nothing routine about a launch.

Twelve days later, on March 17, Vanguard finally succeeded at launching a satellite. But the computers didn't have much time to ruminate on the navy's success. Explorer 3 was due to lift off just nine days later. Their lives had become a whirlwind of calculations, trajectories, and late-night launches. In the midst of this craziness, Helen was trying to plan her wedding. Arthur had gotten a job at Bank of America in Pasadena and, with his new financial stability, wanted Helen to join her life with his. The girls were abuzz about the nuptials. In between calculating trajectories they chatted about lace trim, veil length, flowers, and receptions.

The wedding was coming at a busy time but also on the heels of a celebratory year. JPL had made the jump from developing weapons to taking America's first steps into space exploration. In fact, they were already starting to see scientific gains from Explorer.

The cosmic ray counter designed by Van Allen's group in Iowa had detected radiation belts surrounding Earth. While their existence had been postulated, Explorer gave proof that layers of charged particles wrapped around the planet like a blanket. With each additional Explorer satellite launched into space they would map out this radiation, seeing how far it stretched and with what intensity.

But the computers weren't content to work only on satellites. Already, at least on paper, the race to the moon had begun. The women dusted off the calculations they had made for the spurned Project Red Socks. Where once the U.S. government had been quick to reject any of JPL's projects concerning outer space, now, after Explorer's success, the lab had free rein. The confidence spilled into the computer room, where the women were enthusiastic about their new calculations. Helen laughed when she saw one of the girls using her manicured fingernails to draw the curve of a new spacecraft's trajectory. "You're plotting the path to the moon on your fingers," she teased.

Fingernails were a poor substitute for a set of French curves. These were wooden templates cut into elegant swirl shapes that almost resembled art nouveau. Instead of following a circular arc, the templates followed Euler's spiral. This shape, explored by Leonhard Euler in 1744, curves more the farther the line moves away from its origin. It's a perfect transitional curve for a moving object, because when the line is followed, the object's acceleration doesn't jump but increases steadily. For instance, the spiral is useful in calculating railroad curves that protect passengers from the lurching discomfort of an abrupt turn. Each swirl was a little different in length and slope and allowed the computers to connect any of their data points in a smooth curve that described a rocket's trajectory.

Helen owned a complete set of French curves that the women loved and would borrow whenever they could. She didn't start calculating a trajectory with the French curves, though; she began by getting her special 4H mechanical pencils and graph paper. First she'd calculate two rows of numbers: how far the rocket would fly, and how high. This was the hard part, taking hours as she filled up pages in her notebook. Then she'd get out her log graph paper and plot the data. Occasionally, the yellow carbon paper would peek out from under the graph paper, and Helen had to straighten it. Before electronic copiers, carbon paper was the only way she could make duplicates of her work. Hunched over her notebook, she'd look at the first row of numbers. When the rocket reached 5,000 feet across the ground, it would be 7,600 feet high in the air. All that information became a single dot on her graph paper. She'd fill the paper, data points rising higher, just as the rocket might someday climb. The finishing touch was made by taking her set of French curves and connecting the dots.

Helen was easily the fastest computer in the group. In the afternoons the women frequently held computing races. Two or more of them got ready at their desks while the rest of the room looked on. They started with the same equations and were equipped with identical Friden calculators. One of the women would shout, "Go!" and suddenly the room would fill with the clamor of the calculators, the din intensifying as fingers flew over the numbered keys. As the computers rushed to calculate square roots, the mechanical calculators started shaking. Soon the whole room was vibrating. The women yelled encouragement to their colleagues, spurring them to work even faster. Just when it seemed the room couldn't possibly get any rowdier, Helen would raise her hand and yell, "Done!" She'd won again. The women clapped and laughed. They didn't know why they even tried; Helen was unbeatable.

One evening after work, Margie gave Sue a ride. Instead of driving down to their homes in Pasadena, they turned right off the main road and headed into the hills overlooking the lab. They wanted to see how far the road went. They drove up the length of the canyon road, Margie's car barely making it up the steep incline in some places. There wasn't much up there. The dry, brown hills were littered with scrubby bushes, not a flower to be seen. They got out of the car and rambled among the rocks in the fading afternoon light as the sun bounced off the windows of the lab beneath them. JPL looked tiny among the hills; it was hard to believe that so much excitement was contained within the small scattering of buildings. As they reached the crest of the canyon, Sue pointed out the moon, glowing an ethereal white against the darkening sky. It looked fragile, its brightness diluted by daylight. Still, its glow was like a beacon, challenging them to come closer, to uncover its mysteries. Sue and Margie were ready to accept the challenge.

CHAPTER 7
MOONGLOW

Macie and Barbara stood together and threw rice as Helen walked out of the church with her brand-new husband. They swooned over the dress that perfectly hugged Helen's figure, with sleeves to the elbows, the bodice tucking in at the waist, and a beautiful lace train flowing behind her. Helen smiled brightly. At the reception, held at the Los Angeles Hilton, Helen and Arthur gazed at each other as they slow-danced across the ballroom. When the band started playing "Moonglow," from the popular movie *Picnic,* the dance floor filled with men in crisp suits and women swaying in full tulle skirts. Barbara rested her head on Harry's shoulder as candles flickered at the tables and the singer crooned. Everyone was falling in love, not just with each other, but with the moon above.

While Helen was getting married, America's space program was also making it official. On July 29, 1958, President Eisenhower signed the National Aeronautics and Space Act into law. Its goal was "to provide for research into problems of flight within and outside Earth's atmosphere, and for other purposes" and gave Eisenhower four years in which to transfer existing agencies into the new administration. Pickering's dreams for JPL, the hope of becoming a center for space exploration rather than weapons development, were inching closer. With the National Aeronautics and Space Administration established, JPL was aching to begin planetary missions. They were already anticipating how the new administration, by bringing together disparate research groups, would fundamentally change aeronautics research.

Around the lunch table, the computers and engineers talked of little else. Now that they finally had the go-ahead to leave Earth, they weren't content with plotting mere lunar missions. Before the ink establishing NASA was dry, JPL began proposing explorations into deep space. Mars and Venus fascinated in a way that the moon couldn't. After all, telescopes had been trained on the lunar surface for more than three hundred years. The planets, on the other hand, seemed temptingly close, possibly within reach of JPL's rockets. And who knew what might be on them? They might even discover alien life.

It wasn't just at JPL that dreamers were envisioning flights to nearby planets. Mars and Venus held a powerful sway over American imaginations in the 1950s. As our next-door neighbors in the solar system, the two planets had the best chance of supporting life. Scientists knew that the outer planets (Jupiter, Saturn, Uranus, Neptune, and Pluto) were too cold and their atmospheres likely too extreme to support life, while little Mercury, being closest to the sun, was far too hot. Astronomers were looking for a Goldilocks planet like our own, neither too hot nor too cold.

A 1957 Disney movie titled "Mars and Beyond" described this idyllic temperate region: "In this golden zone are the orbits of Venus, Earth, and Mars. There may be life on Venus but we know very little about our sister planet, for her mysteries lie shrouded behind an impenetrable mantle of dense clouds. Beyond the earth, at the outer fringe of life's temperature zone, is Mars, the third planet in our solar system where life could exist." With only telescopes pointing to the planets, it was easy to imagine life lurking next door.

But while some at JPL were ready to move away from rockets, the lab's bread and butter for two decades, and begin designing spacecraft, others felt that the idea of sending probes to Mars and Venus before they had even made it to the moon was a little crazy.

Harry thought Barbara was a little crazy too. It wasn't just her unusual job. "There's got to be something wrong with you," he contended. "You're young, charming, and still not married." At his insistence Barbara started seeing a therapist. Harry would pick her up after each session and take her for coffee. Although she loved Harry dearly, she'd made it clear to him she wasn't quite ready to get married yet.

With the advent of NASA, the competition within America's borders for its dollars was fierce: the military research labs were all jockeying for position and projects. When the air force failed to deliver on two lunar missions, NASA management handed the project over to JPL.

America was desperate to beat the USSR in space exploration. To aid in that goal, JPL began work on the air force's failure, a satellite named Pioneer that would scout the moon. This satellite had been named Pioneer by the air force, although the

231

women referred to it simply as the moon probe. The design was very similar to the audacious Project Red Socks. The engineers and computers swapped out the Redstone rocket designed by von Braun's group for a new Jupiter missile. The newly developed ballistic missile was capable of 150,000 pounds of thrust, about double that of the Redstone. They would need the extra push if they were going to travel 236,000 miles from Earth.

Atop the Jupiter missile the design was essentially unchanged from Explorer. They would use the same spinning tubs of Baby Sergeants, with the spacecraft nestled on the fourth stage. The computers carefully plotted the course of the satellite, determining with precision the necessary timing and velocity to launch Pioneer into orbit. Their head start from Project Red Socks meant that they completed their calculations in record time. Now they could sit back and admire the design. The nose cone was painted in broad black and white stripes that prompted the women to gaily call it the merry-go-round. It perfectly matched the tubs of spinning rockets below it. They watched as crews of mechanics built the spacecraft. What started as shiny sheets of metal slowly grew into a full-fledged probe.

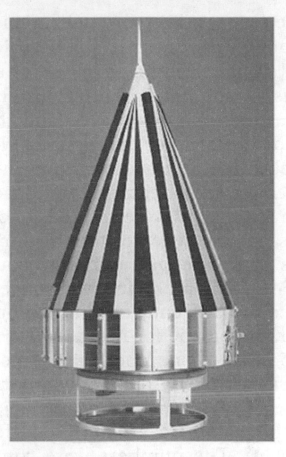

The cone-shaped probe of Pioneer
Courtesy NASA/JPL-Caltech

By December they were ready to give the merry-go-round a go. Pioneer 3 (after 1 and 2 had been air force failures) was set to launch on December 6, 1958. That night Sue's husband, Pete, worried about her. He couldn't understand why she was always working such long hours, and now it looked like she would be there all night. Sue walked into the tiny control room with trepidation. The room was cluttered with tables and seemed oppressively small. She was already nervous — she hated waiting around and just wanted to get started — and then, as she readied herself for the imminent launch, Al Hibbs took a place standing over her shoulder. As the director of the Space Science division at JPL, he wanted to know as soon as possible whether the mission was a success or failure, and only Sue could tell him. Poor Bill Pickering was once again secluded at the Pentagon and counting on an open phone line for news.

As soon as the numbers came racing in, all of Sue's anxiety melted away. Once she was at a desk doing her work, a job she knew she was good at, she could feel the tension lift. The numbers were coming in fast, and Sue's pencil was racing across her paper, barely able to keep up with the data. There was no time for her to break out the Friden; she had to do it all by hand. By calculating the rocket's speed and direction, she was determining its escape velocity. She knew that, whether launching a missile or a marshmallow, you have to reach 11.3 kilometers per second (or about 25,000 miles per hour) to escape Earth's gravitational pull. It was the middle of the night, and Sue was desperately trying to determine if Pioneer 3 would reach this magical number.

In addition to computers made of skin and bones, a new processor had arrived at JPL. IBMs had, so far at least, not fared well in the lab. The engineers and computers preferred to do their calculations by hand, not relying on the massive machines, which had too many glitches to be trustworthy.

The IBM 704, the latest of its kind, had arrived at JPL just in time for Pioneer 3. To differentiate it from its human counterparts they simply called it the IBM. It was huge, weighing over thirty thousand pounds and needing a specially constructed room of its own. At a cost of $2 million, it wasn't cheap either.

Sue found the behemoth the computers were in charge of very sophisticated. Using a keypuncher, they wrote simple programs on punch cards that they would feed into their digital counterpart. The new machine was more powerful than the IBM 701. Instead of cathode ray tubes it used magnetic core memory, which was faster and more reliable. It employed floating-point hardware, allowing for more complex math than its predecessor. Not that they used it much. None of the engineers trusted the

IBM, which was constantly in need of repair. Unfortunately it shared the same vacuum-logic circuitry as the 701. Because of this, the machine generated an enormous amount of heat, causing a tube to burn out every hour or so and shutting the whole system down. But even when it was working perfectly, the engineers and computers didn't put much faith in the IBM. Their spacecraft was too precious to leave to the whims of new technology. The expensive, gigantic piece of equipment frequently sat unused.

On the night of Pioneer 3's launch, they tried to use the IBM only briefly before giving up on it. It was far too slow for this kind of work. Besides, the group in the room could feel confident in the calculations only when a real person was doing the math. Sue wasn't worried when the IBM struggled; she knew it would come down to her hand-drawn computations to predict the mission's success or failure.

Things weren't looking good. The Jupiter missile stopped firing prematurely. Calculating like mad, Sue shook her head. It wasn't going to make it. With the first-stage malfunction, there was no way the other stages could give the spacecraft enough thrust. She was sad to see the Pioneer rise up 63,500 miles before falling back down to Earth.

It was 6 a.m. by the time Sue left the lab. She was dead on her feet, exhausted from the night's work and its devastating finale. When she got home, Pete was watching the morning news as they began reporting on the failed launch. She suddenly jumped up, hardly believing her eyes. "Those are my numbers!" she cried, pointing to the calculations she had done just the night before, now written in chalk on a blackboard. She couldn't believe it; her work had made the news.

After the failed launch, however, there was a salve for the wounded feelings at the lab: JPL had officially been made part of NASA. Although JPL's success with Explorer in January would have seemed to make the transfer inevitable, in fact a delicate negotiation had taken place among the new space administration, the army, and Caltech. With these talks still in the works, NASA opened its doors in October without a scientist in its ranks. Pickering was holding out for Congress to designate JPL the "nation's space laboratory." But while the legislature wouldn't give them the high-status label Pickering sought, Abe Silverstein, the new head of NASA's Office of Space Flight Programs, made up for it by handing the lab a juicy new assignment. Under the NASA umbrella, JPL would be responsible for planning and executing crewless lunar and planetary missions in addition to developing the rockets needed to get there.

In December, Eisenhower signed an executive order putting JPL under the direction of NASA. Thankfully they would continue to be managed by Caltech, which gave them the same freedom and independence they had enjoyed when they were part of the army. The computers were joyous about the change. They loved the idea that they would no longer be called on to make weapons and delighted that they would be taking part in further scientific exploration.

It was Christmas 1958, and Harry surprised Barbara with a tree strung with lights and covered in decorations for her apartment in South Pasadena. She was thrilled with it; Harry was so romantic and spontaneous. After she got her coat on, they headed off to the lab's Christmas party.

It seemed to be NASA-themed that year. JPL celebrated their new affiliation with shiny paper rockets, stars, and moons hanging from the ceiling. The jazz orchestra played with gusto as the staff and their dates danced around the rented hall. They joked and laughed with their colleagues but avoided conversation about Pioneer as much as they could. It wasn't easy, but they wanted to keep the night carefree. As the drinks flowed, Barbara reminded the single girls to be on the alert. After their long days of working under intense pressure, JPL's parties could be loose and a little wild. Even in the midst of their revelry, the girls liked to look out for one another.

Thinking back on the year, the staff exulted in the success of Explorer, yet the failed launch just weeks earlier left a bitter taste in their mouths. As Barbara sang Christmas carols with the crowd, her emotions were mixed. However, when she looked at the man standing next to her, she realized she had finally made up her mind. She loved Harry and was ready to marry him. *Whatever the new year brings,* she thought, *at least we'll be together.*

On January 2, 1959, a small sphere could be seen streaking across the sky toward the moon, dragging an orange glowing tail of sodium gas. The gas had been purposely added to increase the satellite's visibility from Earth. It passed by the moon, coming within four thousand miles of its surface, as close as any human-made object had ever ventured, before swinging into the sun's orbit. Later named Luna 1, the spacecraft had been designed to land on the moon. Although it didn't make it quite that far, it was still an impressive win for the Soviets. They boasted that their spacecraft was now a planet, while the computers at JPL grumbled in frustration at the news. They were clearly losing the space race.

On the first anniversary of Explorer 1, in January 1959, a glittery affair in Washington brought Pickering, von Braun, and Van Allen back together in the capital. Von Braun was easily the most famous of the three and used to being the center of attention at such parties. Yet tonight he was grumbling. While JPL had swiftly become part of NASA, von Braun's group at the Army Ballistic Missile Agency, in Alabama, was going to be phased out. NASA wanted to chop the staff in half, holding on to the employees it wanted while shutting down the rest of the operations. Von Braun was not taking the decision well. He had made a public plea for funds — $50 million to $60 million to preserve his group and keep pursuing the big rockets — but he didn't succeed. Other research groups were also facing corrosion. NASA was transferring 157 employees from the navy's Vanguard team to what would become the Goddard Space Flight Center, in Greenbelt, Maryland. Former competitors JPL and the newly minted Goddard would now form the nucleus of NASA space science.

Another celebration was happening back in California. Margie Behrens was getting married. She was twenty years old, and her family had been anticipating her marriage since she finished high school. Macie knew that Margie, a good Catholic girl, would likely be starting a family soon. Macie and the other women thought highly of Margie and fretted over her decision, thinking her too good for her new husband, an engineer at JPL. To tempt her to stay at the lab, Macie sent Margie to learn programming on a brand-new machine: the Burroughs E101.

The device's capabilities lay somewhere between the massive room-filling computers, such as the UNIVAC and the IBM 701 and 704, and the Friden calculators the women used every day. The big, clunky machine was the size of a desk and very noisy. Margie used a crude assembly language to program it: she stuck pins in a pinboard that sat cradled atop the mechanism. Advertisements for the Burroughs E101 boasted, "Pinboard programming saves 95% of manual computation time!" In addition to its adoption in aerospace engineering, it was also used to forecast U.S. presidential election results. The E101 was made up of eight pinboards, each holding sixteen different instructions. By putting pins in the board, Margie entered the calculations she needed. The women all found the machine painfully slow. It could do twenty additions or four multiplications a second but regularly suffered from breakdowns. Nevertheless, Margie thrilled at using the new technology.

Meanwhile, JPL and von Braun's group were collaborating on Pioneer 4. On March 3, 1959, the spacecraft launched. This time the first-stage rocket worked perfectly. Back at the control room in JPL, the computers and engineers waited. It would take four and a half hours before the probe passed the moon. The Microlock tracking system that had occupied so many of the computers' hours worked perfectly. Pioneer 4 joined its Soviet counterpart and began orbiting the sun as a second artificial planet. A few days later, in the wee hours of the morning, they received the last signal ever from Pioneer 4, now more than 400,000 miles away. As the probe traveled on its orbit, the computers considered in amazement the fact that it would be another

Advertisement for the Burroughs E101

twelve years before it passed within 1 million miles of Earth.

Although Pioneer 4 was a success, there

was a general feeling that the mission had fallen short. JPL had won out over their competitors at the air force, whose two Pioneers had failed utterly, but lagged behind the USSR. The discontent wasn't just about competition. The staff of JPL, from Pickering to the engineers to the computers, felt driven to begin exploring the planets. Pickering in particular saw the lunar missions merely as a means to test their equipment.

If they were going to explore the solar system, the engineers recognized, they would need a better tracking system for their satellites. They proposed a deep-space network that could command and track all American spacecraft. JPL already had a few tracking stations — in Florida, California, and Puerto Rico — that were responsible for transmitting initial trajectory data from every launch at Cape Canaveral. The cornerstone of the network was the tracking station in California. The huge dish antenna, eighty-five feet wide and weighing 120 tons, was located at Goldstone Dry Lake in the Mojave Desert, east of Pasadena. Goldstone had proven its worth by catching Pioneer 4's signal from the greatest distance: 409,000 miles from Earth. But now they needed to hear even farther into space.

Barbara was about to get her first peek at Goldstone, the large dish that had provided her with so much data. She had just been promoted to supervisor of the computers. Macie was retiring, and everyone was sad to see her go. She had been there so long that it felt like the end of an era. Still, she was in her late sixties and had modestly declared that she "just can't keep up with the young women anymore." Barbara, who had been acting as a supervisor beside Macie for years, was her natural replacement.

Not everyone agreed with the decision, however. One of the engineers, Bill Hoover, grumbled about Barbara's promotion, believing that a man should be put in charge of what was a critical part of their operations. "She's just going to get married, get pregnant, and then quit," he complained angrily.

On her first visit to the Mojave as a new supervisor, Barbara had little time to think of such tactless comments. Instead, she and the engineers discussed plans for the deep-space network, envisioning three stations harboring giant radio antennas, similar to the one at Goldstone, that could be set up in far-flung locations around the world, ready to catch signals from distant space. When the beacon from a spacecraft dipped below one antenna's horizon, the next antenna would pick it up. The Goldstone antenna would be a central component of the design, and new stations would be built in Australia and Africa.

While Barbara was making these exciting strides in her career, her personal life was also evolving. On February 21, 1959, after making him wait four long years, she finally married Harry Paulson. Standing outside the church together and cheering as loudly as they once had for Explorer's launch into orbit were her close friends from JPL. Barbara couldn't have been happier. She only wished her mother were there to see the fulfillment of what she had always wanted for her.

Marriage didn't change Barbara's work ethic. It did, however, change her nickname. She had never liked being called Barb or Barbie and preferred that her colleagues call her Barbara. Now, with the addition of her married last name, her initials were BLP. It wasn't long before she became "Blip" around the lab. Blip spent the same long hours training new computers and working on trajectories. Their next goal was clear, and she eagerly anticipated the calculations. JPL had come in second to the Soviets in launching both the world's first satellite and the first craft to fly by the moon. Perhaps they could beat the USSR in becoming the first to land on the moon's surface.

Despite the historic nature of the task, those at JPL found little in the project to admire. There was a feeling among the supervisors that they were simply using the technology out of the box instead of pushing the limits of what they could do. NASA wanted a moon lander quickly, without frills or finesse. To meet both NASA's requests and their own desires, JPL resolved to work on the moon and planet missions simultaneously. While friction flared between JPL and NASA, the women worked on trajectories for moon landers alongside the more grandiose plans to send probes to Mars and Venus. The excitement over the planetary missions was palpable, and the computers found themselves swept up in it.

One morning, Barbara chose her outfit with particular care. She paired a dark, calf-skimming A-line skirt with a cardigan covering her collared shirt. She slipped on her favorite peep-toe heels and smiled as she put on the three strands of pearls Harry had given her as a wedding present. When she arrived to work, all the girls congratulated her, and one of them pinned a showy corsage to her chest. With her friends and colleagues cheering her on, she walked up to Bill Pickering and shook his hand. "Thank you for the decade of service," he said warmly as he handed her a shiny gold pin commemorating the years Barbara had worked at JPL. Addressing the staff, Pickering talked of her hard work on the missions and said he hoped she would stick around for many more decades. Barbara grinned; the last year and a half had been wonderful. She had watched as Explorer flew toward the heavens, had gotten the promotion of her dreams, and had married the love of her life. What more could she possibly ask for? One thing was certain: she never wanted to leave the lab.

Successful tests of the Ercoupe rocket plane in 1941. Above, Barbara Canright is third from left. (Courtesy NASA/JPL-Caltech)

Aerial view of JPL in 1950 (Courtesy NASA/JPL-Caltech)

The computers, 1953. First row, left to right: Ann Dye, Gail Arnett, Shirley Clow, Mary Lawrence, Sally Platt, Janez Lawson, Patsy Nyeholt, Macie Roberts, Patty Bandy, Glee Wright, Janet Chandler, Marie Crowley, Rachel Sarason, and Elaine Chappell. Second row: Isabel deWaard, Pat Beveridge, Jean O'Neill, Olga Sampias, Leontine Wilson, Thais Szabados, Coleen Veeck, Barbara Lewis, Patsy Riddell, Phyllis Buwalda, Shelley Sonleitner, Ginny Swanson, Jean Hinton, and Nancy Schirmer. (Courtesy NASA/JPL-Caltech)

Barby and Richard Canright, 1940 (Courtesy Patricia Canright Smith)

The lunch stand at JPL, 1947 (Courtesy NASA/JPL-Caltech)

Bill Pickering crowns Miss Guided Missile 1955. (Courtesy NASA/JPL-Caltech)

The intimate atmosphere of the laboratory regularly brought employees together for merriment, particularly at the lab-wide dances held each spring and fall and during the December holidays. (Courtesy NASA/JPL-Caltech)

The computers at work, 1955. Helen Ling is sitting at the second desk, left side. Barbara Lewis is on the phone at the back, and Macie Roberts is standing on the right side near the window. (Courtesy NASA/JPL-Caltech)

Barbara Lewis (Paulson) is on the far left as second runner-up for Miss Guided Missile 1952. The other two women, from left to right, are Doris Mahon and Judith Buckhave. (Courtesy NASA/JPL-Caltech)

Jazz orchestras were a popular addition to the dances regularly held at JPL. (Courtesy NASA/ JPL-Caltech)

A January 1958 press conference following the successful launch of Explorer I, with Bill Pickering, James van Allen, and Wernher von Braun holding a model of the satellite aloft (Courtesy NASA/ JPL-Caltech)

Computer Phyllis Buwalda with members of the Explorer I team at JPL, 1958 (Courtesy NASA/JPL-Caltech)

Celebration for Explorer I at JPL, 1958 (Courtesy NASA/JPL-Caltech)

Bill Pickering crowns the Queen of Outer Space in 1964. As JPL's mission changed, so did the name of its beauty contest. (Courtesy NASA/JPL-Caltech)

Tracking lunar missions with the troublesome IBM 704 in 1959. Note the punch cards used for programming. (Courtesy NASA/JPL-Caltech)

Data reduction for firing of Pioneer 4. Computer Phyllis Buwalda shown in white blouse, 1959. (Courtesy NASA/JPL-Caltech)

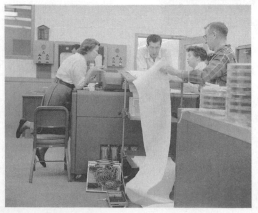

Sue Finley, 1957
(Courtesy Susan
Finley)

From Caltech
handbook for
new students,
1957. Sue Finley
is seated on the
right. (Courtesy
Susan Finley)

Helen and Art Ling,
1958 (Courtesy
Helen Ling)

Barbara (Lewis) Paulson receiving her ten-year pin from Bill Pickering in 1959 (Courtesy NASA/JPL-Caltech)

Barbara and Harry Paulson, 1959 (Courtesy Barbara Paulson)

Sylvia Miller, 1973 (Courtesy NASA/ JPL-Caltech)

The Paulsons with daughters Karen and Kathy (Courtesy Barbara Paulson)

Analog computer equipment in the old Space Flight Operations control center, 1960 (Courtesy NASA/JPL-Caltech)

Tracking spacecraft position in the control room during the Venus flyby, 1962 (Courtesy NASA/JPL-Caltech)

Helen Ling working on Mariner 2, 1962 (Courtesy NASA/JPL-Caltech)

The Mariner 2 team, 1962. Melba Nead is seated in the front row and Helen Ling is standing in the second row. (Courtesy NASA/JPL-Caltech)

JPL Mariner 2 float in the 1963 Rose Parade (Courtesy NASA/ JPL-Caltech)

The new Space Flight Operations Facility, 1964 (Courtesy NASA/JPL-Caltech)

First picture of Mars, captured in pastels, 1965 (Courtesy NASA/JPL-Caltech)

Planning the Grand Tour in 1972, from left to right: Roger Bourke, Ralph Miles, Paul Penzo, Sylvia Lundy (Miller), and Richard Wallace (Courtesy NASA/JPL-Caltech)

Helen Ling's twenty-fifth anniversary party at JPL, 1979. First row, left to right: Sue Finley, Merrilyn Gilchrist, Barbara (Lewis) Paulson. Second row, left to right: Irene Smith, Helen (Chow) Ling, Sylvia Lundy (Miller), Mary Nixon, Judy Wakely. Third row, left to right: Cynthia Lau, Suzanne Cheeve, Victoria Wang, Linda Lee, Kathy Thuleen, Margie (Behrens) Brunn, Joanie Jordan. (Courtesy Barbara Paulson)

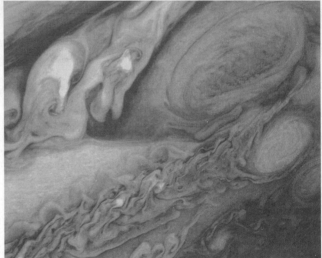

The big red dot of Jupiter as photographed by Voyager 1, 1979 (Courtesy NASA/JPL-Caltech)

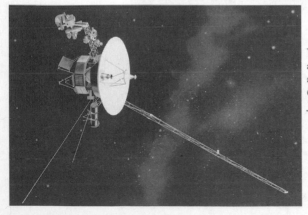

Voyager 1 in space, as imagined in an artist's rendering (Courtesy NASA/JPL-Caltech)

Saturn's rings as photographed by Voyager 2, 1981 (Courtesy NASA/JPL-Caltech)

Uranus as photographed by Voyager 2, 1986 (Courtesy NASA/JPL-Caltech)

Chuck Berry playing "Johnny B. Goode" at JPL in celebration of Voyager 2's reaching Neptune, the last stop on the Grand Tour (Courtesy NASA/JPL-Caltech)

Neptune as photographed by Voyager 2, 1989 (Courtesy NASA/JPL-Caltech)

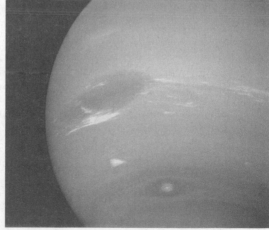

Barbara Paulson (front row, center) and the Magellan sequence design team (Courtesy NASA/JPL-Caltech)

Pale Blue Dot, as photographed by Voyager 1, 1990 (Courtesy NASA/JPL-Caltech)

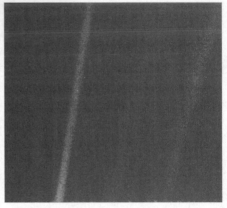

Sylvia Miller with Mars Pathfinder rover airbags taken on July 4, 1997, when the spacecraft successfully landed on the red planet (Courtesy NASA/JPL-Caltech)

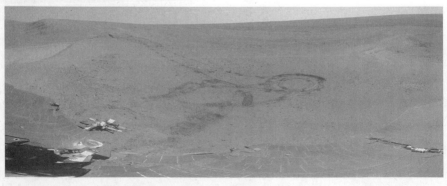

Sue Finley and Barbara Paulson, 2003 (Courtesy Barbara Paulson)

Sylvia (Lundy) Miller's forty-year anniversary at JPL, 2008 (Courtesy NASA/JPL-Caltech)

Barbara Paulson (with microphone) in 2013 (Courtesy Nathalia Holt)

Sylvia Miller (with microphone) in 2013 (Courtesy Nathalia Holt)

Panorama of Mars taken by the Opportunity rover, which continues to roam over a decade after it landed (Courtesy NASA/JPL-Caltech)

The computers in 2013. Standing, from left: Nancy Key, Sylvia Miller, Janet Davis, Lydia Shen, Georgia Dvornichenko, Margie Brunn, Kathryn Thuleen. Seated, from left: Victoria Wang, Virginia Anderson, Marie Crowley, Helen Ling, Barbara Paulson, Caroline Norman. (Courtesy Nathalia Holt)

Helen Ling (on right) in 2013 (Courtesy Nathalia Holt)

Sue Finley in 2013. She is NASA's longest-serving woman and has worked at JPL for fifty-eight years. She won't retire until her latest mission, Juno, orbits Jupiter. (Courtesy NASA/JPL-Caltech)

■ ■ ■ ■

PART III
1960s

■ ■ ■ ■

Barbara Paulson

Helen Ling

Susan Finley

Sylvia Lundy (later Miller)

CHAPTER 8
ANALOG OVERLORDS

Barbara lightly rubbed her belly. The doctor had just left the room. In her hands she held a small piece of paper with a date scrawled in the doctor's loopy cursive: October 1960. She couldn't believe it: she was going to be a mother. She stood up and looked in the mirror, wondering if she looked any different. She thought about Harry; he was wild for a baby and would be thrilled at the news. Married life had been blissful. She spent her days in a job she loved and at night she had Harry to come home to. Now everything was going to change.

Barbara got dressed slowly, her mind racing. As she slipped on her kitten heels, she felt overwhelmed. She was thrilled about starting a family, and yet her mind wandered back to the lab. Her whole adult life, ever since she was a teenager, had been spent within JPL's walls. She was now a supervisor with responsibilities. It would be hard to say good-bye.

Unlike other pregnant women she had seen leave the lab, she couldn't simply pack up her things and disappear. Her position was too critical to the lab's success. She discussed the best course of action with her boss, Dr. Clarence R. "John" Gates, who had a PhD in electrical engineering. It was a mark of distinction among the engineers, who were not required to have a graduate-school degree. Congratulating her on her impending motherhood, Gates helped devise their plan. Barbara would work right up until it was time for her to give birth.

The atmosphere at JPL was tense. Just a few months earlier, in September 1959, the Soviets had sent up Luna 2. The spacecraft flew for thirty-six hours before crash-landing on the moon and becoming the first man-made object to land on another celestial body. Now the Soviet Union was boasting of its superiority over the United States. Americans could hardly believe that on the surface of the moon, far above their heads, Luna 2 had placed titanium pennants printed with the USSR emblem. Once again, JPL was playing catch-up.

In December 1959, they suffered another setback. NASA shut down Project Vega, an audacious plan that called for a rocket capable of launching several probes all at once, one bound for the moon, one to Venus, and one to Mars. The computers had spent hundreds of hours working on the project, and the lab had spent nearly $17 million building a new, powerful rocket system. Pickering had planned that 1960 would be devoted almost entirely to Project Vega. Now that the project was canceled, they needed to devise something new.

Since plans for the last launch vehicle JPL would ever devise — and the "propulsion" in the jet propulsion lab — were finished, NASA decided the lab would focus exclusively on spacecraft for lunar and planetary missions. Not that the computers minded; working on spacecraft was more exciting anyway.

With their schedule wide open, JPL hastily made another plan. They would launch five lunar probes, called the Ranger series, in 1960 and 1961. Venus and Mars probes, called Mariner, would follow in 1962. It was easy to get the engineers and computers excited to work on the probes to Venus and Mars, but the moon probes fell short on sparking enthusiasm. With Project Vega now dead, there was worry that the underfunded Ranger's lunar program might also be on the brink of being cut.

The engineers and computers made their plans over popcorn in the computer room. It had become a gathering place. With the sun slanting in through the large windows, the room was cheery in the afternoons, and the engineers often wandered in to start a conversation. The fact that the room was filled with young women didn't hurt either. No one was quite sure how the tradition started, but by now it was firmly established. At 3 p.m., the smell of popcorn wafted into the corridor, tempting the engineers to poke their heads out their doors. The computers took turns making it in the tiny kitchenette down the hall. As they talked, they ate the popcorn out of a transparent globe that had been cut in half, the hemispheres still marked with latitude and longitude lines.

They discussed the lunar missions in terms of technical considerations, but their voices became elevated only when they started talking about the planets. "Why go to that hunk of lifeless rock when we can explore Mars and Venus?" said one of the engineers, a kind, chubby Belgian fellow named Roger Broucke. He sketched out a mission on a piece of paper, a rocket that released a whole set of probes, each bound for a different planet. In one launch they could explore the solar system. "We can send one to the moon too," he said, almost as an afterthought.

"Well, we'll need a much more powerful rocket for that, Bubbles," Barbara replied with a laugh.

Some of the men hung out so often in the computer room that the women gave them girls' names so they would fit in. Poor Roger was given the unfortunate nickname Bubbles, while Len Efron had been rechristened Leona. Laughing at these pet names, the women jumped into the conversation. With their expertise in calculating trajectories, they estimated how powerful a rocket they would need to get to Mars and Venus. They playfully considered how they would put the rockets together and how many stages it would take to make such a long journey.

The lack of enthusiasm for the Ranger probes was problematic. Yet the finish line for the space race was clear. A human footprint etched into the surface of the moon — which might last a million years or more, far from the effects of gravity and erosion — would be the step over this finish line. It was only a question of whether this footprint would be left by a Russian or an American. But for the United States to achieve the ultimate win in the space race, they first had to get a probe up there. The lab needed to refocus if it was going to help America beat the Soviets.

The computers certainly couldn't help but show interest in the seven astronauts selected for Project Mercury: Walter M. Schirra Jr., Donald K. "Deke" Slayton, John H. Glenn Jr., Scott Carpenter, Alan B. Shepard Jr., Virgil I. "Gus" Grissom, and L. Gordon Cooper Jr. Project Mercury, the States' first foray into manned spaceflight, had three goals: to orbit a manned spacecraft around Earth, to investigate man's ability to function in space, and to recover both man and spacecraft safely. Impressed by the group, Wernher von Braun described them in a letter to Pickering: "They are the most wonderful bunch of people you've ever seen. No daredevils by a long shot, but serious, sober, dedicated and balanced . . . but they deeply resent the suggestion that they are human guinea pigs rather than engineering test pilots." Along with millions of young women across the country, the computers swooned over the handsome group of men.

Barbara was too big for swooning. She was seven months pregnant and, despite her fatigue, was still happily making it to work every day. However, she hated the long walk from the parking lot up the hill to the lab, which left her huffing and puffing. Parking had become a problem at JPL. Unlike in the old days, when employees took the streetcar up to the gate and parking was plentiful, now everyone drove. The lot was bursting at the seams not only with employees but also with visitors, contractors, and politicians. Most days, Barbara found herself having to park at the far end of the lot. With her poufy maternity wear, she felt like a giant circus tent hiking to work in the mornings. Citing her pregnancy, she applied for a better parking spot. She was feeling clever about her maneuver to get one of the coveted spots when the administration replied to her request. "You have to stop working immediately, today," they told her on the phone. "We can't have a pregnant employee." Saying it was for "insurance purposes," they fired Barbara.

It was a blow. In a daze, she looked around the room at the women who were both her subordinates and her friends. There was no time to even say good-bye. She wondered what would become of the missions she had worked so hard on, deprived of her passion and expertise. A decade of her life was vanishing before her eyes. At home she cried as Harry held her. "I thought I was worth more than that," she said between sobs. In the space of a phone call, Barbara had gone from invaluable supervisor with a long career to unemployed pregnant wife.

JPL was reorganizing since becoming part of NASA. The computers were still human and still literally had a hand in every project. In recognition of Helen Ling's importance, management made her head of the newly organized computer department, now called Mission Design. She had won the respect of both the engineers and the other women. Comprising the women that Macie and Barbara had hired and trained, the computer department soon became known as Helen's girls. Frequently the engineers referred to them as "computresses," but the women bristled at the term. They called themselves the sisterhood.

Within the computer group, interlopers began to appear. These stealthy intruders were new IBMs, far more advanced than their massive predecessors. The women couldn't believe how quickly the technology was advancing. Instead of vacuum tubes, the new computers used transistors, small, three-pronged gadgets, first made out of germanium but soon afterward silicon. In addition to amplifying electrical inputs just as vacuum tubes did, they acted like switches, turning on and off, and thus vacillating between two binary states, zero and one. The transistors were much more efficient than the tubes, able to work faster with less energy and taking up far less space. They could also be integrated onto a circuit, forming a chip. That chip was then connected with fine gold wires to a resistor and a capacitor. The women would take the backs off the new IBMs to admire the neat rings of gold inside. They called them the small computers, since they could fit on a desk rather than requiring their own room. The large, vacuum-tube IBM held its place of honor in its own room next door, still in daily use, but the Burroughs E101 was already starting to collect dust.

The new digital computers still couldn't do much. Even basic arithmetic was sluggish. Compounding this problem was the fact that the engineers were suspicious of the technology. Having a human being perform the calculations was the only way they could feel confident in the math.

While Helen was taking charge of both the women and the machines, men were leaving Earth. On April 12, 1961, Yuri Gagarin became the first human in space. He orbited the planet aboard the Soviet Vostok 1. Helen was shocked to see the headline MAN IN SPACE. She couldn't believe they had lost yet again. Less than a month later, on May 5, Alan Shepard sat perched atop a Mercury-Redstone rocket in a capsule he named Freedom 7. He blasted off from Cape Canaveral, rising 116 miles above Earth on his fifteen-minute, twenty-eight-second trip. However, unlike Gagarin, he didn't go into orbit.

Although the Redstone rocket powering the spacecraft was simply a stretched-out version of Juno, the launch vehicle that propelled Explorer into space, the women felt little personal connection to the mission. While JPL was focused on unmanned missions, the new Space Task Group based in Houston was tackling crewed ones. Dr. Max Faget, an engineer in the newly formed group, designed the spacecraft that would carry humans into space. He would eventually work on all the crewed ships, from Mercury to Apollo to the space shuttle. The task group's designs were sent from Houston to a private contractor. McDonnell Aircraft constructed the cone-shaped Mercury capsule, barely big enough for Shepard's five-foot-eleven frame. The capsule weighed only a third as much as its Russian counterpart but was also less durable. While the Vostok could survive in space for a week, the Mercury spacecraft could barely last twenty-four hours.

So while launching a man into space and bringing him back safely was a big accomplishment for the Americans, in many ways it was a hollow victory. Whether in manned or unmanned missions, the USSR was far ahead. There was hardly a staff member at JPL who didn't feel the burning desire to beat the Soviets.

Helen was doing a little burning of her own. She had prepared data analysis for one of the engineers, Charles "Chuck" Vegos. As a joke she burned the edges of the pages that were printed with the data before handing them over to Chuck. He looked at the pages, rimmed in orange and black, in shock. He was speechless until Helen started laughing. "Well, we're in the data reduction business," she said, a wide smile on her face. The room filled with laughter, and Chuck recovered when Helen handed him the real data, intact.

Data reduction started with the women wading through exceptionally large sets of raw data from the performance of the rockets being fired in Florida and California. The rows of numbers were a nonsensical mess until the computers transformed them into simplified, meaningful information. Helen summed up the relationship between engineers and computers with the phrase "Engineers make up the problems and we solve them." Solving the problem meant finding trends in the data sets and reporting on their findings. The computers' calculations would help determine the maximum possible weight of a spacecraft and its various possible trajectories.

The computers' deft abilities also greatly influenced spacecraft design. However, the new ship the engineers were designing for, Ranger, apparently weighed too much. New test data were underwhelming, showing the rocket's ascent to be less powerful than the computers had originally calculated. The group now needed to trim off a whopping seventy-five pounds. Worse still, time was running out. A firm launch schedule, starting in July 1961, had already been set by NASA. The pressure to get to the moon was intense.

While the Soviet Union had already landed on the moon, America's lunar program was lagging behind. JPL had designed the sophisticated new Ranger spacecraft with a tall antenna, solar power, and a camera to capture images of the surface of the moon. An Atlas-Agena rocket would launch it. The Atlas missile had first been designed by the U.S. Air Force to launch an eight-thousand-pound thermonuclear warhead, and it was gigantic, standing seventy-five feet tall. Despite its size, the rocket was sprightly, featuring a "balloon structure" that kept it lightweight. It contained three engines, two of which dropped off soon after flight, making the load that much lighter. The upper stage of the launch vehicle was an Agena rocket, designed secretly by the air force. The combination had the potential to be powerful, although it was still untested. Because of this, the first two Ranger missions wouldn't even try to get to the moon; these two launches were solely for testing.

For the Ranger missions, the engineers had decided to try a new kind of trajectory. Previously, all spacecraft had been launched in a straight shot to the destination, but as a result, they had to fight directly against gravity, wasting fuel. This gravity drag limited the size of the spacecraft and magnified any errors in the computers' aim. To limit losses, JPL would first launch Ranger into orbit around Earth and then, when the spacecraft was in the right position, perform a midcourse maneuver in which a second rocket would fire, sending the ship to the moon. It was a daring strategy, and the women composed their new trajectories with care.

One month after the ship's design was frozen in place and the trajectories set, the team at JPL received some unpleasant news. The Ranger spacecraft, once seen as grossly overweight, could stand to gain a few pounds. In fact, cutting the seventy-five pounds from the cone-shaped structure had been a mistake. In the rushed frenzy to capture the moon, they had shed needed weight. Ranger would have to leave Earth in an emaciated state, not an ideal beginning for the perilous mission.

Running a month late, on August 23, 1961, the first Ranger blasted off from Cape Canaveral. The Atlas missile performed well and launched the spacecraft into a low orbit around Earth. Next, the upper stage, the Agena, was supposed to reignite to send the rocket into a higher orbit. But a faulty switch circuit prevented this from happening, stranding the spacecraft in low orbit. It was a poor place to test Ranger, since the spacecraft traveled through a ninety-minute day-night cycle, not optimal for the solar-powered ship. It performed as well as it possibly could, unfolding its solar panels and straightening itself out into its unusual three-axis design, like a giant tripod in the sky. The mission, however, was mostly a failure. The ship plummeted to its doom on

August 31.

Even on the ground, the air force's Agena rocket was causing trouble, and JPL had to push the next test of Ranger to November because of problems they encountered with production and reliability. But when November came, the Agena once again failed to reignite, and Ranger, so carefully built in Pasadena, burned up in the atmosphere a mere six hours after its launch. At JPL the engineers and computers were frustrated. If Project Vega hadn't been canceled, it would be the Vega rocket they had designed powering the upper stage. They couldn't help but feel that if they were using their own rocket, they would have better luck with it, or would at least be in control of their failures. It was easy to blame a rocket that had been designed by the air force and built by a private contractor, the nearby Lockheed Corporation, for their troubles. While they waited for the kinks in the launch vehicle to be fixed by Lockheed, the engineers and computers found themselves drawn to the Venus and Mars missions.

Far away from the failures of the Ranger, Barbara was about to give birth. As the due date grew nearer, Harry wished for a girl. He was forty and not sure he could keep up with an exuberant boy who might be even

269

more rambunctious than he was as a child. Barbara didn't have a preference, but as the days passed, she was getting impatient for the baby to arrive.

Barbara's water broke in the wee hours of October 9, 1960, and she and Harry headed for the hospital. While Barbara struggled through a long labor, Harry was desperate to find a television. The hours dragged on in the little waiting room, crowded with other fathers, and his mind turned to baseball. When Harry mentioned the World Series game to Barbara's obstetrician, he confessed that he too was desperate to see it, and they searched until they found a TV. It was Game Four, the Pittsburgh Pirates versus the New York Yankees. Absorbed by the game, the pair kept their eyes on Yankee Stadium, where the game remained scoreless until the bottom of the fourth. Mickey Mantle struck out and Yogi Berra ground out before their teammate Bill Skowron hit a home run. The game suddenly had become a nail-biter when the doctor was called back into the delivery room. Harry snapped back to reality. He was about to become a father.

As the Pirates narrowly beat the Yankees, 3–2, Barbara cuddled her baby girl, who had weighed in at nine pounds six ounces.

Harry wasn't allowed in the same room as the baby; fathers weren't given the luxury of holding their little ones so soon. Instead he fell instantly in love as he watched her through the glass of the nursery, mesmerized. They named her Karen Marie.

Barbara cradled Karen in her arms, breathing in her newborn smell. She looked in her eyes and felt an intense love unlike any she had ever experienced. Once home, Karen happily cooed in her parents' embrace. Still, Barbara had her hands full. The baby was so much work. Luckily, Harry did his share. He fed her bottles and swaddled her in blankets. He changed her diapers in the middle of the night, dipping the heavy cloth in the toilet before putting it in the big, stinky bin the diaper-delivery service gave them. One night he was so exhausted he fell asleep while rinsing the diaper. Barbara found him on the bathroom floor and couldn't hide her giggles as she shook him awake, the dirty diaper still in his hand. The nights were the longest. They paced the halls of their small one-bedroom Pasadena apartment, singing lullabies to try to get Karen back to sleep. Sometimes Barbara stopped at the window and looked out at the night sky. The moon and stars were out there, shining brightly, but her future was no longer tied to exploring them.

Helen had barely finished congratulating Barbara when she realized she was pregnant too. She was excited but also worried that she wasn't ready to be a mother. She had just started her job as supervisor and didn't want to leave. Exhilarated by the news, Arthur supported his wife and promised her he'd do whatever she needed to make things work. With no maternity leave available, Helen and Arthur had to plan carefully. If she took a leave of absence, her job wouldn't be waiting for her when she got back. Employers argued that too many women vanished after taking a leave. Instead, she would use her saved vacation time and sick leave to be home with the baby. When those ran out, she'd come back to the lab.

Patrick was born in 1961, only months after Barbara's baby. Helen was in love, gazing in awe at his soft round cheeks and tiny fingers and toes. But as much as she adored their child, she missed the lab. She wanted to have it all: the experience of motherhood and a fulfilling career. Seven weeks after giving birth she was back at JPL. She was thankful to have her family living close by. Her mom was able to watch Patrick while she was at work. Because Helen was confident that he was in good hands, it was easier to take up where she had left off. And now that she was back at JPL, she knew she needed people she could rely on — she needed Barbara.

When Karen was seven months old, Barbara got a phone call. "Merrilyn Gilchrist's leaving. Do you want to come back to work in my group?" Helen asked. Barbara gave it some thought before answering. In 1960, a working mother was the exception to the rule: only 25 percent of married American mothers with children under the age of eighteen were in the workforce. Especially for mothers of infants, pursuing a career was considered peculiar. On the other hand, Barbara certainly missed the lab and her work there. And while the computers had to work late nights during a launch, most of the time the hours were flexible. She also thought about Harry. He wanted to change jobs and had been planning to go back to school to obtain a real estate license. If she worked, it would take some of the financial pressure off them. With a mix of excitement and nervousness, Barbara called Helen and told her yes, she'd come back. Then she started calling babysitters.

Barbara found she wasn't the only computer returning. Melba Nead, one of the first ones hired at JPL, was also back. Melba

273

had left JPL in 1950 to work for North American Aviation and was now bringing her expertise, gained from years of working in private industry, back to the lab. In the intervening years she had learned modern computer programming, applied the software design to the development of nuclear-reactor codes, and become a full-fledged engineer.

And there were more new girls. Janet Davis and Joanie Lee both started in the lab. Helen was off the day Janet interviewed, and Janet had found meeting with Dr. Gates intimidating. She had just graduated with her master's degree in math from the Carnegie Institute of Technology, today known as the prestigious Carnegie Mellon University, world-renowned for its engineering program. Her credentials were impressive, and she was a natural for the job. Dr. Gates, however, on hearing that she was a newly-wed, was contemptuous. Although he hired her, he added dismissively at the end of her interview, "You won't last long." It was something that would not have happened under Barbara's or Macie Roberts's leadership. Joanie, a recent graduate from the University of Southern California with a degree in mathematics, fared better. Perhaps her unmarried status made her appear a more stable candidate to Dr. Gates.

The women were now hard at work on the Mariner program, the favorite child at JPL. Similar to Ranger, it used an Atlas-Agena launch vehicle, but unlike the moon probe, Mariner was bound for Mercury, Venus, and Mars. Everyone was excited to work on it.

The Mariner program would construct ten spacecraft, all bound for Earth's closest neighbors in the solar system. The design would be similar to that of Ranger, with solar panels that opened up to face the sun and provide continuous power, and a large antenna that would point back home. The spacecraft didn't spin like the Pioneer moon probes but, as in Ranger, were stabilized by a three-axis system. Engineers developed Mariner and Ranger side by side, and the rival projects, despite the obvious closeness in their designs, were creating tension. While the engineers were divided into Ranger or Mariner teams, the computers were united, working on the missions simultaneously.

Still, the women were feeling the tension between work and home life. Helen found herself exhausted at the end of the day, struggling to find the energy to cook dinner and take care of the baby. Her parents, getting on in years, were having trouble keeping up with the infant's demands, and Helen worried that she and Arthur would have to find different child care. Barbara also found the schedule of a working mom hectic. Harry would drop off Karen with the babysitter in the mornings while she went into the lab early. In the afternoons, she couldn't wait to see her baby but was soon overwhelmed with the day-to-day chores that awaited her at home. There was no happy balance, only the will to see things through.

By January 1962, JPL was ready to launch another lunar probe. Ranger 3 blasted off from Cape Canaveral, bound for the moon. At least that was the plan. Almost immediately, things began to go wrong. Only two minutes after takeoff, the staging of the Atlas missile went haywire and the engine cutoff did not occur on schedule. Instead, the rocket accelerated off course. Then the guidance system of the Agena rocket malfunctioned, sending Ranger even farther off its trajectory. It was clear they weren't going to land on the moon, but the engineers at JPL thought at least they could use the spacecraft's instrumentation to explore deep space. Unfortunately, when they sent the command to turn the system on, the onboard computer died. It was a complete disaster.

As those at JPL tormented themselves about the failed Ranger, Sue Finley had just received some happy news. She'd been trying to get pregnant and, ironically, had been taking birth control for three months under the guidance of her doctor, who believed the pill would help regulate her cycles.

The pill was brand-new in 1960, and Sue was among the first in her generation to benefit from it. For the first time, women had the medical means to control when they became pregnant. The arrival of the tiny tablet of hormones marked the beginning of two decades of revolution in gender equality and the rise of feminism worldwide.

For Sue, the pill was a godsend, but for a different reason than for most. Coming off the pill, she got pregnant right away. She was filled with emotion, elated at the prospect of becoming a mother but terrified of losing another baby. At the same time, she had fallen in love with her work. Now the idea of leaving JPL saddened her. *I'll just take a leave of absence,* she thought. She wasn't ready to let the lab go.

As Sue was contemplating leaving, changes were afoot. The women were learning FORTRAN, a new computer-programming language. The name FOR-

TRAN, they would learn, came from "Formula Translation," since the program was ideal for translating mathematic equations into code. Barbara and Helen found the language exceptionally easy to learn, especially with the Caltech classes that JPL sent them to.

FORTRAN was a string of simple commands and could program nearly any computer. The women wrote out their program on paper in much the same way they set up their equations by hand. The difference was that they used only the specific commands the computer could recognize. They then took their notebooks to the keypunch.

The keypunch looked like a typewriter but with special buttons that allowed holes to be made in punched cards. The cards were rectangles, about 7 1/2 inches long and 3 1/4 inches wide, made of thick, stiff paper with long rows of repeating numbers, 0 to 9, running down their length in eighty tightly packed columns. To run a complex set of calculations, whole decks of cards were needed. Like the pages of the women's notebooks, each card contained lines of mathematical functions.

Most of the computers had never used a typewriter — only secretaries at JPL used those — and didn't even know how to type.

Punch cards used by the women to write programs

But they quickly learned how to work the keypunch. Just as each number on the keypad of a phone can be used to type in letters, the keypunch used a code to translate each letter of FORTRAN into a number. When Helen pressed A on the keypunch, the machine loudly leaped into action, feeding the card into the machine and punching a hole in the 7 on the card. Line by line as Helen typed her commands into the keypunch, the letters transformed into a punched pattern. If she made a single mistake on the keypunch there was no salvaging it; the card had to be thrown away, and she had to start over with a fresh card.

When Helen had accurately entered the

full set of commands from her notebook, she wasn't quite done yet. She still had to compile her code. Just as is done today, Helen's source code — written in her programming language, FORTRAN — had to be compiled so that the computer could recognize it in its own language, the binary code of zeroes and ones. Each line of assembly code translated into one instruction in binary machine code. While Helen could translate the punches in the cards into the equations they stood for, the IBMs could not. She had to run all the cards through a special machine called a compiler.

Navy rear admiral Grace Brewster Murray Hopper and her team at Remington Rand, in New York City, produced the first compiler in 1952. That machine, the A-0, and later the A-2, translated mathematics into computer code. Hopper knew that for digital computers to become mainstream, people couldn't be expected to write in binary code. Instead she had to find a way to communicate between humans and computers. The compiler was the answer: a translator between man and machine. It was the beginning of computer languages.

The compiler technology was brand-new and had to be specific to each computer language. "Nobody knew anything. They [compilers] didn't exist! Everything we did we invented on the fly," said Lois Haibt, a programmer at IBM who built the core of the FORTRAN compiler in the late 1950s.

Helen ran her cards through the FOR-TRAN compiler, which then produced a second set of cards containing the running program in a language the IBM could understand. The first set of cards was for her; she and the other women could pass them back and forth and see how the code had been written. The second set of cards was only for the IBM. This deck was then loaded into the computer, which would run the operations and give Helen the output she needed. When it was all done, Helen put the cards away in cardboard boxes. You never knew when you might need to run the program again.

The engineers viewed the IBMs with suspicion, while the women embraced the new technology, largely because of their hands-on experience in using the machines. The world of programming kept drawing them in, expanding in both complexity and scope.

In 1960, a new girl had started in the computer room. She didn't have the best work ethic. She was prone to unexpected flare-ups and overheating. The new girl was an IBM 1620 who took up her own desk in a nook adjoining the computer room. It didn't seem right that the new computer didn't have a name. A sign on the outside of her door read CORE STORAGE, so they christened her Cora and spoke of her as one of the group. Cora needed the air to be chilly, so inside her room it was freezing cold. Even when it was 100 degrees outside, the women got in the habit of bringing sweaters to the lab in deference to their wired companion.

Within IBM, the 1620 had another nickname: the CADET, or Computer with Advanced Economic Technology. The programmers there jokingly referred to the machine's limits by saying the acronym stood for "Can't Add, Doesn't Even Try."

Despite its drawbacks, Barbara smiled as she read the nameplate that hung outside the computer room, listing each member of the Mission Design department. HELEN LING, SUPERVISOR graced the top, while the rest of their names, including her own, followed. Beneath them she added a nameplate that read CORA. The IBM computer was officially part of the family.

Cora was getting a lot of use as the team worked on Mariner. The competition to reach Venus was intensifying. When the women needed motivation, they wandered over to an engineer's desk where a picture of the Soviet Venera 1 hung. The USSR's first mission to Venus, in early 1961, had failed, but the picture was a reminder that if they wanted to be first, they needed to hurry.

The computers charted a course for the spacecraft. It would fly by Venus, carrying scientific equipment capable of detecting the neighboring planet's atmosphere. They constructed the spacecraft in pairs so that even if one mission failed, they would have a backup. Second chances were important, since Mariner would be the first spacecraft to fly by another planet. The excitement among the computers was building. They watched as the ship was constructed, impressed with the solar panels that reminded them of butterfly wings. They said good-bye to their baby as the spacecraft was packed up and sent off to Florida.

On July 22, 1962, Mariner launched. Immediately, the mission went awry. First the Atlas antenna malfunctioned, and for the first minute mission control couldn't detect its signal. Without a detectable signal, a smoothing function from the internal guidance system was supposed to kick in, keeping the spacecraft headed in the right direction. Instead, the launch vehicle wildly overcorrected, forcing the rocket off course.

The internal guidance system didn't work properly because of a simple transcription error. When the handwritten guidance program was transcribed in Florida, a superscript bar was mistakenly left off the program. That one mistake meant that the program wasn't able to correct the rocket's course. Both the hardware failure of the Atlas antenna and the software bug in its guidance system meant that Mariner was completely out of control. No one could predict where it would wind up; it could slam into the Atlantic Ocean or it could veer off and crash into a town. With only seconds remaining before the stages separated and Mariner could no longer be destroyed, the range safety officer made the difficult decision to order the destruct signal. Built into every launch was a self-destruct button. In case the rocket headed for a residential area instead of space, explosive charges were placed on the vehicle. The range safety officer, a member of the air force, was put in the unenviable position of having to decide when the rocket had deviated so far off course it had to be destroyed. When the decision was made, the spacecraft that they had invested so many hours in was blown up, only minutes after it was launched.

The women in Mission Design were upset, but they didn't have time to waste on self-pity. If they wanted to get to Venus they had only weeks to get there. The Mariner program had been designed to take advantage of Venus's relatively close position to Earth during the summer of 1962. Unlike in the typical picture of the solar system, which shows the planets moving around the sun in perfect, uniform circles, the orbits are actually far more complex. The planets move in unique ellipses, their speed and direction varying as they make their way around the sun. Because of this, the computers knew, they couldn't simply point a rocket at Venus and fire it. Instead they had to determine how the spacecraft would bend around the orbits of both the sun and Venus and plot a precise trajectory. Earth, Venus, and the sun had to be flawlessly lined up, but an alignment so perfect happened only once every nineteen months. If they wanted to catch Venus, they had to send Mariner 2 up right away.

The women worked late nights and weekends on Mariner, desperately checking their trajectories and programs. The hours were exhausting, especially for new mothers Barbara and Helen, but their paychecks were worth it. As hourly employees they were both earning impressive incomes, outstripping their husbands, thanks to the long hours Mariner required.

At Cape Canaveral the air force had little time to assign blame for the Mariner 1 accident. The man who had left the bar out of the program, and who had since been promoted, apologized. They moved on. The Atlas antenna was fixed and the guidance system reprogrammed. On August 27, 1962, Barbara sat in the control room and felt the strange, frenetic energy that filled the room before a launch. The late launch nights were hard on her little family, yet so worthwhile. She knew she wouldn't be able to do any of it without Harry. While she worked late, he rushed around, picking up Karen from day care, then feeding and bathing her, and putting her to bed with a kiss.

Barbara thought of the family moments she was missing but quickly had to focus and prepare for what they all hoped would be a history-making launch. At 11:53 p.m. in California, she watched the Teletype data roll in. Sitting with paper and mechanical pencils, she began to calculate the position of the rocket. Suddenly, an electrical short occurred in the Atlas rocket and the whole launch vehicle began to roll, spinning once a second as it flew through the sky. Luckily the range safety officer wasn't worried enough to destroy it, and the group watched as the Atlas flew, completely unresponsive to the guidance system. Then, as mysteriously as it started, the short fixed itself. From then on everything went smoothly, and they were amazed at their luck. However, it would be months before they would learn whether the spacecraft would make its groundbreaking flight past Venus. Barbara thought of their Mariner 2, out exploring the universe alone, while Harry picked her up. It was the middle of the night and Barbara, exhausted, was feeling lucky to have a ride. She worked late so frequently that Harry had ingeniously constructed a baby cot carefully nestled in the backseat of their Peugeot so he could bring Karen along when he ferried Barbara home. The French car often drew snickers from the neighbors, who whispered that it was a sure sign the new father was a beatnik. Harry laughed off such comments; he loved the little car, unusual as it might be. Barbara did too, and as she got in that August night, she caressed her sweet daughter, snuggled in blankets.

While the Mariner program seemed to have turned things around, the lunar missions were floundering. The Ranger program had already suffered four failures and now, only a few months after the Mariner 2 launch, they were about to fail again. There were grumblings from NASA that perhaps an academic lab wasn't the best place to organize missions and that the work should be transferred to a private contractor.

At JPL they knew that not only were their jobs on the line, but the entire manned space program was depending on them. While JPL tried to keep up, the Mercury Seven were finishing their training. The astronauts were completing multiple missions orbiting Earth, all of them successful. At the same time their launch vehicle was coming along nicely. The Saturn rocket, developed by von Braun's team at the newly minted Marshall Space Flight Center in Huntsville, was speedily going through development and testing. Based on the Jupiter-C, developed by JPL and von Braun, Saturn would be far more powerful. It had to be if it was going to carry humans into space. It seemed everything was progressing as it should, with one glaring exception: the Ranger program. If they couldn't land a spacecraft on the moon, how could they send men there?

The pressure was mounting on September

12, 1962, when President Kennedy spoke at Rice University. "We choose to go to the moon," he said to the crowd. Yet it seemed JPL was choosing Venus instead. With the lab's attention divided, it was questionable whether either mission would succeed. Still, Barbara was happy to hear the president pledge to put the space program into high gear. Her cheeks flushed with pride when he mentioned their work at JPL: "The Mariner spacecraft now on its way to Venus is the most intricate instrument in the history of space science. The accuracy of that shot is comparable to firing a missile from Cape Canaveral and dropping it in this stadium between the forty-yard lines."

With support for the space program soaring, it was hard to watch Ranger 5 fail only a month later. For some unknown reason the power malfunctioned on the spacecraft and the batteries ran down. It missed the moon by 450 miles and instead started circling the sun. However, the timing was fortunate, since Americans were suddenly too worried about nuclear war to care about missions to the moon.

For thirteen days in October 1962 the world seemed on the brink of disaster. When an American spy plane spotted nuclear-missile-site construction by the Soviets in

Cuba, President Kennedy placed a blockade of American ships around the island. Cuba was cut off from the world. Addressing the nation on October 22, Kennedy said, "My fellow citizens: let no one doubt that this is a difficult and dangerous effort on which we have set out. No one can foresee precisely what course it will take or what costs or casualties will be incurred." It seemed the world was accelerating toward nuclear war.

The roots of the Cuban missile crisis were tangled up in American rocketry. In 1961, Americans had deployed Jupiter nuclear missiles to Turkey, adjacent to the Soviet Union. And these medium-range ballistic missiles were developed by none other than Wernher von Braun at the Army Ballistic Missile Agency.

At last, Kennedy brokered a deal with the Soviets. They would dismantle their weaponry in Cuba in exchange for a pledge from the United States not to invade the island. In addition, the United States would dismantle its missiles in Turkey. The tensions between the two countries were lessened, at least for the moment.

Although nuclear missiles had temporarily swallowed up public attention, it was clear something in the moon program had to change. The Ranger program chief at JPL was fired, as were several engineers. The whole program was put on hold until they could figure out what was going wrong.

Meanwhile, Mariner 2 was getting closer to its goal. On Halloween it lost one of its solar panels, and by the middle of November the poor ship overheated, its temperature gauges hitting the upper limit of its sensors. Yet it kept on course, limping along to Venus.

While Ranger floundered and Mariner soared, Sue was experiencing the highs and lows of new motherhood. She alternated between overwhelming joy and sleepless despair. The days ran together, so that often the milk delivery was her only clue as to the day of the week. Sue could feel her life bending around her son, Ian. Everything else was slipping away. When he was six months old, Helen called, asking if she'd like to return. She looked at her baby's wide, toothless grin and didn't think she'd ever go back.

Janet Davis was about to leave too. Fulfilling Dr. Gates's prophecy, she was eight months pregnant and knew she would have to quit soon. She hid the pregnancy as best she could, wanting to work right up to the end. When she wasn't crippled by terrible morning sickness, she was hungry all the time, constantly snacking at the lab, doughnuts being one of her favorites.

Sometimes at night, Janet would look up at the bright speck of light in the sky and wonder what was there. Venus was so easy to see, a dazzling spot that popped up next to the moon. The women wondered what could be on the planet that spun next to Earth whose atmosphere, entirely obscured by clouds, was impenetrable to high-powered telescopes. They had discussed some of the crazy theories out there, laughing at the idea that the whole planet was a hot, steamy jungle with alien dinosaurs roaming its surface. As Carl Sagan said, "Observation: I can't see a thing. Conclusion: Dinosaurs." Her hand on her belly, Janet looked up at its twinkling light and thought, *Soon enough, we'll know what you're hiding.*

The moons and planets remained mysterious. Space was uncharted territory, the stuff of science fiction. Though Mars and Venus, our closest neighbors in the solar system, held the highest hopes for alien life, most Americans believed even the moon might harbor life. With its basic characteristics, such as temperature and the presence or absence of water, still unknown, it was easy to get lost in fantasy. Hollywood heightened imaginations, producing a steady stream of sci-fi movies in the 1960s with such titles as *Twelve to the Moon, Journey to the Seventh Planet, Twenty Million Miles to Earth,* and *Visit to a Small Planet.* Since the only tangible data were those collected from telescopes, the idea of alien creatures hiding in the craters of the moon or in jungles spread across Venus seemed plausible.

Helen would be one of the first to find out how close these imaginings were to reality. On December 14, 1962, Mariner made its closest approach to Venus. Helen and Melba were anxiously waiting in the control room, and they had good reason to be nervous. They couldn't be sure if the high temperatures on board the spacecraft had fried its ability to scan the planet. They stood by a large light board on the wall of the control room and hastily wrote equations while tracking the position of the ship. Data began to pour in from the Teletype, the roll of punched paper tape curling under itself. The data came coded in seemingly endless rows of letters: ZXXDRDDRXOS. They worked quickly, calculating the ship's position mostly by hand but also using the new desk-size IBM 7090.

As Mariner closed in on Venus, yet another

glitch occurred. The control system on board the ship malfunctioned, and the team at JPL had to manually transmit the command for the encounter sequence to begin. As the ship received their command and began to scan the planet, the team members looked at one another in amazement. They were communicating with a spacecraft that was thirty-six million miles away. Helen focused on the task at hand. With data flowing in so quickly, she could spare little time to contemplate the moment's importance.

In the control room that night, three distinct groups nervously awaited word of Mariner's fate. The engineers assessed the operation and position of the spacecraft, looking carefully at the mechanical performance of the ship, while the scientists awaited the data the spacecraft would send back. The computers stood in the middle, their programming simultaneously reporting the ship's condition and position while unveiling the scientific data. All the information sent back by the spacecraft about Venus's atmosphere, magnetic field, and charged particle environment would be relayed to Earth in a river of radio signals hitting the high-gain parabolic antenna at Goldstone before being converted to usable data by the women's telecommunications programming. How well the groups balanced their separate interests would determine not only the current mission's success but also how well they worked together in the future.

Around 11 a.m. a strange, chordlike sound was heard as they established radio contact with the spacecraft. Hearing the sounds as they were picked up at the large dish antenna at Goldstone, Bill Pickering said, "Listen to the music of the spheres." For forty minutes, they did. Data gushed in as Mariner, using infrared and microwave radiation meters capable of breaking through the planet's dense cloud cover, scanned Venus. They held on to the signal as long as they could, mindful that each additional minute was giving them a wealth of information. Finally, Mariner's orbit pulled it away from the planet. Helen sat back in awe. She couldn't believe they had really done it. Out there, soaring through space, was a ship following a path she'd helped map out. Not only that, but they'd beaten the Soviets. It was their first win in the space race, and the victory was precious to all of them. Mariner would inch toward the sun before sending out its last signal on January 3, 1963. After that, JPL would lose contact with it forever as it became just another piece of space junk spinning around the sun.

While Mariner 2 was sending out its farewell signals, the women watched the Rose Parade on New Year's Day 1963. One of the floats was a giant planet Venus, constructed in yellow flowers with the words "Venus to Pasadena" written on it in red roses. They watched as a replica Mariner spacecraft, just like the one they built, floated above the big ball of flowers.

While the computers took pride in their history-making accomplishment, their jobs were in peril. They had been hearing tales that the digital computers they programmed were swallowing up jobs across NASA. At the Dryden Flight Research Center, in nearby Palmdale, California, the human computers were being laid off, despite their long-standing working relationships with the engineers. At the NASA Langley Research Center, in Virginia, the group of computers was similarly shrinking. The more reliable the IBMs became, the greater the threat to the human computers. One of the engineers ominously told Helen, "Your jobs will be gone soon." All she could do was work harder than ever. Yet in a world where engineers were men and computer programmers were women, everything was about to change.

CHAPTER 9
PLANETARY PULL

Helen stared at her beautiful baby girl. She gently nestled her daughter in her arms and stroked her silky, dark hair. She was perfect in every way. Helen was already in love with the little girl she and Arthur had named Eve. Her arrival, so soon after their first child, Patrick, sent Helen's orderly household into complete disarray. Having two little ones was a challenge. She struggled to keep up with her suddenly mobile son as her newborn mewled to be held. Although feeling the pull of her children, Helen didn't want to lose her job. She loved the work and knew that she couldn't take off much time. Eve was six weeks old when Helen returned to the lab, leaving the two infants with their grandmother. Yet almost immediately Helen knew it wasn't going to work. Two babies were simply too much for her parents to handle. They were going to have to figure out something else. "We'll work swing shifts," Arthur suggested. It was the best solution. Helen worked early while Arthur worked late. They saw little of each other as they passed back and forth, the days and nights melding into one exhausting stretch of time.

Helen's home life was not the only source of stress. The team at JPL was still struggling to get the Ranger program off the ground. Five successive failures had plagued Ranger, and its poor execution had humbled the project in the eyes of NASA, especially when compared to its flashy counterpart, Project Apollo. While Apollo trained its astronauts in the "vomit comet," an airplane designed to simulate the effects of weightlessness, Ranger couldn't even capture an image of the lunar surface.

From its earliest days, the Ranger project lacked the grandeur that distinguished Apollo. In early 1960, JPL's program director had named Ranger after his Ford pickup truck. At the same time NASA's chief of Space Flight Programs, Abe Silverstein, was choosing titles for the manned missions to the moon, saying, "I was naming the spacecraft like I'd name my baby." He chose the Greek god of the sun, Apollo, whose name seemed to match the lofty ambitions of the program.

The mission's goal, as defined by President Kennedy in 1961, was to "land a man on the moon and return him safely to Earth." To accomplish this, Apollo would send a three-man spacecraft into lunar orbit. Once it was circling the moon, a second spacecraft, the lunar module, would bring two astronauts down to the surface, leaving one man in the cone-shaped command module. All three astronauts would return to Earth in the command module, parachutes slowing their descent as they splashed down into the ocean. Despite their differences, Ranger and Apollo were faces of the same coin; they were both headed to the moon, one with men aboard and one without. While Project Apollo steadily advanced, NASA worried about their inability to get a lander on the moon. They needed Ranger to work.

Mechanical problems continued to vex the lunar lander, but the women gave the project little thought. They were running ahead, not looking back, as they began work on a project far more exciting: the first mission to Mars. Much as Mariner 2 had successfully flown by Venus, Mariner 3 would fly by the Red Planet. There was one striking difference in the missions: the distance from Earth to Mars was 140 million miles, roughly four times farther than to Venus. They were able to attempt such a feat only because of Mariner 2.

Mariner 2 had been an unqualified success. The mission gave not only the scientists but the entire world a peek through Venus's clouds. Yet, instead of finding a jungle teeming with alien life, as predicted in glossy magazine articles, they found temperatures and pressures far too high to sustain any life at all. Unlike Earth and all the other planets of the solar system except Uranus, which rotate in a counterclockwise direction, Venus rotates clockwise on its axis. The women were amazed at how slow this rotation is: a single day on Venus takes up 243 Earth days. The long day means that the planet has no magnetic field. On Earth the hot metal core at the center of the planet, combined with its spin of one revolution every twenty-four hours, generates our magnetic field. The liquid iron, nickel, and other metals surrounding the core swirl, thanks to the Coriolis effect.

This effect is named for French scientist Gustave de Coriolis, who in 1835 described how water follows a curved trajectory when it encounters the rotating motion of a waterwheel. The effect explains why hurricanes rotate counterclockwise in the

Northern Hemisphere and clockwise in the Southern Hemisphere. At Earth's core, whirlpools develop from the swirling liquid metal. Because of the Coriolis effect, the spiraling metal moves in the same direction, generating electrical currents and, ultimately, a magnetic field. Although Mariner discovered that Venus likely has a metal core, which may even be partially liquid, without a faster spin to get it going, it generates no magnetic field. And without a magnetic field, the planet is unable to form the protective cushion of an atmosphere such as that necessary for sustaining life on Earth.

JPL would use a similar design to Mariner's for its spaceship to Mars, this time with a camera on board. It would be propelled using the same Atlas-Agena launch vehicle and, just like the Venus missions, it would be constructed in pairs, the twin spacecraft ready for launch within weeks of each other. If one failed, at least they would get another try within a short period.

They didn't have much time to launch the spacecraft. As with their challenge with Venus, they had to schedule the launch to catch Mars when it was closest to Earth. While the Venus missions had a fifty-day launch window, the women calculated the

Mars missions would have to be launched within twenty-seven days. Otherwise, it would be another two years before they would get another chance. It was going to be tight.

The team would send the ship into Earth's orbit to circle the sun before mission control performed a risky midcourse maneuver to send the spacecraft on a course toward Mars. They estimated the journey would take seven and a half months. The computers drew up theoretical trajectories, mapping the direction and speed needed at each critical juncture. They were plotting the longest interplanetary mission ever devised, one that would carry the spacecraft more than 180 degrees around the sun. For the women it was like shooting an arrow at a moving target.

The computers aimed the spaceship by calculating its altitude and azimuth. The altitude was the height of the ship's path off Earth's surface, while the azimuth, like a compass, measured the angle relative to true north at which the ship arced along the horizon. The ship would leave the ground and enter Earth's orbit before flying into a transitional elongated ellipse. A boost of its rockets, millions of miles from home, would then send the ship flying toward Mars in a path around the sun. It was important that the ship didn't crash into Mars.

Normally, all equipment was sterilized before entering space. If scientists wanted to find alien life, they had to be careful not to first contaminate the foreign planet. Otherwise how could they distinguish Martian life from the microbes carried by earthly machines? But unlike the case with previous missions, the Mariner 3 equipment would not be heat-sterilized before launch. Given how long the ride to the Red Planet would take, JPL engineers didn't want to subject the equipment to the deteriorating effects of extreme temperature. Therefore, they designed Mariner 3's trajectory so that the chance of its hitting Mars (and possibly contaminating it with Earth germs) was remote.

While JPL planned the mission, disaster struck. It was just another weekday morning in November 1963 when the news came over the wire. Shots had been fired at President Kennedy's motorcade in Dallas, and everyone in the lab was glued to the radio. No one could possibly work. Only nine months previously, Kennedy had awarded the lab's first director, Theodore von Kármán, the country's inaugural National Medal of Science. Packed into a room that contained the engineers' offices, the women held hands. When the news anchor announced that Kennedy was dead, they held one another, in shock and sobbing. They knew that neither the country nor the fledgling space program they belonged to would ever be the same.

A month after Kennedy's assassination, JPL unveiled a shiny new piece of the space program. Christened the Deep Space Network and known as the DSN, the network of large dish antennas was capable of maintaining a two-way connection between spacecraft and the new Space Flight Operations Facility at JPL. It had taken two years to build the SFOF (pronounced "ESS-fof"), a three-story structure that boasted more than two hundred television displays and thirty-one consoles, enough to support tracking from the DSN and serve as a backup for Project Apollo, which was controlled at the NASA center in Houston. From 1963 on, the facility would serve as NASA's control hub for all interplanetary and deep-space communication. It would receive signals from the antenna located at Goldstone, where Barbara had visited, as well as those in Australia and South Africa, to follow a spacecraft far into the reaches of space. Although a spacecraft transmits at low power, with roughly the same signal strength as a refrigerator lightbulb, the huge curved antenna dishes could concentrate the weak signal. The new network meant that when a spacecraft took a picture, even from millions of miles away, the surge of digital data in the form of ones and zeroes could be caught and sent to the new control room at JPL. In commemoration of the signals streaming in, a plaque was put up in the SFOF reading THE CENTER OF THE UNIVERSE.

Completion of the DSN was critical to advancing the Mars missions. Yet the pressure to launch the next Mariners while the planets were aligned, combined with JPL's partiality for the project, meant that Ranger wasn't always getting the attention it needed. Ranger 6 was launched in January 1964. JPL "parked" the spaceship in Earth's orbit as planned before sending it out toward the moon. On February 2, the ship neared its planned crash site: the Sea of Tranquility. In the SFOF, engineers and computers waited patiently as the cameras warmed up, already anticipating the thousands of pictures that would be taken as the spacecraft plunged toward the lunar surface. President Lyndon B. Johnson was listening in the White House while officials waited in a special NASA control room in Washington. Suddenly, a strange female voice came over the wire: "Spray on Avon cologne mist and walk in fragrant beauty." Officials were dumbfounded. Surely this wasn't coming from the moon. A technician righted the error. He had accidentally crossed the feeds from the ongoing Queen of Outer Space contest (formerly the Miss Guided Missile competition) at JPL. The embarrassment paled in comparison to what the technicians felt when the cameras didn't turn on. There were no images of the moon to broadcast. Once again, the mission had failed. With this disappointment, JPL worried that the project would be taken away from them and that their standing at NASA had been forever damaged.

A few days later, after the results were tallied, Pickering crowned the winner of the Queen of Outer Space at the annual dance at JPL. The lab's becoming part of NASA had changed not only their mission but also the name of their beauty contest. Pickering was still contemplating what NASA administrator James Webb had said to him back in D.C.: "One more flight. You've got only one more flight." This last Ranger mission would determine JPL's entire future. The gravity of the situation made the lighthearted pageant seem a little dull this year. As Pickering made his way to the stage, the crowd began to clap, slowly at first but then building in intensity until everyone got to their feet, surrounding their boss in a standing ovation. In the warmth of their confidence, Pickering picked up the microphone and said, "We're going to fix this. We're going to make it work."

Barbara applauded Pickering, full of respect for her director and enjoying what she assumed would be her last beauty contest. Her focus was on Mariner. She didn't work on Ranger, so her thoughts lingered on her Mars trajectories. At the same time she was thinking about her family. She was pregnant again. She worked as long as she could, up until she was eight months pregnant and waddling around. This time she didn't apply for a better parking spot; she wanted to be sure she wouldn't lose her job prematurely. When she left she felt a twinge of sadness. It was unlikely she would be able to come back, since they couldn't hold her job for her. With more new IBMs arriving, the women could even be on their way out.

The human computers worried that their fate would be like that of the women who worked as switchboard operators at JPL. Beloved among the lab's telephone operators was Sally Crane, who joined the lab even before Barbara, in the mid-1940s. Sitting at the switchboard, she witnessed a complete revolution in JPL's telecommunications as manual operations switched over to completely electronic ones. Sally held on to the outgoing technology during her last years at JPL before retiring in the 1970s. With the advent of automated operations, the number of switchboard operators in the United States fell 43 percent between 1947 and 1960. It was the beginning of the fall, with hundreds of thousands of switchboard jobs eliminated by new technology. The trend was enough to make anyone working with computers nervous.

Helen was fighting against the menace of obsolescence. She was still hiring women as computers, but the definition of the position had changed. Her team had become NASA's first computer programmers. The women still worked closely with the engineers, almost all of whom were men, but it was no longer enough for them just to be good at math. They needed to know how to build, fix, and run programs on the IBM computers, something the engineers rarely did. Widening this divide, JPL kept the women's skills up to date with programming classes. So, while at other NASA centers women's jobs were fading into the past, the women of JPL were becoming more indispensable than ever with their expertise in computing.

Meanwhile, the lab had figured out why the cameras hadn't worked on Ranger 6. The problem lay in a midflight ignition that had caused an electrical short in the camera system. With the design issues resolved, everyone looked ahead to Ranger 7. Surely, after six miserable failures, this would be the one. It had to be.

The launch of Ranger 7 took place on a hot, humid afternoon in July 1964. The control room at JPL was tense. Everyone knew that their jobs, and even the fate of the lab, were in jeopardy. To lighten the mood and distract everyone from the pressure, one of the engineers, Richard Wallace, known as Dick, decided to pass out peanuts. Whether it was the good-luck peanuts or simply the hard-won lessons from six failed missions, the launch went off flawlessly. But it wasn't time to celebrate yet; the ship had to successfully reach the moon's surface.

A few days later, in the early morning of July 31, Helen sat in the gallery of the new SFOF. The room was packed as everyone anxiously awaited news. As the spacecraft made its deliberate death plunge toward the moon, the cameras warmed up. Suddenly, thousands of images began to pour in. The room erupted in cheers, and everyone jumped from their seats in excitement. Those at JPL were the first to see what the surface of the moon looked like up close. The images revealed a large, dark plain speckled with craters. Seeing this desolate realm stirred happiness in the hearts of the women. They had finally done it.

Now that they had landed a spacecraft on the moon, even if it was a crash-landing, they had to decide where to send the next Ranger. Although a soft landing might seem the next logical step, gently landing a spacecraft wasn't one of their objectives. Since the program was primarily a recon- naissance mission, they wanted to get as many images as they could. They had to pick an area where a three-foot-long land- ing pad would fit, in preparation for Apollo. Everyone at JPL had an opinion, and staff debated whether the Sea of Tranquility, the Alphonsus crater, the Mare Vaporum, Sinus Medii, or Oceanus Procellarum would be chosen. The perfect site would balance the scientific goals of JPL with the needs of the Apollo program.

It was the start of a long tug-of-war between scientists and engineers at JPL. The two groups would constantly have to compromise, vacillating between often-opposing goals: the desire for scientific exploration on the one hand versus the development of new technology on the other. During the Ranger missions, Eugene Shoemaker, a U.S. Geological Survey scientist and astrogeology teacher at Caltech, was constantly tugging on the rope. Shoemaker's specialty was astrogeology — a melding of astronomy and geology — and he brought critical expertise to the science team at JPL. He tried to persuade mission managers to move Ranger 8 closer to the moon's clear, sharp shadow line, the defining edge that separates day from night. The edge, also called a terminator, moves slower on the moon. A day on the moon is equal to 28.5 days on Earth. Just as the low light of a sunset can make for dramatic pictures on Earth, Shoemaker believed, the low angle of the sun would create a contrasting light for the cameras. Engineers, however, argued that there might not be much light at all, which would jeopardize their ability to obtain pictures. The engineers won the round, but Shoemaker kept fighting and ultimately prevailed for the next mission, Ranger 9. The images

Image of the moon from Ranger 9 with shadow line separating day from night visible on bottom Courtesy NASA/JPL-Caltech

were as stunning as promised, but the relationship between scientists and engineers continued to be strained.

While NASA administrators and JPL scientists discussed landing sites, they were also gearing up for the Mars missions, only a few months away. A few weeks in November were all they had to make Mariners 3 and 4 a success. As they had before, the women watched from a glass-box balcony that looked down on the assembly area while the Mariner spacecraft were constructed. Men in long white coats, caps, and gloves tinkered with the ships. They attached four large solar panels and a crowning antenna before testing all the systems. Watching the designs come together before their eyes was both thrilling and frightening for the computers. They could never be sure if these creations were headed for greatness, would explode into a million pieces, or would simply become floating space junk.

On the evening of November 5, Mariner 3 was ready to go at the former Cape Canaveral, now known as Cape Kennedy. It sat atop the Atlas-Agena rockets on the same launchpad from which Ranger 7 had so recently experienced its success. The team in the control room wasn't superstitious, but just in case, peanuts were again passed out. While the launch went smoothly, only an hour later there was trouble. No power was coming from the solar panels. The shroud covering the spacecraft hadn't jettisoned as planned and was now keeping the solar panels from opening. Repeatedly they sent commands to Mariner to drop the pesky piece of fiberglass, but it was too late. Mariner 3 was destined to become space debris.

Now the shroud was all anyone could talk about at JPL. Just as a corpse is wrapped in a funeral shroud, the spacecraft was wrapped up to protect it during the rocket's ascent through the atmosphere. The shroud was first introduced during the Juno tests, in which a simple strip of aluminum was used. The trick was to make the covering aerodynamic enough not to interfere with the flight, yet strong enough to protect the ship within. Composite materials such as fiberglass soon drew favor, since they were both light and rigid. However, Mariner 3 showed JPL that fiberglass was problematic. The difference in pressure between the shroud's skin and its honeycomb fiberglass core had prevented the covering from being properly jettisoned. They had to come up with a solution, and fast.

They designed a new shroud, made of metal this time to avoid the pressure problem. Because this changed the weight of the ship, the computers suddenly found that everything had to be recalculated. Modifications would have to be made to the rockets, and therefore the trajectories would have to shift as well. They had only weeks to accomplish everything. The computers worked around the clock as they put the finishing touches on Mariner 4. If they didn't succeed this time, it would be a two-year wait until they could shoot another spacecraft to Mars.

On November 28 the pad was ready, and the peanuts were passed out. The ship bolted into the sky, the shroud jettisoned, and the solar panels deployed. Just when it seemed that everything was in place for the journey, the space probe fumbled as it got its bearings. The guidance system on board was the first to navigate by the stars. It required that the ship lock on both the sun and the star Canopus. Canopus was chosen because, as the second-brightest star in the sky, it was easy to find. But the ship's onboard electronics were finding too many bright stars. At JPL, they determined that the guidance system was confusing a few paint chips that had flecked off during deployment with stars. From the ground, the technicians at JPL watched as the guidance system repeatedly locked on to the wrong stars, until, finally, they were able to get the sensors to detect Canopus. Mariner was on its way to the Red Planet. They would have to wait seven and a half months before they knew whether it arrived.

While the Mars mission was monopolizing the attention of those at JPL, the need for moon missions was greater than ever. Ranger 8 reached the moon on February

20, 1965. As the spacecraft plummeted to the surface near the Sea of Tranquility, it sent back thousands of high-resolution photographs of the moon as well as video. At JPL the women watched breathlessly as the moon came closer and closer, the grainy images gradually becoming clear. The bizarre surface staggered its observers, with its strange rolling hills and smooth contours that made way for craters atop craters.

Geologists at JPL would have preferred a rockier surface, ripe for scientific exploration, such as the lunar highlands. The highlands form the intriguing spots on the moon that appear bright from Earth. Instead, the landing site near the Sea of Tranquility was chosen for its usefulness to Project Apollo. Finding a flat surface was critical for safely landing crewed spacecraft. The Ranger 8 mission was a success; the pictures showed a surface that looked smooth and strong enough to support the Apollo lander.

Barbara sat watching the television as live video from the last Ranger was broadcast. She was exhausted from running after her girls all day long. Karen was four years old, while Kathy was about to celebrate her first birthday. Between the two, Barbara was kept on her feet. Despite her fatigue, she couldn't believe her eyes when she saw the robotic spacecraft crash into the moon. Along with millions of other Americans, she was mesmerized by the sight of the moon craters rushing toward her. Barbara felt a far-off pride as she thought of her friends at JPL, and yet the moment didn't belong to her. She hadn't worked at JPL in a year. Her time as a computer seemed distant now that she was absorbed by the demands of home and family.

Helen also felt tired. It wasn't easy balancing a career with her two little kids, not yet in school. Her hours at work were getting longer as Mariner 4 approached Mars. She was constantly recalculating the trajectory, ensuring that their computations were correct and preparing for the ship's midcourse correction. Many Americans believed that Mars was a sister planet to Earth, likely to be a home for intelligent life. Around the turn of the twentieth century, the astronomer Percival Lowell published three books about life on the Red Planet, basing his conclusions on his sighting of "canals" when observing Mars through his telescope. Although he wasn't the first astronomer to see long, thin channels cutting across the surface, his descriptions of them and the Martians who made them were vivid. The world anxiously awaited the first views from the probe, and many were certain they were about to see the first glimpses of alien life.

On the evening of July 14, 1965, Mariner sailed by Mars. For twenty-two minutes Helen sat in the uncomfortably quiet control room as the data rushed in. Unlike the situation with the Ranger missions, where they could watch the images as they arrived, Mars was too far away. The digital image data came in as strips of paper that had to be processed by IBMs to produce images. The team members couldn't possibly wait that long. They decided to construct their own picture. They printed out the strips of data on ticker tape and hung them on the wall. Each number in the data corresponded to the brightness of its pixel, short for "picture element." The colors ranged from light to dark on a scale of twenty-five to fifty. When Dick Grumm, one of the engineers, went to buy chalk, the clerk told him they didn't have any, but he could use pastels instead.

Using brown, red, and yellow pastels, the engineers made up a key for how the numbers should be colored and got started. It was like a giant paint-by-numbers, and Dick was careful to follow his color key. It wasn't an easy project: the image was two hundred lines of two hundred pixels per line, an impressive amount of coloring to do. Meanwhile, the public relations folks at JPL were getting nervous. How could they keep the media away from the pretty artwork and make them wait for the official black-and-white images? It turned out they couldn't. Not only were Helen and the engineers excited by the early glimpse of Mars, but so were the television crews. They filmed the hand-drawn picture and broadcast it to the world; the first-ever image of Mars was radiant in red and brown pastels.

The formal black-and-white images were processed over the next few days. They revealed no canals of an alien civilization. Instead the planet was littered with craters reminiscent of the moon's. It looked like a desert. An editorial in the *New York Times* declared, "Mars is probably a dead planet." Yet at JPL hope still remained that a future mission might uncover some remnant of life, perhaps clinging to a crater or bubbling in a warm spring.

In the midst of the Mars excitement, Barbara once again got a call from Helen. They needed her at JPL, and Helen asked, "Wouldn't you like to come back?" Barbara missed both the lab and the companionship and said she'd be thrilled to return. She was already thinking about potential babysitters. Coming back the second time, she found the computers had grown even more sophisticated. To regain her skills she took programming classes offered at Caltech and sponsored by JPL. The lab's association with the university was convenient in keeping the computers, both living and wired, up to date. The women frequently took programming-language courses and also held classes in the lab. Helen was always first in learning the programs, eager to pass on what she had learned to her staff.

Barbara's friend Kathy Thuleen was back after having kids as well. In a society where only 20 percent of mothers with young children worked outside the home, the women at JPL bonded over their new babies at lunchtime. The talk naturally flowed from the moon to Mars to first words and first steps. While chatting over developmental milestones, they could feel the mood changing in the lab. The engineers were asking them for analyses of increasing difficulty and allowing them greater independence. With their growing responsibilities, the computing section's work was finding its way into numerous publications, although they were rarely credited in academic journals. Roger Bourke, one of the engineers, felt the injustice. He wondered what he could do to include his colleagues, hindered only by gender. At the same time that they were being denied the full recognition they deserved, it seemed to the young mothers, their work was more important than ever.

Kathy was working closely with Roger, analyzing the mountain of data that Mariner 4 had sent back to Earth. Hovering between the engineering and scientific worlds at JPL, they were uncovering the mysteries of the Martian atmosphere. They discovered that the atmosphere was only one half of 1 percent as dense as Earth's and that the polar caps that resembled the North and South Poles of Earth were actually frozen carbon dioxide. They determined that, like Venus, Mars lacked a robust magnetic field. However, unlike Venus, which lacks a magnetic field due to its slow rotation, Mars owed its weak magnetic field to its solid core. Without liquid metal that swirls charged particles, like that at the core of Earth, Mars was left without the protection from the solar wind that an atmosphere provides.

The more responsibility Kathy gained in her work — calculating the Martian ionosphere and gravitational effect — the more enthralled she became. Roger recognized these contributions by adding her name to their next paper, which detailed the altitude-control system on board Mariner 5. Kathy gasped when she read "Kathryn L. Thuleen, engineer" on the title page. She had never seen that word, *engineer,* after her name before.

Kathy was at her desk with one of the Mariner calculations when she got a frantic call. It was their babysitter. "Your son's up in a tree and can't climb back down," the sitter cried. "I don't know what to do." Kathy didn't know what to do either. Her husband was only ten minutes away, so perhaps he could leave work. The couple fretted over the phone until they finally thought to call a friend of their son's. The young boy was able to coax their child down, and all was well. Still, Kathy felt the nagging guilt of being a working mom. It was horrible to think she wasn't there when she was needed.

Luckily, JPL was willing to bend to her and the other mothers' needs. Kathy and Barbara both got to the lab early in the morning, often startling the deer that wandered through the parking lot looking for breakfast. They conscripted their husbands to drop the kids off with the babysitter. In the early hours they enjoyed the quiet, with the only sounds those of their pencils scratching across paper and the quiet hum of the IBMs in the room next door. In the late afternoon, they rushed home, eager to spend time with their children. The flexibility JPL gave them to shift their hours as needed, coming in early and leaving early, was invaluable. The job was never about sitting at a desk from nine to five. Instead, it was about getting the work done.

While the women were getting the support they needed at work and home, a new JPL project — the Surveyor program — was created to support Project Apollo. The engineers joked about putting a sign on its back, FOLLOW ME, to help keep the astronauts on course. Its goal was to produce a spacecraft that could softly land on the moon instead of crashing into it. If they were going to send men up there, they would have to learn to land them gently.

The Surveyor looked like a long-legged white tripod with two large solar panels at the top. Attached to the body of the ship, just above the tripod legs, were steerable rocket thrusters, the first of their kind. Using radar and an autopilot system, the engines were able to slow the ship down considerably, making a soft landing possible. An antenna was mounted near the panels to transmit images from the two television cameras housed below. Even though by now Ranger 9 had been launched and success-fully transmitted live video from the moon's surface, there was considerable nervousness about broadcasting Surveyor's delicate landing and photography live. On May 30, 1966, the launch went as planned. Two and a half days later the women watched as the lander approached the moon. The thrusters on board the ship fired as planned, slowing it from nearly 6,000 miles per hour to just 3. The spacecraft softly landed on the lunar surface. At JPL, one of the television net-work people leaned in to Bill Pickering and said, "Oh, by the way, we're live all over the world." Although he always knew the event would be broadcast live, the words shook Pickering; it had to work. An hour later the ship started taking pictures. The mission was flawless.

The next Surveyor mission wouldn't go as smoothly. During the midcourse correction, which had been carefully plotted by the women, one of the rockets failed to fire. The spacecraft tumbled out of control. It was a frustrating setback, especially since the first Apollo mission was slated for launch in mere months.

In preparation for the first mission, the Apollo crew had a practice session in January 1967. The cone-shaped Apollo command module sat atop a giant Saturn rocket, divided into two stages to form a launch vehicle powerful enough to lift men into space. The test was a launch simulation, with conditions as close as possible to a real launch: all components assembled and systems up and running. Dressed in their white and silver space suits, three astronauts — Gus Grissom, Ed White, and Roger Chaffee — crossed the red metal bridge and climbed into the command module. The hatch was shut behind them, and they drank in the rich atmosphere, approximately 100 percent oxygen. They lay back flat in their seats and looked up at the controls.

It was a long day of testing in the cramped space. Nearly eleven hours later the astronauts were gearing up for the simulated final countdown. The count was held at T minus 10 minutes as they resolved a communications problem that had popped up. Everything seemed to be operating normally until the launch team at the blockhouse suddenly heard a voice yell, "Fire! We've got a fire in the cockpit!" The next words came through garbled as crew members ran to rescue the astronauts. The flames started slowly but picked up before curling underneath the hatch door. Feeding on the oxygen-rich air, the fire consumed the command module. The rescuers were too late; the men inside were already dead.

The accident was nearly Apollo's undoing. The emotional toll of this loss of life caused several NASA officials to resign, unable to resume their work. Some feared that Congress might cancel the Apollo program, especially after a congressional investigation placed part of the blame for the accident on NASA's failure to report problems with Apollo. Ultimately, investigations by NASA and Congress would find that a spark ignited accidentally in the capsule, likely near Grissom's seat. Because of the oxygen-laden atmosphere and abundance of flammable materials inside, the fire quickly raged out of control. Tragically, the hatch door was too cumbersome to open quickly and prevented the astronauts' escape. The three men had asphyxiated in their space suits, their bodies protected from the flames around them but deprived of air to breathe.

Barbara and her colleagues were horror-struck when the news made its way to JPL. The three young men reminded them of their husbands, especially since they were roughly the same age, in their thirties and forties, with young children at home. It was heartbreaking. The Apollo program was put on hold, and a feeling pervaded the country that perhaps landing a man on the moon was reaching too far. Yet at JPL the tragedy had the opposite effect. They had to make the next Surveyor mission a success. The manned missions needed a boost of confidence, and it was up to them to show that the landing could be performed safely.

With the Apollo disaster at the forefront of their minds, the team watched Surveyor 3 blast off from Cape Kennedy in April 1967. Following its planned trajectory, the ship made two big bounces on the moon's surface before settling down in a crater. Unlike the previous Surveyors, this one was equipped with a shovel. It dug small trenches and scooped up dirt, placing it in front of the camera. Back at JPL, more than two hundred thousand miles away, Margie Behrens worked late that night in the control room, reducing the data that came in from the spacecraft. This meant that she converted the stream of data from analog to digital, revealing the texture and strength of the materials that made up the moon.

Margie and the team at JPL were pioneers in digital-image processing. Using FOR-

TRAN and later a program called VICAR, they programmed the IBM 7094 to convert each square of the analog image, taken by cameras pointed at the moon, into dots, or pixels. For JPL it was a necessity. Without digital processing, the terrain of the moon and planets was an indistinct blur. By compensating for distortion in the digital data, they could produce clean, crisp images.

Surveyor 3 had provided the first in-depth look at the composition of the moon and discovered a landing site well suited for an Apollo spacecraft. The success of the lunar lander lifted spirits, giving Americans hope for manned missions there.

Even as Barbara marveled at these new developments, she was enjoying the fruits of other advances right at home. Sitting at her desk, calculating new trajectories for their planetary missions, she ran a finger over her pantyhose. The hosiery was brand-new, uniting panties with nylons for the first time. For decades, Barbara had worn her stockings with a garter belt like any proper woman as she headed to work or went out in the evening. To put it mildly, it was a pain.

The garter belt was uncomfortable, often digging into a woman's stomach and legs. Pantyhose came about in the late 1950s when Ethel Boone Gant had had enough. She told her husband on an overnight train from New York City to their home in North Carolina that she wouldn't be accompanying him on trips any longer. She was pregnant, and the tight garter belt was far too uncomfortable to bother with. Yet she couldn't leave the house without her hosiery. Her husband, Allen Gant Sr., ran a textile company and wondered if he could use his expertise in the industry to solve her problem. "How would it be if we made a pair of panties and fastened the stockings to it?" From that conversation, Panti-Legs, later known as pantyhose, were born and began lining shelves in 1959. They started catching on in the 1960s, when the increasingly popular miniskirt couldn't cover the edge of garter belts and new fabrics made them far more comfortable and convenient.

While Barbara didn't intend to start wearing miniskirts, there was a new style she wanted to try. She loved the beautiful pantsuits she saw in store windows and would stop to admire the slim-fitting outfits, displayed in a plethora of colors and designs. But she wasn't brave enough to buy one to wear to work yet.

Barbara was happy to see Margie again. She was back after having had three babies in three years. She'd found a neighbor who could watch the children during the day. They chatted about their children but also about the new fashions. One day they noticed that Bill Pickering's secretary was wearing a pantsuit. "Well, surely if she's wearing one we can get away with it too?" Barbara said to Margie. They bought the pantsuits and wore them to the lab, feeling both beautiful and slightly scandalous. They had never worn slacks to work before.

While trying out their new fashion-forward outfits, they were also debugging programs. A computer bug was a problem in the code. The term had been coined by Thomas Edison and then popularized by navy rear admiral Grace Hopper while she worked as a research fellow at Harvard University. On the evening of September 9, 1947, the operators of a Mark II computer at the university were having trouble with the machine. Upon investigating, they found a moth trapped in the relay points of a panel. They jokingly taped the dead insect in their lab notebook, noting "First actual case of bug being found." After that night they loved to kid that they were debugging their computer program, and the term spread.

Debugging a program at JPL in the 1960s

simply meant talking through the problems. Margie would sit with Barbara, and they would run through the programs one command at a time. With each line of code she explained her reasoning. "I divided the integer here," Margie would say. Each equation, each string of text, was thought through logically. As Margie described the program aloud step-by-step she would usually come across the error herself. Even if she didn't catch it, her friend Barbara was there listening and would be sure to spot it.

But while Margie could rely on her colleagues at work as much as ever, at home she could feel her marriage slipping away. Her teenage fantasies of romance had subsided into apathy. She and her husband were an ill-matched couple who couldn't seem to get along. The worse her marriage got, the more she felt the need to work. She knew that if they were to split, she'd need her financial independence, made possible by her job at JPL.

Leaving the lab at the end of the day, she laughed when another computer said to her, "Now we go home and really work." It was said in jest, but Margie knew it was only too true. Day after day, she would get home from the lab and rush to make dinner, give the kids a bath and get them to bed, then wash the dishes and do the laundry. At 10 p.m. she'd get into her pajamas and feel exhausted from head to foot. Being a working mother was always hard, but unlike Barbara and Helen, she didn't have an equal partner at home. The man she chose at nineteen had no interest in helping out around the house. Margie sighed and wondered how much more she could take. She knew something had to give.

Against the dark blue of a morning sky on April 4, 1968, Apollo 6 blasted off into space. There were no men inside; instead this flight would test the ability and safety of the three-stage Saturn-V rocket launch vehicle. The launch suffered from setbacks: first, just two minutes after liftoff the frame of the rocket vibrated dangerously. Meanwhile, a manufacturing flaw meant that structural panels began to fall off the lunar module adapter. Then two of the five second-stage engines didn't fire and the third stage didn't ignite at all. Still, the Apollo spacecraft reached a peak of 13,810 miles above Earth. The command module, where astronauts would one day sit, splashed down safely in the Atlantic.

But there would be no celebration. An hour after the crewless spacecraft fell into the ocean, Martin Luther King Jr. was fatally shot in Memphis, Tennessee. The assassination stunned the country. Barbara, Margie, and their team struggled to understand why this tragedy had happened. It was difficult to keep their minds on space when things on Earth were falling apart.

CHAPTER 10
THE LAST QUEEN OF OUTER SPACE

The wind whipped through Sylvia Lundy's hair, and the sun sparkled on the windshield. Sylvia smiled as the little car rumbled down the road. She loved exploring in the summertime. She couldn't be sure what was ahead, and yet she was leaving everything behind. Any road trip in the Volkswagen Bug was a gamble, but this trip, all the way from New Jersey to California, was a real adventure. For the first time, Sylvia was leaving her family home. She looked over at her new husband behind the wheel and tenderly touched his hand. The newlyweds relished the freedom of the open road. They got lost, driving down dirt tracks, the map becoming worn and crinkled as the miles accumulated. They visited family and then picked cities on a whim; as long as they were heading west, they didn't care how they got there.

Sylvia had always loved to travel. Even as a child she felt the lure of leaving familiar places. After her family moved to Rio de Janeiro when she was only three, her older sisters wrestled with the language and culture, but Sylvia slid right into their new life. Her father had a doctorate in public health from MIT and was working for the U.S. government, bringing his knowledge of epidemiology and sanitation to educators. Her mother graduated with a degree in education, having taken many classes in chemistry and math. While Sylvia's father earned his PhD in Massachusetts, she had taught school, supporting him. In Brazil she was busy running the household. She took the girls' education seriously and worried a little about Sylvia, who wasn't a very good reader.

They moved to a house on the beach in Ipanema. Close in age, the three girls — known affectionately as Berta, Barbie, and Sally — built sandcastles together and splashed in the water. The white-sand coast stretching into the dark azure surf was spectacular. But while the warm water tempted them, the massive, powerful waves made swimming dangerous. The beach so terrified the girls that they sometimes had nightmares about being pulled down by the surf.

The family fell in love with Brazil, taking

visitors on tours of Rio, including to the top of Mount Corcovado to see the famous Christ the Redeemer statue. Sylvia's father traveled around Brazil for work while the rest of the family stayed in the capital city, the girls attending English schools. Although their father was hoping for a transfer to India, four years later they moved again, this time to Mexico City. With the move, their parents were getting more serious about the children's education. Sylvia felt the expectation that one day she would follow in her father's footsteps and earn her doctorate. In preparation, as her mother tucked her in at night, she gave Sylvia math puzzles to solve. Sylvia would fall asleep with the numbers still running through her mind.

Sylvia was almost nine years old when they moved back to the United States for her father's work. Only a few weeks after moving to New Jersey, he collapsed from a heart attack. His heart was weak, possibly made weaker from their time living at high elevation in Mexico City. His death was devastating; the girls desperately missed him.

Now it was up to Sylvia's mother to support the young family. She got a job as a secretary to the assistant dean at Douglass

College, the prestigious all-female sister school of Rutgers University. Her hands full and with three girls to educate, Sylvia's mother knew that if she worked for the university she could send her girls to college tuition-free. The perk motivated the once-itinerant family to put down roots. The sisters became known in the college town as "the girls from Ipanema," every bit as graceful and lovely as in the popular song.

Sylvia lived at home while attending Douglass. She still wasn't a great reader, but she loved math. She loaded up on advanced courses in calculus. For some classes she went to the all-male Rutgers, rushing to the bus to get to her physics class on time. By her senior year, Rutgers was offering a new class: a full-year course in computing. Sylvia loved it. She learned programming on an IBM 1130, and although it was complicated, it also felt like a game or an enormous puzzle whose pieces she needed to fit together. Her teacher was a systems engineer at IBM, an inspiring mentor named Mrs. Droege.

Sylvia was doing more than earning her degree. She was also falling in love. She had been dating David, a Rutgers student and an engineering major, since her freshman year, and now that she was graduating, marriage seemed inevitable. Both her sisters had married immediately after finishing college; now it was her turn. She and David married in June 1968 and then took off for California, where David planned to study engineering at Caltech.

Once in California, Sylvia started looking for a job. A friend at church mentioned a section called Mission Design at JPL and suggested that Sylvia apply. When it came time for her interview, Helen Ling was out that day, so Barbara Paulson filled in. Her warm, friendly manner made an immediate impression on Sylvia. She knew she wanted to be part of Barbara's group.

Barbara was impressed with Sylvia's math degree and experience in FORTRAN and told Helen they needed to hire her. Although JPL had rejected Sylvia's formal application for reasons unknown, Barbara saw her worth. They offered her a job, and Sylvia officially became one of Helen's girls.

It was 1968, and the women were gearing up for another go at Mars. Mariner 6 and 7 would be the latest craft to fly by the Red Planet. The computers eagerly plotted the spacecraft's trajectories and programmed the instruments that would probe the planet from space in search of extraterrestrial life. Helen was doing contingency planning, just in case something went wrong with the ship and they had to reroute it. She plotted out new paths using star maps. Instead of the latitude and longitude used to plot location on Earth, Helen used the celestial co-ordinates, declination and right ascension, to plot positions. She drew the contours on cumbersome eleven-by-seventeen-inch charts, spending long hours on the project even as she hoped that her work would never be used.

Margie was also putting in long hours. She was uniting data from all over the lab to improve signal strength between JPL's spacecraft and the ground. One of her duties was to send out memos to keep the lab abreast of their progress. It was the first time she had taken direct ownership of a project, and she was proud of seeing her name on the updates sent all around the lab. Because of her involvement in this project, she got the nickname dB counter, since signal strength was measured in decibels, or dB. She laughed at the new moniker; *at least it isn't Bubbles,* she thought to herself. She also worked closely with the spacecraft-assembly facility and wrote programs to convert the data collected on tape from the spacecraft's photographic equipment into information the image-processing lab could turn into pictures. Her software was working well. Her marriage, however, was over.

Margie's friends at JPL had been right: she was too smart for her husband. She had tried her best but couldn't save her marriage. In the wake of her divorce, Margie felt lonely and isolated. She worried about her four children. Although she felt as though she was the only person in the world splitting with her partner, divorce was actually experiencing a surge of nearly 50 percent in the United States. When California's Family Law Act passed in 1969, it made no-fault divorces possible in the state. And it wasn't just in California — across the country, laws allowing couples to separate solely because of "irreconcilable differences" were opening up the option to divorce, especially to women who felt trapped by marriage. As Margie grappled with her decision, she thought, *I'll still have my kids and my job.*

Sue Finley, on the other hand, felt nothing. Her mind was slipping away from her. She had been home for six years taking care of her two boys, and while she loved them both dearly, she felt she was going crazy. She tottered along, trying to keep it all together, but she was overwhelmed by feelings of fear and anxiety. She began meeting with a psychologist, who listened to her patiently and then prescribed an unusual therapy. She didn't need clinical treatment, he said; what she needed was to return to work. "It'll be better for the children," he explained. Sue nodded. She was ready to go back. Having a job she was proud of and doing work she was good at made her feel strong and purposeful. She loved being a mother more than anything, but she had missed that feeling.

In the six years since Sue had left the lab, much had changed. To prepare, she spent months studying manuals, trying to catch up with the new computer-programming languages. FORTRAN 66 had become an industry standard. For the first time, every new IBM could use the same computing language instead of programming being unique to each machine. As she immersed herself in the new technology, Sue could feel the sense of madness drift away. Returning to JPL and her friends, she was thankful to have no feelings of guilt at leaving her children. Her psychologist had told her this was a medical necessity, and it also helped that so many of her colleagues were working mothers. She turned to Helen, Barbara, and the recently returned Merrilyn Gilchrist when she needed support.

While Sue was regaining her sanity and her life in the lab, men were about to walk on the moon. On July 20, 1969, Neil Armstrong and Buzz Aldrin were the first humans to tread on another planetary body. The computers' fingerprints were all over the historic mission. Their legacy began with the rocket that flew the men up there. It blasted off in stages, a technique made possible by the women's computations for the world's first two-stage rocket, JPL's Bumper WAC. The rocket itself was a successor to the one they had helped advance for the Explorer satellites. A special propellant that needed no ignition fueled the Apollo rocket. The computers had helped develop this novel substance, called hypergolic fuel, when working on liquid propellants for the Corporal. Of course, the Ranger and Surveyor missions they had recently launched were key in determining landing sites for the Apollo missions. And when Neil Armstrong stood on the surface of the moon and said, "That's one small step for man, one giant leap for mankind," the voice transmission back to Earth was received because of tracking stations in California and Australia, part of the Deep Space Network that the computers had worked on so faithfully. Apollo 11 was the culmination of a thousand successes, each one building on the next, stretching up into the beyond.

The women watched the first steps on the moon with the same mixture of awe and wonder as millions of other Americans. Yet modestly, they didn't think about their own handiwork in making it happen. Instead, they were lost in the magic of the moment, glued to the grainy images on their televisions, scarcely believing their own eyes.

Nine days later, it was time to see Mars. Mariner 6 was about to meet the Red Planet, in what JPL called a planetary encounter. Margie waited nervously in the control room. It was the first time they would be able to see live images from another planet, thanks to the high-rate telemetry system she had helped program. Data came streaming in from the spacecraft to the giant antenna at Goldstone as it flew only 2,000 miles from the surface of Mars and more than 40 million miles from Earth. It was late at night, but Margie wasn't sleepy. As she watched the images coming in real time, excitement coursed through her. Each image revealed new details. The poles, similar to our own North and South Poles, jumped out in white, giving the planet an Earth-like appearance. As the spacecraft got closer, however, the cameras showed a strange topography the scientists called chaos terrain. There were cratered deserts, strange collapsed ridges, and mysterious concentric circles that looked like huge bull's-eyes.

The information JPL was gaining about Mars was beyond anything they had learned before. While cameras captured the alien terrain, spectrometers and radiometers were analyzing the Martian atmosphere. The new scientific experiments revealed a planet that, with its craters, resembled the moon superficially but otherwise was quite different. The mission quashed any hope of finding complex life on Mars. Temperatures were freezing, and there was very little oxygen in the atmosphere and no vegetation to be seen. Mariner 6 revealed an ancient planet with an extremely thin atmosphere.

It was a blow not only for scientists, some of whom had mistaken a seasonal dust storm for vegetation coming back to life in the Martian spring, but also for popular culture. It flew in the face of what H. G. Wells wrote in *The War of the Worlds:* "The vegetable kingdom in Mars, instead of having green for a dominant color, is of a vivid blood-red tint." The fascinating and frightening aliens who populated Mars, famous in both movies such as *Invaders from*

Mars and *The Day Mars Invaded Earth* and books like Ray Bradbury's *Martian Chronicles,* were not a possibility.

Yet the dream of finding another world capable of supporting life was not so easily crushed. There was still a chance that simple life-forms might lurk somewhere on the planet. Just as bacteria live in extreme conditions on Earth, such as in volcanic vents and the ice of Antarctica, as we know they do today, it was possible that similar life could be found on the alien planet. The problem was, JPL would have to get much closer, dig into the planet, and take and analyze samples to find it. This would require a much more complex approach. The need to discover life on Mars, to find companions in the universe, was fast becoming an obsession, one that would persist for decades.

Sylvia had little time to appreciate the beauty of Mars. She was going to night school, and her days had become a blur of work, school, and home. Everyone at JPL, especially Helen, had been encouraging her to get her master's in engineering. Twice a week she attended a three-hour class. She enjoyed the coursework and loved the fact that many of her teachers were engineers from JPL. On the other nights, she tried to keep up with her homework. It wasn't easy. She and David were living in a furnished one-bedroom apartment that was cramped and had no dishwasher or other modern amenities. At least its small size meant she didn't have much to clean. However, the other household chores — all the grocery shopping and cooking — left Sylvia overwhelmed. David was busy at Caltech, with no time for these tasks. Under the weight of her daily life, it seemed inevitable that something would break.

Although Sylvia joined JPL during the age of IBM, in the lab the women were still hand-plotting, manually calculating each spacecraft's trajectory before drawing the path in their notebooks. She had never performed that kind of work before, and some of the women laughed at her as she struggled to put mechanical pencil to paper. The paper was thin, so Sylvia tried not to make mistakes. Whenever she erased, which was often, the eraser tore tiny holes in the paper, evidence that she needed more practice.

Sylvia wasn't just calculating on paper. She was programming for what promised to be the most exciting project at JPL yet: the Grand Tour. The audacious project would take advantage of a rare event due to take place in the late 1970s: a once-every-176-year alignment. This occurrence would bring the outer planets of the solar system close to one another at just the right times, shrinking what was a thirty-year voyage to Neptune to one of only thirteen years. JPL wanted to send two probes bound for the outer planets: Jupiter, Saturn, Uranus, Neptune, and Pluto. An untested maneuver called gravity assist, like a giant game of leap-frog through the solar system, would make this possible.

Dick Wallace, the engineer who introduced peanuts to the control room, explained the concept to Sylvia. "It's like a big gravity slingshot," he said. He described how a spacecraft can gain speed as it approaches a planet because the planet's gravity pulls on it. Since the planet is also orbiting the sun, the spacecraft can borrow some of its orbital angular momentum. Therefore, if you sent the spacecraft on the right trajectory, it would curve around the planet, getting faster and faster as it flew away. If they plotted the trajectories perfectly, they could send their probes all over the solar system. Because of gravity assist and the upcoming alignment of the planets, they could accomplish this exploration with significantly less fuel, and consequently less cost, than previously believed. JPL pitched the project to NASA, highlighting the budgetary advantages.

In November 1969, Apollo 12 approached the moon. Charles "Pete" Conrad and Alan L. Bean were looking out the window as they neared the surface. When the lander made a wide turn, Pete couldn't believe what he saw dead ahead. There was Surveyor 3, whose mission had ended two years earlier. The astronauts picked up the pieces of the robotic spacecraft whose success, although dimmed by time, had paved the way for men to walk on the moon. They packed up the parts, exactly as they had been specially trained to at JPL, and placed them in the ship. Surveyor 3 would be the only lunar space probe to make its way back home.

With the 1960s coming to a close, a new president was in the White House. It was clear to the computers that Richard Nixon saw NASA not in terms of its scientific value but as a partisan political pawn, and specifically as a Kennedy endeavor. This was evident when, soon after taking office, Nixon shut down a NASA lab in Cambridge, Massachusetts, and slashed the space agency's budget. The Grand Tour was canceled.

JPL wasn't giving up on their plan to explore the solar system. They couldn't let the rare planetary alignment pass them by. Following the cancellation, a small group of engineers met in secret one weekend. They had to come up with a low-cost way to make the Grand Tour possible. Sylvia worked on the programming challenges. Instead of splitting the mission into two probes, each bound for different planets of the outer solar system, they would design a spacecraft and trajectory that could tour all of them in one astounding expedition. The group worked into the wee hours that weekend, devising trajectories and exploring the programming that would govern such a trip.

Their biggest challenge was figuring out how to fly by Saturn. They had to calculate the path perfectly if they were going to get enough momentum to make it the rest of the way to the other outer planets. Sylvia started writing a program called post-E, which stood for "post-encounter." Their plan was coming together. By Monday morning Sylvia felt the thrill of success. They had come up with an ambitious but feasible plan that significantly cut costs, and her boss, Roger Bourke, was now presenting the scheme to NASA administrators. She crossed her fingers and hoped the meeting would go well. She wanted to continue working on the program.

While Sylvia was devising a Grand Tour of the solar system, her marriage on Earth was faltering. Just like Margie, she reacted by delving deeper into her work, finding comfort in the challenge of uncovering the mysteries of the universe. Her work stood in contrast to the tedious daily strife with her husband. They didn't have any children; if she was going to leave, she should do it now. Pulled between her career and her marriage, she knew she couldn't possibly save both. Working late at night in the lab, she would think about David and his long hours spent only a few miles away, at Caltech. It seemed strange to her that two people who shared a home and a life could know so little about each other. Suddenly her feelings were clear; she had to leave him.

Along with Sylvia's and Margie's marriages, a tradition was ending at JPL. The lab's last Queen of Outer Space beauty contest was held. The competition and dance seemed to belong to a different era. Even to Barbara, once a runner-up when the contest was known as Miss Guided Missile, the event seemed outdated. As the final winner was crowned, protests over gender equality were sweeping the country.

350

The year 1970 marked the fiftieth anniversary of the Nineteenth Amendment, which gave women the right to vote. In recognition, the National Organization of Women held a Women's Strike for Equality. The strike took place in forty states, with twenty thousand people marching up Fifth Avenue in New York City. They held signs declaring WE ARE THE 51% MINORITY and HOUSEWIVES ARE SLAVE LABORERS. The protests put pressure on Congress to pass the Equal Rights Amendment, which would constitutionally guarantee equal rights for women. Their role was changing so quickly that many women were left bewildered. A female real estate agent watching one of the protests told *Time* magazine, "I don't know what these women are thinking of. I love the idea of looking delectable and having men look at me." Although the changes prompted confusion for some, the effects of women's liberation were spreading everywhere, even to the offices of JPL.

The women's titles were shifting. Known as computers since the lab's inception, they were now officially engineers. It was a breakthrough as big as landing on the moon. Their work had been steadily increasing in importance for years, and now they had the title to match their experience. For women like Helen, Barbara, and Margie, who had worked there for years, it was worth far more than anything a beauty pageant title could possibly bestow.

Armed with her new professional title, Margie was working on Mariner 10, which would visit both Mercury and Venus. On its way to the smallest planet of the solar system, Mercury, the ship had to pass behind Venus. The problem was that if the spacecraft was behind the planet, the engineers couldn't detect its signal or correct its course. Margie had to find some kind of solution. She devised a strategy wherein the radio signal from the ship would bend around the planet as long as the spacecraft was oriented toward Earth. She carefully calculated the position of the spacecraft and that of the antennas back home. With her team, she also figured out how to use Venus's gravitation to her advantage. Falling toward the sun is relatively easy, but if you want to visit Mercury you can't drop too fast. Like a restraint, the pull of Venus would slow the ship so it could orbit the planet closest to the sun. It would be the first mission to use gravity assist. When Margie struggled with some parts of the program, she did what she had always done — asked the other women. She loved having her friends to rely on. Using all the components of the DSN, she was able to map out a trajectory that would allow Mariner to make the first exploration of Mercury

Sylvia was also working on the project, creating computer animations to visualize where the ship would travel. With these, she helped plan the ship's trajectory. Where would the spacecraft go after orbiting Mercury? One idea came from an unusual source: a visiting Italian engineer named Giuseppe Columbo. At a conference on Mariner 10 in 1970, held at JPL, Columbo suggested that they might be able to achieve a second encounter around the planet. Working with the other engineers, Sylvia found Columbo was right and calculated a trajectory that allowed Mariner to loop around Mercury a second time, to capture even more of the planet with its cameras.

Margie and Sylvia watched as Mariner 10 launched from Cape Kennedy on November 3, 1973, bound to study the atmosphere and surface of Mercury. It would be months before either knew if her plan had worked.

Meanwhile Helen was devising a plan of her own. Although she and the other women were grandfathered in as engineers, all new hires for that department had to have a degree in engineering. Engineering programs were only just starting to accept women as students — Caltech's had done so in 1970 — but while the doors were finally open, few women were walking through them. That year, women earned fewer than 1 percent of engineering degrees nationwide. Given this, JPL's new requirement meant few women would qualify. Helen enjoyed being a mentor to the women in her group and wanted more for them, so she came up with a simple plan. She would find intelligent women and get them in the door by hiring them as programmers. Then she would encourage them to get advanced degrees in engineering. While they went to night school, she'd teach them to succeed within the framework of JPL. Between their aptitude and her guidance, a generation of female engineers would emerge in the lab.

On a warm, sunny summer afternoon, a dozen of the JPL women and their families met at the beach in Malibu for a picnic. The breeze coming off the ocean tangled their hair as they laid out blankets and beach chairs. From their bags and baskets they unpacked drinks, sandwiches, and fruit. The warm sun felt like heaven against their skin. They frolicked in bathing suits, some sporting stylish new bikinis, as they dipped their toes in the water before running screaming back to the warm sand. Between the heat of the sun and the penetrating cold of the water, they felt intensely alive.

It was a day to celebrate their accomplishments. While protesters were demanding equal rights for women across the country, the women at JPL had created their own equality. They had formed the lab in their own image, building an environment welcoming to women, where their work and contributions were every bit as valued as those of their male counterparts.

A transistor radio, containing the same technology that made their IBMs hum, played the Beatles while the women, with baby oil rubbed on their bodies, let the California sunshine soak into their hair and skin. They raised their drinks high and toasted one another, then their newest spacecraft. "Here's to Mariner," they cried. "Here's to the Grand Tour." Their ships were traveling millions of miles away, and even on Earth, within the confines of their little town of Pasadena, they were breaking new ground. Yet there was another frontier they had yet to conquer. The solar system was out there, waiting to be explored, if only they could persuade NASA to let them do it.

PART IV
1970s–TODAY

Barbara Paulson

Helen Ling

Susan Finley

Sylvia Miller

CHAPTER 11
MEN ARE FROM MARS

Barbara Paulson at Christmas was like a cyclone: you either got swept in or you got out of her way. She didn't care that there was no snow on the ground or that California was in the grip of a December heat wave. She was going to get everyone in the holiday spirit. She decorated, brought in cookies, and made sure everyone was ready for the gift exchange. No names were allowed on the presents; instead you wrote a poem that would subtly tell the group both whom the gift was for and from. The tradition prompted groans every year, but enough of the women, particularly Sue Finley and Barbara, loved it enough to keep it going.

As Barbara was whirling around the office, Dick Wallace, Sylvia Lundy's boss, brought a huge roll of chicken wire into the room. "What are you doing?" asked Barbara. "You'll see," he replied. He started forming the thin, malleable wire into a giant cone that reached all the way to the ceiling. Dick was always bringing the women something, and not just peanuts for their launches. In the spring he would fill the room with camellia blossoms from his yard and in the winter help decorate for the holidays. "There you go, there's your Christmas tree," he said with a big grin. The women laughed, admiring it. They took bunches of green tissue paper and threaded them through the holes in the chicken wire. Then they draped the tree with colored lights. A few homey ornaments also made their way onto it, all fashioned from odds and ends they found around the lab. They giggled at its funny shape and unusual decorations. One of the engineers, Paul Muller, popped his head into the room, looked at the tree, and muttered, "Highly inflammable." As soon as he was gone, the women roared with laughter. If they could annoy Muller, it was definitely worth it.

Muller was a complainer. He whined that the women monopolized Cora, the IBM 1620. Cora's time had become valuable now that computer programs were finally taking precedence over hand-plotting. Unfortunately for Muller, the women had priority on Cora since they were responsible for 90 percent of the lab's computer programming. The men were just beginning to dip their toes into the technology, and they lagged behind their female colleagues.

While those at JPL immersed themselves in emerging technology, Apollo missions were beginning to feel routine. On April 10, 1970, the news that the Beatles were breaking up far overshadowed the Apollo mission scheduled to take place the next day. Despite the lack of attention, Apollo 13 lifted off Earth smoothly and was on its way to the moon. But only two days later, an oxygen tank aboard the ship exploded two hundred thousand miles from Earth. Soon after astronaut Jim Lovell said, "Houston, we've had a problem," the world became riveted.

At mission control in Houston, NASA flight controllers acted heroically, abandoning the original mission of landing on the moon and transforming the lunar module into a lifeboat. Even at JPL, where manned missions weren't part of the repertoire, the crisis brought things to a standstill. The women waited anxiously for news that the three astronauts had safely splashed down in the Pacific Ocean. When on April 17, they made it, with bright orange-and-white-striped parachutes slowing the module's plunge into the water, the lab in Pasadena burst into cheers and hugs. With the safe return of the astronauts, the "successful failure" brought attention back to NASA, though not necessarily the attention the space agency was looking for. The accident changed how manned space exploration was perceived, earning Apollo a dangerous reputation.

Barbara contemplated the bravery of the astronauts as she made her way to Building 180, the tallest at JPL. At the top, on the ninth floor, was director Bill Pickering's office, while Barbara and her colleagues had their offices on the third floor. Despite their groundbreaking promotions, there remained a gulf between the men and women — not only an economic divide, since the men did earn more, but also a physical one. Most of the male engineers they worked with were in Building 230. Although they saw each other daily, working on problems and eating lunch together, the groups sent data between the two buildings using messengers. The women were starting to have fun with the mail. Like children sending notes across the classroom, the men and women started up a harmless flirtation in the missives flying back and forth.

Most of the girls were being silly; they had

no intention of actually dating their colleagues. Margie's flirtation, however, was becoming serious. While some of the women shook their heads at her dating another engineer, Derry Lee Brunn captivated her. She couldn't forget her abysmal first marriage to a onetime JPL engineer, yet here she was, ready to try again.

Margie wasn't thinking only about men; her mind was also on Mars. In the first days of February 1974, Mariner 10 passed Venus, circling around it just as anticipated. As the ship flew near the planet, it began sending back close-up images. Margie was afraid they would lose the spacecraft's signal and not be able to pick it up again. However, as she had hoped, Mariner swung away from cloudy Venus and flew by Mercury a month later. Their first views of the tiny planet revealed a cratered, dead surface. There was no atmosphere, in the traditional sense, at all. Instruments on board the ship confirmed the planet had a dense, iron-rich core but surprisingly also detected a magnetic field. Scientists had thought the planet too small to generate one. As if assembling a giant puzzle, they put eighteen of the ship's images together to form a clear picture of the surface. In crisp black and white they could see craters atop craters;

Mercury looked battered and bruised. Without an adequate atmosphere, the planet has no protection from the impact of large debris such as meteorites. To Margie, though, it was beautiful. She had never felt more proud of a mission, even as the ship ran out of fuel and its transmitter was turned off, dooming it to incessantly orbit the sun.

Mariner 10 proved to JPL that they could use the gravity of one planet as a slingshot to send a spacecraft to another. It was an important milestone as they geared up for the Grand Tour. Although it had been canceled just the year before, Sylvia and her colleagues resurrected the program, albeit with one-quarter the original budget. It was now called Mariner-Jupiter-Saturn 77, or MJS 77. Their dreams for the mission, however, were still grand. Although the official goal of the project was an encounter with Saturn, the team wasn't content with the shortened journey. They were determined to explore the solar system and planned for the spacecraft to keep traveling as long as possible. To make this happen, they needed Sylvia to work on her post-E computer program, which would direct the ship after its encounter with Saturn, swinging it out to Uranus and Neptune. Writing the program was so much fun that Sylvia could hardly call it work. She came into the lab each morning excited to get started.

The trajectory they came up with was a waltz around the planets. The spacecraft would swing around its biggest partner, Jupiter, passing between its moons before being swept up by the next partner, Saturn. From there it would spin around Uranus before being flung off to Neptune. Sadly little Pluto, like a wallflower never asked to dance, was too far away to be included. Sylvia's programming made sure the ship swung in line with the movement of the planets it passed, so that instead of using fuel, it would simply be thrown from one planet's gravitational field to the next. Each step of the elegant dance was carefully choreographed.

While the program plotted a course, a successful flight still relied on humans. Flight technicians at JPL's mission control needed to send signals to the ship at specific waypoints using the Deep Space Network. These midcourse corrections necessitated some fuel being carried on board to fire the thrusters while batteries powered by plutonium-238 would generate electricity. Besides this, gravity assist would do all the heavy lifting. The team published their audacious route in 1972, clearly defining the mission. The publication overwhelmed Sylvia; she could hardly believe it. Titled "Mariner Jupiter/Saturn 1977: The Mission Frame," it both opened and closed with quotes from *2001: A Space Odyssey* by Arthur C. Clarke, a nod to the mission's grand aspirations. But for Sylvia the real excitement lay in seeing her own name included in the list of authors. It was her first publication, and she looked with pride at the trajectories within, the result of the group's hard work and dedication to the Grand Tour. Along with her name was a picture of the team. Sylvia, resplendent in white, sat smiling among her co-authors: four male engineers.

As Sylvia plotted a path through the universe, Helen was looking a little closer to home. She held in her hands a picture of Earth taken from space. The famous photograph, *The Blue Marble,* was taken during Apollo 17, the last manned lunar mission, in 1972.

Despite Apollo's accomplishments, public support for it had never been particularly strong. During the 1960s, most Americans didn't believe the manned lunar program was worth the cost, with the exception of one poll taken immediately after Apollo 11. In 1965, only 39 percent of Americans thought that the United States should do whatever necessary, regardless of cost, to be the first nation on the moon. Now, with victory behind them, support waned further. The Apollo program was seen as expensive and unnecessary, especially with the country plunging deep into debt from the ongoing Vietnam War. In 1970 the budget for NASA was cut 17 percent, an odd reward for the program that had just won the space race. The next year, just after the Apollo 14 launch, two hundred African-American protesters held a March Against Moon Rocks at Cape Kennedy. One of the leaders, Hosea Williams, was quoted in the *Rome* (Georgia) *News-Tribune* as saying, "We are protesting our country's inability to choose humane priorities." Many, especially in the wake of the Apollo 13 disaster, shared his feelings.

At NASA, it was generally expected that the program would run to Apollo 20, but that hope soon faded. After the success of Apollo 15, the first to include a three-day stay on the surface and a lunar rover, President Nixon considered canceling the program altogether. He worried that another disaster like Apollo 13 could be detrimental to his 1972 reelection campaign. Finally, he was persuaded to allow Missions 16 and 17 to go ahead. But it was clear there would be no more. All told, six missions had carried twelve men to the lunar surface. But even with its many successes, only 41 percent of Americans in 1979 felt the Apollo program had been worth the cost. It was time to move on.

With the end of Apollo, the Nixon administration began reconsidering NASA's future. Shooting expensive rockets into the sky, never to return, was untenable. In this atmosphere, the Space Task Group proposed an ambitious program composed of a space shuttle, space station, and manned missions to the moon and Mars. It was too much. The proposal belonged to a different era, one in which NASA was still expanding. However, the idea of the space shuttle appealed to Nixon. Unlike the space station and the crewed missions, the shuttle oozed practicality. It was a shift away from space exploration and toward application. With reusable rockets and a trajectory that wouldn't extend beyond a low Earth orbit, it had the possibility of making space travel available to everyone. The idea behind it could be traced to Wernher von Braun's vision for space discovery, termed the "von

Braun paradigm" and first described in the 1950s. Bizarrely enough, this vision was rooted in von Braun's World War II background. He based the design for the space shuttle on the Nazi Amerika Bomber project, a winged rocket that would ascend to suborbital space before dropping bombs on New York City.

With these unlikely beginnings, the White House reviewed the Space Task Group's proposal. With a shrinking budget, cost-effective projects had priority. The first project Nixon approved was Skylab, the initial NASA space station, which had the double advantage of being relatively cheap and already developed. The operation employed what NASA called its Apollo Applications Program, which planned to use the leftover hardware from Apollo to support new missions. Carved out from the third stage of one of Apollo's unused Saturn rockets, and including such features as a workshop and a solar observatory, Skylab launched in 1973. It was supported by the Marshall Space Flight Center in Huntsville, von Braun's old stomping grounds. However, the retired rocket scientist was no longer in Alabama; instead, at sixty-one, he was grappling with a cancer diagnosis.

It was NASA's first experiment maintain-

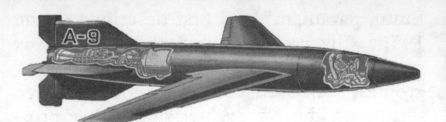

Von Braun's Amerika Bomber, illustrated in 1947 (Popular Mechanics)

ing human life in space, with one crew prepared to spend eighty-four days aboard the station. It wasn't, however, the first space station launched from Earth. The Soviet Union had launched one two years earlier. That mission, Salyut 1, ended in tragedy. In June 1971, after spending a record twenty-three days in space, the three-man crew was headed back home, speeding toward Earth in their reentry capsule. Outwardly, the Soyuz 11 mission capsule showed no damage, so it was a shock to the recovery team when they opened the hatch and found all three of the cosmonauts dead. They later determined that a pressure-equalization valve in the capsule had opened prematurely, sucking the air out of it and exposing Georgi Dobrovolski, Vladislav Volkov, and Viktor Patsayev to the vacuum of space, making them the only humans in history to have perished outside of Earth's atmosphere.

Although it was an unfortunate accident caused by mechanical failure, the Soviets were wary of confirming the cause of death. They would only go as far to say that the casualties were "being investigated" and offered no details. With Skylab set to launch soon, NASA worried that extended time in space could be fatal. There was no way to be sure space was safe. It would be two years before the Western world was told the cause of the Soviet mission's demise.

In addition to Skylab, politicians viewed the shuttle program as cost-effective. The reusable "space bus" had the potential to ferry astronauts and equipment safely into outer space and back. Designs for the project began to pour in from private contractors, and in 1972, Nixon approved the winning design. Cost dominated the discussion while safety considerations took a backseat. The juicy $2.6 billion contract went to California-based North American Rockwell, a decision Jean Westwood, chair of the Democratic National Committee, decried as a "calculated use of the American taxpayers' dollars for [Nixon's] own pre-election purposes." The influx of jobs in the Golden State would certainly help Nixon's chances of grabbing its fifty-five votes in the electoral college, although it probably didn't hurt that Rockwell was the lowest bidder.

NASA set a hasty launch date for the shuttle: 1978. It would be composed of an orbiter, a massive fuel tank, and rocket boosters. The orbiter was designed to ride piggyback on the fuel tank. It launched like a rocket but then, after the fuel tank separated, it could glide back to Earth. Its design was familiar, resembling a typical airplane, and the hope was that the shuttle would eventually carry the astronauts with the same ease and comfort in which people rode commercial airliners. Once launched, the rocket boosters would separate from the shuttle, falling into the ocean, where a boat would recover them. The fuel tank, on the other hand, would be jettisoned over the atmosphere, destined for disintegration.

As both Skylab and the space shuttle got the green light, other projects were struggling for approval. In 1973, Nixon canceled plans to put a large Earth-orbiting telescope in the sky. The device, later known as the Hubble Space Telescope, was still in development, and the hope had been to launch it from the space shuttle. Astronomers had long dreamed of a telescope that was free from the distortions of Earth's atmosphere, allowing faint objects to be resolved more clearly than ever before. Although it had yet to be built, much less to deliver a single image, its cancellation provoked a strong response. A massive lobbying effort, fueled by astronomers and non-astronomers alike, reversed the decision. The Marshall Space Flight Center would assemble the telescope while the Goddard Space Flight Center would develop its scientific instrumentation.

While all the proposed projects were defining a new generation of exploration at NASA, the massive budget for the space shuttle made the project especially prominent. Many at JPL saw it as competition. With the NASA budget shrinking, they knew that every dollar going to the shuttle was one less for exploration of the solar system. In the new funding climate, the engineers worried that the Grand Tour would get pushed aside.

Although JPL was focused on exploring other planets, the *Blue Marble* photo of Earth hung all over the lab. Against the black of space, the ball of blue shone, the African continent and the south polar ice cap clear beneath whirling white clouds. Familiar as the image was, it also brought home the fragility of our planet. With Earth Day celebrated for the first time in 1970, the view of Earth from space drew attention to environmental issues. As Helen looked at the picture she found herself drawn to the oceans she had been assigned to work on, their deep blues covering most of Earth's surface.

Helen was working on a project called SEASAT, which would collect data on Earth's oceans. The satellite, launched in June 1978 from Vandenberg Air Force Base, in California, could measure sea surface winds and temperature, wave heights, and the ocean's topography, employing sophisticated instrumentation that included a radar altimeter, a microwave scatterometer, and the first use of synthetic aperture radar in space. In its orbit, SEASAT was able to cover 95 percent of Earth with its remote sensing every thirty-six hours, peering into the oceans with even greater detail than they had anticipated. It was so sensitive it could even detect the position of submarines simply from the wake they left as they moved. Then, in October, a massive short circuit rocked the satellite, rendering it inoperative. Despite this blow, Helen was excited about the extensive data they had gathered. The mission was just the beginning, opening the door for a string of radar satellites that would be launched to study Earth. The radar system pioneered by SEA-

SAT would also make its way onto the space shuttle.

Meanwhile, Barbara was hard at work on a project called Viking. For the first time, they were planning to land a spacecraft on Mars. Although the chances of finding complex life on the planet had been crushed by Mariner, they still held out hope that a simple alien life-form, perhaps something like Earth's resilient bacteria, known as extremophiles, might inhabit the Red Planet. To find such creatures, the ship was designed with a robotic arm capable of digging up soil and analyzing it within its own contained laboratory. The data would then be sent back to Earth. In keeping with tradition at JPL, the mission was designed as a pair of spacecraft, providing two shots at success.

The team designed each Viking to break into two pieces: an orbiter and a lander. The orbiter would survey the planet for a landing site and then drop the lander. The lander would deploy its parachute and sink safely to the surface. The orbiter would continue on its way, studying the Martian atmosphere while also acting as a relay station for the lander on the ground below.

Barbara considered the options for Viking's flight to Mars. She worked on different trajectories as they considered which path would be most successful. The mission would take place while Mars was farthest from Earth, 206 million miles. This would be a striking difference from the Mariner Mars missions, which had made a six-month journey. Viking's journey would be an epic eleven months. To maintain contact at such a fantastic distance, JPL had to carefully align the ship's trajectory to all six stations of the DSN, each equipped with huge dish antennas. Because Viking was 206 million miles away, it would take twenty minutes to send a message and another twenty to receive a reply. Barbara wrote computer programs that sent the ship all the way around the sun but never out of range of the DSN. Her maps resembled the delicate spiral of a seashell, with the ship curving out from Earth's orbit, bending around the sun, and then joining Mars in its orbit.

Barbara knew that even once they got the spacecraft to Mars it wouldn't be easy going. The orbiter would take pictures of possible landing sites, but when it came time to drop the lander they would have to do so blindly, unsure exactly what the little robot would land on. It was distressing to think that all their work could be for nothing if the lander crashed onto uneven terrain. Barbara watched from California as each of the two Viking spacecraft launched in Florida in August and September 1975, only a month apart.

While Barbara kept an eye on Viking, Helen was spending her evenings at the swimming pool. She loved sitting on the bleachers and watching her daughter, Eve, swim. Next to her was a big stack of work. As Eve practiced with her team, Helen worked out the kinks in her programs. She looked up every once in a while and watched her daughter's powerful kick. Eve was strong and beautiful, and Helen was proud of her. Life wasn't always easy for Helen's children. Their mother's work sometimes felt like another child who needed constant looking after. But though Helen's attention was sometimes divided, her kids were always foremost in her life.

Their home life was simpler now with kids in school, and now that Arthur was at JPL alongside his wife. He worked with the mechanics at the lab, and the couple shifted their schedules as needed around the kids' activities. They especially wanted to support Eve's exceptional ability in the water. Luckily, Helen could lug her printouts with her. Her programs ranged widely in scope, since she had her hand in just about every project.

When she wasn't writing the programs herself, she tried to spot her colleagues' mistakes. She thrived on the details of the work, which made her an excellent supervisor.

Kathy Thuleen was going to miss Helen. She was pregnant for a third time and leaving the lab. She loved being an engineer and had never enjoyed more responsibility than she had in the previous two years. Programming was precious to her. She had two young sons and wished she could come back after having this baby too, but her husband was being transferred to San Diego and they were moving. She knew she would never find another job like the one she was leaving. The group gathered for a teary farewell lunch, everyone wishing Kathy luck.

While Kathy anticipated her baby's arrival, the women looked ahead to Viking's encounter with Mars. The ship reached the planet on June 19, 1976, and the orbiter began taking pictures as planned. Around 6 p.m., Helen and the team anxiously awaited the images, which they would use to select a landing spot. They came in slowly, line by line on the television screen, and everyone crowded around, desperate for a closer look. With the first photograph there was cheering and excitement. Unlike the paint-by-numbers pastel picture that had formed their first view of Mars, this image was clear and detailed. Soon, though, their excitement faded into shock. This wasn't the Mars they knew. The pictures showed lava flows and deep craters stretching across the surface. It was far more cratered than the Mariner images had led them to expect. The rocky terrain was forbidding, hardly the spot to land a robot. "We need you," one of Helen's colleagues said, turning to her. Helen could see that a new computer program was going to be necessary if they were going to land safely. They wouldn't have much time.

They had originally planned to land Viking 1 on Mars on July 4, 1976. It would be a grand gesture in celebration of the United States bicentennial. Now they would have to push back the date. They couldn't wait too long; once the second Viking arrived at Mars they would need to switch their attention, and the DSN, to the new spacecraft. Everyone was spending sixteen- to eighteen-hour days trying to understand the complex geology of Mars. The engineers and scientists had to work together closely to find a spot big enough for the lander but near enough to what they thought might be flowing water. Caltech students and interns were counting the craters one by one while they fed the raw numbers into new computer programs. The scientists reviewed the computer analysis and tried to make sense of it. Some of the students were surprised by how much of the operation required human interaction. They expected to see supercomputers instead of people doing all the work. Senior scientist Harold Masursky good-naturedly responded to one inquiry: "Computers are just like wearing shoes. You need them when you are walking on gravel, but they don't get you across the gravel."

Nancy Key was trying to get across the gravel. She spent the country's birthday working late in the lab. Viking needed the women computer programmers, as well as most of the JPL staff, and few employees could take the holiday off. As July Fourth fireworks went off, she heard distant thuds that proclaimed celebration. The black sky filled with color and smoke. Some of the women went to the windows to look, opening them wide so they could stick their heads out. Then they went back to work.

A warm night's breeze swept in through the open windows. Nancy noticed black ash dancing on the gusts of air and floating through the room. "What's happening?" she asked. The women looked outside and saw the hillside ablaze. The fireworks had ignited the dry canyon shrubbery. They debated what to do. "Well, the fire doesn't look too big," one of the women said. Nancy agreed. With their Martian robot circling millions of miles away, they were too consumed with calculations to worry about fires. They stayed where they were, and luckily the fire was soon put out.

Using the computers' analysis, the scientists picked the safest spot they could find. On 5 a.m. on July 20, 1976, they sent down the lander. The mood was tense. The lander dropped, and its parachute opened. But with no live pictures, they had no idea if the robot was headed for a safe parking spot or a jagged rock that would destroy their work. There was nothing to do but wait while the robot slowly floated down to the surface. Then came the words they had been waiting for: "Touchdown, we have touchdown." The room erupted in celebration. Nancy couldn't believe they had made it. Amid a flurry of hugs and kisses, the first image ever taken from the surface of Mars came through at JPL. The view of the rocky surface confirmed the danger of the landing site. They wouldn't find out until the next day, when the first color images of the planet came in, how lucky they had been. A huge boulder that stood only thirty feet away would have caused the lander to tumble and fall.

The first color picture from the surface of Mars was rocky and red. The sky was a curious dusky-salmon color. The Red Planet was living up to its name. But the lander wasn't there just to take photographs; it was looking for chemical evidence of life. Two months later a second lander would join in the search. What the Vikings found on the surface of Mars led to more questions than answers. While one set of experiments designed to detect metabolism from microbes living in Martian soil was positive, other tests were negative, igniting controversy. Conspicuously absent were organic compounds in the soil, suggesting that the planet harbored no life at all.

While Barbara and her colleagues pondered the future of the Mars missions over lunch, a man with floppy dark hair sat down at a table nearby. They all knew who the visiting scientist was. Carl Sagan had taken part in the missions at JPL for years — Mariner, Pioneer, Viking — and he seemed to have a hand in everything they worked on. Everyone knew he was extremely bright and friendly. Barbara smiled across the room at him.

Sue joined them at the lunch table. She

was easing back into her routine. Coming back to work had been good for her — she loved her work and her friends. What was hard was going home. She adored her little boys but struggled with her husband. After fifteen years of marriage she couldn't go on. As she wrestled with the decision, she kept thinking, *I don't want my boys to think this is what marriage is like.* She no longer valued stability above all else; instead she wanted to give her sons a home without strife. The decision was painful, but she decided to go forward with a divorce and hope for the best.

Far from her worries at home, Sue was working on computer programs for the Grand Tour. She and Barbara were using the Exec 8 operating system on the UNIVAC computer and programming in FORTRAN 5. It was the latest in computing technology. They were working with Charley Kohlhase, an engineer and Voyager's Mission Design manager. He was an old friend from the early Mariner missions. Kohlhase and the project manager, John Casani, weren't fans of the clunky moniker MJS 77, the working name of the Grand Tour mission, so they scribbled alternatives on a blackboard: Nomad, Pilgrim, Antares. None of them worked. Finally, the name Voyager, pulled from a defunct Mars mission, stuck. It felt right.

The team analyzed thousands of possible trajectories to determine Voyager's path through space. The engineers never seriously considered including little Pluto in the trajectory. While their once-in-176-year alignment was perfect for exploring Jupiter, Saturn, Uranus, and Neptune, it would take a once-every-600-year alignment to travel to Pluto as well. Just getting past Saturn was going to be a challenge. In fact, they had to be careful not to mention their plans to visit Uranus and Neptune outside the lab. The engineers knew that Congress had barely approved this mission and that if they proposed extending the tour, the entire operation could be in jeopardy. Instead, they would proceed in secret and hope to get authorization after leaving Saturn.

Voyager was such a massive effort that everyone had to pitch in. Overwhelmed with work, they fretted over possible mistakes. Gentry Lee, the section manager, stressed the importance of checking their work by introducing the term "proper paranoia." While Barbara could still remember the rush of excitement in JPL's early days, when the computers raced to get their calculations from their notebooks to the rockets firing in the test pits, nowadays they checked and rechecked their equations before passing them along to be implemented. So the women repeated the phrase to one another, the words becoming a mantra of mindfulness as they scrutinized their calculations.

When there was a rush job and they needed to program quickly, Kohlhase would burst into the offices and ask for Helen. With the perfect combination of speed and precision, she was always his choice.

While the women were reaching for the edges of the solar system, there was trouble in the space closer to home. Skylab, the first space station, was struggling. Two of its rocket thrusters sprang leaks, and due to unusually high solar activity, a rescue became impossible. After orbiting Earth for six years, the station had to be abandoned. Commander Jerry Carr, one of the last astronauts to leave Skylab, was saddened by the departure, later saying of the space station, "It had hung together beautifully for us, and we kind of hated to leave it." On July 11, 1979, Skylab fell to its doom, the atmosphere breaking it up and scattering it over the Indian Ocean and Australia. However, before its untimely end, it had proved that humans could live and work in space. Skylab was an important stepping-stone in the development of the modern International Space Station.

As expensive equipment fell from the sky, Sylvia, now armed with her master's degree in engineering from West Coast University, was becoming a star at the lab. Plucked out of Helen's group and working with Dick Wallace, she was building a reputation as an extremely talented engineer. Her programming on the Voyager mission was meticulous, producing elegant trajectories for the twin ships. Sylvia's task was especially difficult; she needed to plot a path close enough to Jupiter's moons and Saturn's rings to use their gravity while still staying in the proper alignment to fling the spacecraft out to Uranus and Neptune. To hedge their bets, the team charted a course for Voyager 1 that would take a shortcut through the solar system, getting closer to Jupiter and Saturn, while Voyager 2 would wind its way around more slowly, flying by both Uranus and Neptune. To accommodate this plan, Voyager 2 would actually be launched first.

At the end of May 1977, Sylvia and her date sat in a movie theater watching the blockbuster *Star Wars.* Sylvia was tired, and her mind kept drifting back to a computer program that wasn't working properly. It was hard to let go of the code and relax; she went over the broken commands again and again. Suddenly a view of the stars filled the screen. It was the splendor of outer space, as imagined by George Lucas, and Sylvia was entranced. She giggled at R2-D2, amused at the difference between robots in movies and those in the lab, and reveled in the quirky characters in the bar scene. Along with everyone else in the theater, she became lost in the story. Later, as they left the dark movie theater for the bright light of day, she felt energized. It was as if she had a secret, shared only by those at JPL. She was about to see the real outer space, a view that needed no special effects from Hollywood.

There was one NASA icon who would not live to see the majesty of Voyager. Wernher von Braun succumbed to pancreatic cancer on June 16, 1977, at the age of sixty-five. His legacy of mighty rockets would live on in the exploration of the solar system when, two months later, Voyager 2 sat atop a powerful Titan-Centaur rocket at the launchpad at Cape Canaveral. It was early morning, and those at JPL were full of nervous energy. The women knew this was their one shot at the Grand Tour. The planets wouldn't align like this again for another three lifetimes.

Almost immediately things began to go wrong. First the onboard computers failed on the launchpad. Thankfully, this was a quick fix, and they were ready to begin again. In four-foot-high digits, the iconic launch clock at Kennedy Space Center counted down to zero. A billow of white smoke appeared as the rocket set off, lifting slowly from the ground. As expected, the launchpad became consumed in clouds of exhaust that engulfed everything and everyone, almost as if the sky had descended upon the earth. A luminous white light, the result of aluminum oxide exhaust from the rocket boosters, blinded observers. In mere minutes the whole thing was out of sight.

As the rocket carried the spacecraft up through the clear Florida sky, the ship began to get confused. Like humans who find themselves in the throes of a wild spinning sensation, Voyager was suffering from mechanical vertigo and unable to get its bearings. Bruce Murray, JPL's new director, called it an anxiety attack. The engineers at JPL watched helplessly. If they rebooted the system it might never reorient itself. The entire mission would be a wash as the probe forever sought direction in the vastness of space. Instead, they waited, hoping the computer system would fix itself. Soon, its fault-protection programming kicked in and the ship righted. Yet only an hour later there was another hiccup. The semi-autonomous Voyager, dealing with another orientation failure, shut down communications with Earth. JPL mission control was nervous; the robot had a mind of its own. Then, seventy-nine minutes later, Voyager found its bearings, communications came back up, and the ship was finally on its way to Jupiter.

The second Voyager launch was even more of a nail-biter. It took place on September 5, just sixteen days after Voyager 2's liftoff. Although it was the second Voyager to be launched, it was named Voyager 1, since its arc through space would leapfrog the spacecraft past its twin, delivering it to Saturn first. The day started out promisingly. The sky was a clear, dark blue in Florida while dawn had yet to break in California. It didn't matter to the team at JPL; they were huddled inside, waiting for the countdown. At 8:56 a.m. in Florida, in a fiery flash of light and exhaust, the rocket carrying the ship lifted off. Sluggishly at first, then rising steadily, it soon disappeared, a coil of smoke in the cloudless sky the only evidence of its path.

Something was wrong. On both coasts

they watched as the rocket rose slowly through the atmosphere, a little too slowly. At Cape Canaveral, two JPL staff members were particularly concerned. Charley Kohlhase turned to John Casani and said, "We may not be making it. We're not getting enough velocity." If the spacecraft couldn't reach escape velocity, its tour of the solar system would be a short one. It would pop into Earth's orbit, caught in the clutches of gravity and unable to travel any farther. They were running out of both propellant and time. The ship had already eaten through twelve hundred pounds of fuel it shouldn't have needed. The culprit was a tiny fuel leak in the propellant line. In California, the mood was tense. They sat helplessly; there was absolutely nothing they could do. Then, with 3.4 seconds of propellant left, the rocket made it, breaking the chains of gravity before the first-stage Titan fuel tanks fell away. Relief washed over the entire team. Voyager 1 had reached a high enough orbit.

Now the engineers and computers turned their attention to the second-stage Centaur rockets, which they knew contained extra fuel, enough, they hoped, to push the ship onto its path to Jupiter. Yet burning through all this fuel until the tanks were empty carried a risk. The walls of the fuel tanks were thin strips of stainless steel, no thicker than a dime. The tank was built like a balloon, kept inflated only by the presence of propellant. The design was ideal for keeping the weight of the rocket down. However, once the tank ran dry, the walls would collapse in on themselves, possibly ripping apart at the seams as they did so. If this happened, an explosion could be sparked that would destroy the ship.

Flight controllers at mission control waited as the rocket coasted into the anticipated position and then fired the Centaur rockets again. For a second time, they got lucky. Within seconds before the tanks emptied completely, the ship sailed into the correct orbit to make it to Jupiter. The tanks, nearly empty, dropped away.

The ultimate interstellar journey had begun. Equipped with scientific instruments, cameras, and a gold-plated copper record designed by Carl Sagan and his colleagues, Voyager was off. The record was a message in a bottle, containing such diverse sounds as crashing surf, birdsong, greetings in fifty-five languages, and an eclectic ninety minutes of music. Helen and her team wondered what mysteries the spacecraft might uncover as it set out to explore the universe.

CHAPTER 12
LOOK LIKE A GIRL

The size of the storm made them gasp. The red spot that represented the maelstrom was as big as three Earths and vivid in angry swirls. It looked like a giant eye, staring back at the crowd of JPL employees observing it. Among the bewildered spectators in the lab's auditorium were Barbara Paulson, Helen Ling, and Sylvia Lundy. They couldn't believe they were looking at Jupiter. The colors of the planet's atmosphere resembled the light brushstrokes and blurred detail of an impressionist painting, with bands of soft blue and ivory cut by dark red stripes. It was hard to believe those bands were circling the giant planet at speeds of 400 miles per hour. The moons stood out in spectacular glory; on Io, never-before-seen volcanoes, ten times as powerful as those on Earth, erupted in plumes of sulfur. From March 5 to April 13, 1979, Voyager 1 swooped past the Jupiter system, gathering an immense amount of data and nearly nineteen thousand images; it was a decade of discovery condensed into one encounter.

The next year they gathered multiple times in the auditorium, shuffling sleeping bags out of their way. Many engineers, especially the young ones without families at home, camped out in the lab, mesmerized as thousands of images flashed on the screen. Before their eyes, Saturn's rings came through so clear and crisp it seemed you could reach out and touch them. Voyager 2 flew above the rings as the light shone through them, revealing more dazzling loops of ice, dust, and rock than had been thought possible. Some of the rings intertwined, like golden jewelry hoops, while others possessed odd spokes, sticking out like carriage wheels. There were so many rings that eventually Bradford Smith, leader of JPL's imaging science team, gave up trying to keep track of them all for reporters. Exasperated, he told the press corps, "You count them."

The Voyagers left Saturn nine months apart, in November 1980 and August 1981. At JPL, the staff was elated to learn that NASA would keep supporting the mission beyond Saturn. Their stealthy plan had worked; the Voyagers could keep exploring the solar system. Voyager 1 left first, headed directly for the edge of the solar system, while Voyager 2 would make a five-year journey to Uranus before trailing its twin into deep space. Then, disaster struck. The platform on Voyager 2 holding two of its cameras jammed. The cameras kept taking pictures, but only of the endless night of space. JPL couldn't point the lenses to their targets any longer; the mission was in danger of not being able to capture any more of the images it needed. The engineers working on Voyager fruitlessly tried to come up with a way to turn the camera around toward the planets. Then they had a lucky accident. One of the flight controllers mistakenly sent a command to Voyager to rotate the stuck platform at ten times the typical force. The forceful twist did the trick; the cameras could now be inched around at low speed. It seemed that in their frenzy to take pictures, the engineers had inadvertently locked up the system. Now, as long as they kept their movements slow and careful, they could still capture the beauty and mysteries of Uranus and Neptune. They just had to wait for the ship to reach them — only another 1.7 billion miles to go.

The Voyager missions were a tour like

none other and brought the staff at JPL closer together. They gawked as they watched the images streaming into the auditorium and then played softball together, bowled, or went hiking. And Voyager made them incredibly proud. Their hard work and dedication had produced images that seemed too beautiful to be real. As their spacecraft explored the solar system, they couldn't help but be struck by how singular Earth was. Eventually traveling 13 billion miles, the mission made clear that, with its swirls of white clouds sailing above blue seas, our planet was alone in the solar system in its ability to support life. Yet beyond these nine planets, the JPL team felt, they were creeping closer to unexplored galaxies, to a universe filled with the possibility of life beyond the blue marble. The ships just keep exploring, transmitting data back to Earth as they leave the regions touched by our sun and enter the space between the stars. Voyager 1 was the first to enter this interstellar space, with Voyager 2 at its heels. Around 2025 their power, fueled by three batteries filled with a decaying lump of plutonium-238, will run out. Yet the ships will silently continue their journey. For those lucky enough to be part of the team at JPL, Voyager stands as the culmination of their careers — their most beautiful, important accomplishment.

While Voyager opened a new view of the solar system, Helen was continuing to hire women at a rapid pace, albeit at the whim of NASA budgets. "We're a sisterhood," teased Merrilyn Gilchrist as she welcomed the new hires. The sisters cultivated their friendships both in and out of the lab, spending countless hours together.

Although three decades had passed since Macie Roberts began her policy of hiring solely women, Helen was unapologetically carrying on the tradition. When Macie hired new women she had often told them, "In this job you need to look like a girl, act like a lady, think like a man, and work like a dog." In some ways, her advice still rang true. If you wanted to be one of Helen's team, you certainly had to be a woman.

When Macie was hiring Barbara, Helen, and Sue, her view of women in science was as limited as the boundaries of space JPL had penetrated up to that time. She couldn't have dreamed what was ahead for them or foreseen the responsibility they would earn. She certainly never expected to see computers advancing to be Mission Design managers, like Phyllis Buwalda, or leading their own teams on explorations of the universe, like Sylvia.

Helen honored Macie's legacy of hiring bright women with education and experience in math and computer science. Her mentoring encompassed not just the importance of advanced degrees but also the balance of working while raising children. Helen had been following this vision for a decade, watching as her hires worked their way up the ranks, but now she was really stepping up her numbers. Grandfathered in to her position as an engineer, she had no need of a degree, yet she pushed the coursework on every woman she hired.

Sue Finley, on the other hand, had never been a fan of school. She disliked it so much that she had dropped out of college, never to return. So she was surprised to see an envelope on her desk one day — some routine correspondence about a mission she was working on — emblazoned with the words *Dr. Sue Finley.* She picked it up and caressed it lightly. She wasn't a doctor, of course, but the envelope meant something to her. *This is what my colleagues think of me,* she thought with pride. She tucked the envelope away carefully, a prized memento. When she was feeling discouraged she could look at it and be reminded of her value to the lab.

Sue was working on a new mission — a cooperative venture between the French space agency, the Centre National d'Études Spatiales; the Soviet space program; and NASA — to put two balloons, with instruments dangling, into Venus's atmosphere. The balloons were designed to have a short lifetime, only forty-six hours. During their nearly two-day exploration, they would travel a third of the way around the planet, floating miles above the surface. Hanging from each balloon would be a "gondola" containing sensors to measure temperature, pressure, wind velocity, cloud particle density, the amount of ambient light in the sky, and even the frequency of lightning strikes. It would be painted with a white varnish designed to protect the contents from the corrosive sulfuric acid of the planet's atmosphere. The entire apparatus, balloons and gondolas, was hitching a ride on the Soviets' Vega mission, a rocket destined for a rendezvous with Halley's Comet.

Only days apart in June 1985, the balloons were dropped off on the night side of the planet, in an area known as the Mermaid Valley, chosen for its relatively cooler temperatures of only 800 degrees Fahrenheit. At thirty-three miles above the surface, parachutes attached to each Teflon-coated plastic balloon were released, and the balloons soon began to fill with helium gas. Engineers had worried that if they placed the balloons in direct sunlight, the helium inside would explode. Now, in the darkness, the balloons bobbed up and down in the Venusian winds before they began transmitting data.

Though the project would use French scientific equipment and a Russian spacecraft, Sue's expertise on the Deep Space Network was essential. The network had expanded from a few well-placed stations to a grid of communication stations across the globe. She could have scarcely imagined collaborating with the Russians when she started at JPL, at the height of the Cold War, thirty years earlier. But now it was 1985, and the once-warring nations worked together, tracking the weak signal of the balloons. Sue updated the software so the worldwide network of antennas could follow the balloons, the enormous parabolic dishes turning automatically. Unfortunately the program kept failing. She started plugging in the commands by hand, just as she had in the old days. *Some habits die hard,* she thought, smiling to herself.

Hours later in the control room, Sue and

three male team members waited to see if the mission would be a success. The room was dark, and no one made a noise. Instead they kept their eyes trained on the monitor. It was pitch-black, showing no activity. Then suddenly, dots began to appear. The antenna at Goldstone had caught the balloons' signal. Sue couldn't believe her hand-plotting had worked. She started jumping up and down, overcome by excitement and relief after so much hard work. It was the best feeling in the world. When the moment passed she looked around at her colleagues; she had been the only one leaping for joy. She felt foolish only for an instant before she saw her excitement reflected in their smiles.

Along with the successes there was sadness too: Margie was leaving the lab. Her second marriage was falling apart, and she wanted to give the fragile union every chance she could. With six children to care for, she felt she was needed at home. Everyone was sad to see her go. It was as if she had grown up in the lab. Barbara could still picture Margie at eighteen, learning the ropes. Macie had always believed in her, giving her precious opportunities, such as the historic launch of Explorer 1. Thirty years later it was time for Margie to let go.

The women had a farewell party, promising they would keep in touch.

Helen, Sue, and Barbara, however, had no thoughts of retirement. They were too busy. A new mission was monopolizing their thoughts: Galileo. The view from Voyager had whetted JPL's appetite for Jupiter and its mysterious moons, and the women were plotting trajectories that would use the gravitational pull of the moons to power the spacecraft around the planet. At the same time, they were working on how to keep in contact with the spacecraft as it traveled nearly three billion miles. The amount of work was overwhelming. Barbara barely had time to eat lunch. She would run over to the cafeteria and quickly have a chocolate shake and a croissant sandwich before heading back to work. She was gaining weight from her unhealthy diet, but she didn't have time for anything else.

On January 28, 1986, Barbara skipped breakfast and came in to work early. The lab was quiet that morning because almost everybody was watching the twenty-fifth space shuttle launch on TV. There had been far fewer than the sixty launches a year that had been proposed in 1972, when the shuttle project was first announced, yet it was enough to make space travel feel safe.

All over the lab, staff crowded around TV sets, especially excited to see Christa McAuliffe, who would be the first civilian in space, a teacher, aboard the Challenger. Only three years earlier the Challenger had made history when it carried Sally Ride, the first American woman in space. Although JPL worked only on crewless missions and had little to do with the space shuttle, McAuliffe had captivated Helen's girls. She was one of them: a mother of young children with experience and accomplishments that resonated across the nation, particularly with women.

While it was a mild day in Pasadena, in Florida the weather was unusually cold. However, after six delays, everyone was eager for the launch to go forward. At JPL they watched with enthusiasm, knowing that the next space shuttle launch would likely propel Galileo on its journey to Jupiter. Galileo was quietly putting pressure on Challenger. Since the mission was scheduled for liftoff in just four months, a date that depended on the unalterable alignment of the planets, NASA felt especially compelled to get this shuttle off the ground. Another mission was also waiting: the Hubble Telescope was finally slated for a launch in 1986, after multiple delays in development.

The schedule for the shuttle was packed.

While those at JPL admired the grandiose space vehicle, hidden inside the shuttle's boosters was a beautiful eleven-point star, the same design that had its origins in the dreams of a British scientist during World War II and the research performed by the computers at JPL in the 1950s. The star had been an essential part of the shuttle's big booster rockets from the beginning.

The launch at first seemed like any other, with the immense rocket carrying the crew of seven into a clear blue sky. The shuttle ascended, a river of puffy, white clouds billowing from its exhaust nozzle. A little more than a minute later, however, tragedy struck. Across the country, people watched live footage of the shuttle exploding and then breaking apart, the rocket boosters sending white tendrils of smoke twisting through the heavens. Those on board — McAuliffe, Gregory Jarvis, Judith A. Resnik, Francis R. Scobee, Ronald E. McNair, Michael J. Smith, and Ellison S. Onizuka — wouldn't survive.

The disaster was caused by a rubber loop: an O-ring seal in the right solid rocket booster had failed. The Rogers Commission, tasked by President Reagan with investigating the disaster, later found that concerns over the O-ring were raised years earlier by engineers at the Marshall Space Flight Center. A memo sent in January 1978 from the chief of the Solid Rocket Motor branch at Marshall to his superior specifically pointed out problems with the O-ring and stated that proper sealing of the joint maintained by O-ring pressure was "mandatory to prevent hot gas leaks and resulting catastrophic failure." Despite numerous objections, the design wasn't changed. NASA minimized the issue while Thiokol, the manufacturer, stated, "The condition is not desirable but is acceptable."

But as the temperature dropped on January 27, 1986, some at Thiokol had begun to worry. Engineers Allan McDonald and Roger Boisjoly recommended delaying the launch until the next afternoon. They were concerned that the cool temperatures could make the O-rings stiff and degraded, unable to do their job sealing the joint between two segments of the solid rocket motor. Boisjoly had agonized over the O-rings for the past year in his position on the seal task force at Thiokol. On July 31, 1985, he wrote a memorandum about his concerns with O-ring erosion, saying, "It is my honest and very real fear that if we do not take immediate action . . . then we stand in jeopardy of losing a flight along with all the launch pad facilities." Needless to say, with concerns over O-rings foremost, McDonald and Boisjoly refused to sign the launch recommendation the night before liftoff in January 1986. NASA managers overruled their objections, approving the launch. Yet despite the engineers' premonitions, when the disaster unfolded, they were shocked. Their vindication brought only torment.

Watching the explosion at JPL, Sue started to cry; she never wanted to see another launch again. One of the other women went in to tell Barbara, who, concentrating on her work on Galileo, still didn't know. The women were shocked and saddened. They were reminded of the dark day when Apollo 1 had burst into flames on the launchpad. It was now only 9 a.m. and they had a busy day ahead, but no one could work. With the disaster occupying their thoughts, their programming felt trivial.

Their emotions raw, the women headed to the auditorium, where images from Voyager were on a constant feed during planetary flybys. Only a few days earlier Voyager 2 had encountered Uranus. Now they sat in the hushed room as if it were a church. They held hands and watched as images of Uranus and its moons filled the screen, acting as a balm to their shock and hurt.

Uranus was a solemn crescent, with an ocean of boiling water hidden beneath its clouds, while its small moon, Miranda, had a curious pattern of chevrons running across the surface before dropping into deep cliffs. The engineers and scientists were astounded by their first peek at the moon; it was nothing like the dead, cratered surface they expected. Despite only flying by Miranda for five and a half hours, Voyager 2 delivered images that revealed deep chasms, ten times the depth of Earth's Grand Canyon.

It would be more than three years before Voyager 2 reached Neptune. On August 25, 1989, in celebration of the last stop of the Grand Tour, Chuck Berry performed in the JPL courtyard. His song "Johnny B. Goode" was included in the gold record carried by the spacecraft. In the warmth of a summer evening, the staff and their family and friends danced outside. The mood felt carefree as they celebrated the final signpost of the Grand Tour. They had received the last images of Neptune, which shone a bold blue, only two days previously. Amid the bustle of the lab the planet seemed clear and still. Yet behind its calm blue façade were whipping winds, at 1,242 miles per hour the fastest ever recorded anywhere.

After the Challenger disaster, space shuttle missions had been put on hold, so Galileo had to be postponed. The delay meant its trajectory would have to change significantly. Since the ship's course had been carefully plotted to coincide with the position of Jupiter at a particular time, the team would have to start over with a new path. In addition, the original upper-stage rocket selected to carry Galileo and the space shuttle crew into space was now deemed too dangerous. With a different, less powerful rocket substituted, they would have to further alter Galileo's path, no longer plotting a straight line through space but instead relying on gravity assist. Luckily, they had a lot of experience with the maneuver. They'd swing twice by Earth and once by Venus to get enough momentum to send the spacecraft all the way to Jupiter. The three-year trip was now extended to a six-year journey.

Barbara's boss on Galileo was Johnny Driver, and he lived up to his name. He worked long hours and inspired all the other engineers to do the same. Barbara was trying to fix one troublesome part of Galileo's programming. Unlike most of JPL's missions, which were constructed in pairs, Galileo was an only child. Everything relied on the success of the single spacecraft. The number of intercommunicating computer systems made work on the project even more taxing. The challenge wasn't fixing the program but searching through the mass of code to find the troublesome piece. When Barbara finally located it, she yelped in excitement. Her enthusiasm, however, was short-lived. Seeing her success, Driver started to bring the difficult work to her. Above all, simplicity was their priority in building the computer code. Although their objectives were more sophisticated than ever, in some ways coding hadn't changed much from the early days at JPL. They wanted to write a clean code that made it easy to find bugs while using the fewest lines possible.

Of course programming had become more complex. FORTRAN had new capabilities the women could have scarcely imagined two decades earlier. The computer language could manage large-scale programs with far greater capacity and handle errors in the code with better flexibility. The women were learning a new language as well: HAL. It stood for "High-Order Assembly Language" and was in use all over NASA. The women laughed at the name. They would mock the program by speaking to each other in calm monotones like those of the malevolent computer HAL 9000 from the 1968 movie *2001: A Space Odyssey.* Working with HAL and FORTRAN wasn't easy, and the use of the two computer programs only added to the complexity of Galileo's software.

The computers had also changed. Only a decade before, the women had squabbled over scheduling time on massive IBMs, while Helen could still remember the Burroughs E101 that she programmed by inserting pins into holes on a pinboard. Now, amazingly, she and each member of her staff had their own personal computer. The revolution was made possible by microprocessors, tiny pieces of metal slimmer than the strands of hair on Helen's head.

The microprocessor revolutionized computing. People have debated its origins, but the engineers at Intel, specifically Marcian "Ted" Hoff, are usually credited as its inventors. Hoff was working on a desk calculator whose design called for eight separate chips, each programmed with an individual task. Hoff used the term "chip," short for microchip, the tiny yet complex module that replaced the vacuum tube in computing. During the summer of 1958, Jack Kilby, a new employee at Texas Instruments, had come up with the idea for a chip by designing a slim slice of germanium etched with a transistor and all its components. He chose germanium because it is a semiconductor, able to conduct electricity under certain conditions. Later, manufacturers would swap out the superior germanium for silicon, which, because it's composed primarily of sand, is both abundant and cheap.

Despite the advances of computer chips, Hoff saw room for improvement. Instead of having each function of the computer on a separate chip, he wanted to create a multitasker capable of doing it all. Accordingly, he came up with the idea of a general-purpose chip that used erasable, programmable memory. With twenty-three hundred transistors etched into its silicon, the one-eighth-by-one-sixteenth-inch 4004 chip from Intel contained the same computing power as Cora, the massive IBM 1620 that the women considered one of their own and that was put out to pasture in the 1980s with scarcely a good-bye. The women would never form the same attachment to a computer as they had with Cora; the equipment didn't stick around long enough. Technology was moving too fast for them to stop and make friends.

The 4004 chip was the first microprocessor of many to come. Intel advertised the brand-new technology in 1971 as a "micro-programmable computer on a chip." Yet at first they saw the future of the chips tied to their industrial clients; they could not imagine that they were destined to change the computing industry. Soon, though, they made their way into calculators, radios, toys, and, by the mid-1970s, personal computers.

Microprocessors transformed computers from clunky and expensive machines to small and affordable devices. In 1974 Micro Instrumentation and Telemetry Systems introduced the Altair, a build-it-yourself computer kit. With no keyboard and no screen, it didn't do much besides blink lights. Data were fed in using toggle switches, and output came through the blinking pattern of red LEDs on the front of the machine. The company expected to sell only a few hundred of the kits, priced at $395, but instead, within three months, they were backlogged with four thousand orders.

Given the popularity of their microcomputer, in 1975 they took a chance on hiring two childhood friends: Bill Gates, a twenty-year-old student at Harvard, and Paul G. Allen, a twenty-two-year-old employee at Honeywell. The two adapted the BASIC programming language for the Altair, making it far easier to use. The first program was delivered on a paper tape. Now connected to a Teletype terminal, Allen typed "PRINT 2 + 2" and immediately the answer popped out on the paper: 4. The new software was so popular that its users widely copied and distributed it among their friends. Because of this, Gates and Allen found their profits smaller than expected — they were barely breaking even. In response, Gates wrote an "open letter to hobbyists" in early 1976, sent to the Homebrew Computer Club and published in their newsletter, where he declared, "Most of you steal your software . . . Who cares if the people who worked on it get paid." Despite their poverty, Gates and Allen still managed to form their own company, which eventually turned into the empire named Microsoft.

A demonstration of the Altair energized two computer engineers who happened to be part of the Homebrew Computer Club: Stephen Wozniak and Steve Jobs. After Wozniak saw the Altair for the first time, he had a revelation. "The whole vision of a personal computer popped in my head," he said. "That night I started to sketch out on paper what would later become known as the Apple I."

Personal computers, or PCs, soon underwent a revolution, with Apple, IBM, Xerox, Tandy, and Commodore all contributing models. By the 1980s the personal computer had invaded JPL, although it was first met with resistance. Managers initially believed the powerful central computers that made up the mainframe were sufficient for the lab's needs and denied requests for individual computers.

Soon, though, the ease and power of PCs became irresistible. Hewlett-Packard machines found a home on the desks of all technical staff. Coincidentally, with the new computers came a revised office layout. In 1984, the walls of private offices came down, making way for the dreaded cubicle. There was nearly an uprising over the new configuration. Many engineers were frustrated by the lack of privacy, the noise, and the secondhand cigarette smoke. As supervisor, Helen kept her private office, but Barbara was assigned to a new four-person cubicle. She found she didn't mind the change. Two of the engineers she shared space with were new hires, straight out of college, and Barbara loved their enthusiasm.

Barbara was impressed by the new PCs, each with a microprocessor that was able to hold an entire central processing unit on a sliver of silicon. They were a far cry from Cora, which ran at a speed of 1 million cycles per second, or 1 MHz. In contrast, the computers they worked with by the late 1980s ran at speeds of 25 million cycles per second. Both the lab's first computer programs and the women who wrote them seemed like early pioneers. Now they were marching into a new age where computing speed and power were astounding.

The lucky beneficiary of the impressive new technology was the study of Jupiter. While Voyager had flown by Jupiter, learning what it could while heading onward, Galileo was designed to stick around the planet to answer some of the JPL scientists' pressing questions. How could one of Jupiter's moons have active volcanoes while another lay buried under ice? By studying the formation of Jupiter and its diverse moons, they hoped to better understand the formation of the rest of the solar system.

In October 1989, Galileo prepared to hitch a ride on the space shuttle Atlantis before continuing on to the massive planet. Though it wasn't the first space shuttle to follow the Challenger disaster — the Discovery had been launched the previous fall — that tragedy still haunted the women's thoughts. None of them watched as the space shuttle blasted off from Cape Canaveral. To everyone's relief, the launch went off without a hitch, and Galileo sailed off into space flawlessly. The women celebrated their success. Creating the software architecture for the mission had been one of the most trying projects of Barbara's career. Yet there were more challenges to come.

Eighteen months later, disaster struck Galileo. An antenna the size of a moving truck atop the spacecraft wouldn't open. The ship was orbiting Earth after spinning around Venus, gaining enough momentum before its slingshot to Jupiter. Though they tried to free the ribs that made up the antenna's internal structure, the hinges wouldn't budge. Engineers determined that the problem was likely caused by the spacecraft's hiatus after Challenger. After the craft had spent five years in storage, no one had thought to check the lubrication and coating on the antenna's rib apparatus. Without a functioning antenna they were in danger of losing the majority of the $1.5 billion probe's data. The mission would be a complete failure.

All they had left were the significantly less powerful low-gain antennas on the ship. The signal strength on the low-gain antenna was ten thousand times weaker than that of the high-gain ones. As Galileo pointed toward the antennas on Earth, it was like trying to hit a distant target with a squirt gun instead of a fire hose. Since they couldn't improve on the antennas sitting on Galileo, JPL had to make the DSN more sensitive, better able to receive weak signals from far away. Sue wrote a program that created an array, electronically combining the power of the DSN's antennas. She carefully crafted the program to dovetail with the coding of the spacecraft, written six years earlier. It was the first time they had built such software, and everyone was amazed at the array's ability to harness the power of the DSN in a novel way. They held their breath as they waited to receive data from the ship. Incredibly, the array worked. Sue's program saved the mission, and Galileo continued on its way.

The spacecraft made history as it flew through the asteroid belt between Mars and Jupiter, which is punctuated by massive rocks. Already the array was paying off; those at JPL were shocked to find that one of the asteroids they were fortunate to pass en route, named Ida, boasted its own moon. Making it safely through the asteroids, the ship then watched as a comet, the Shoemaker-Levy 9, co-discovered by the same Eugene Shoemaker who worked on Ranger, broke up and dived into Jupiter's atmosphere. In the stunning video and images, it looked as if the planet were being rocked by a series of bombs, the impacts glowing a fiery orange before leaving large, dark scars on the cloud tops.

Finally reaching the massive planet in December 1995, Galileo relayed images of Jupiter and new data about its moons. Falling at 106,000 miles per hour, its atmospheric probe dropped into the planet's atmosphere before deploying its parachute. For fifty-eight minutes the probe sent back weather data, revealing a hot, dry climate with winds of 450 miles per hour. Then it melted into the alien atmosphere. Peering onto the surface of Jupiter's moon Europa, Sue saw firsthand evidence of the saltwater ocean hiding beneath giant ice rafts. Similar traces of salt water were found on the moons Ganymede and Callisto. Volcanoes erupted on Io while thunderstorms rocked Jupiter's atmosphere. Sue watched proudly as the mission returned stunning pictures and scientific data. On September 21, 2003, after fourteen years in space and eight years exploring the planet, Galileo met its end by crashing into the gas giant at over 100,000 miles an hour.

Not every mission could be saved. Sylvia comforted herself with this thought as she lay awake one night and thought of her beautiful project gone awry. She was the Mission Design manager for a Comet Rendezvous Asteroid Flyby, or CRAF. She had spent years planning the exploration, which would study the geological structure of the asteroid Hamburga before flying in formation with the comet Kopff for three years, exploring the comet's composition, atmosphere, and tail. She had even brought in her friends Sue and Barbara to help. Now it was over. It seemed that comets and asteroids weren't sexy enough to get NASA funding. Lying in bed, she felt as if she had invested years of work for nothing.

CRAF was the victim of funding woes. New budget rules outlined by the 1990 White House–congressional budget summit put caps on all defense, domestic, and international spending. With these new cuts, a House subcommittee had to decide between boosting housing and veterans' programs or funding NASA's space station. Amid controversy, the subcommittee opted for the former. When the House later reversed the decision, the subcommittee had to compromise by cutting housing funds and freezing NASA spending. The space station was saved, but all other NASA programs would suffer. Old wounds having to do with NASA's priorities — scientific discovery versus human exploration — were reopened at JPL. Yet even with NASA's "Better, Faster, Cheaper" policy, JPL would preserve the agency's pursuit of science.

Although her project was breaking up, with the crumbs spread out to other missions, Sylvia was finding her second chance at love. She had met Lanny Miller, another engineer at JPL, around the lunch table at the cafeteria. With his PhD in nuclear physics, he was a perfect match for Sylvia and her quick mind. They didn't work on the same projects, but the two had much in common and soon married. Shortly after the wedding they contemplated starting a family — neither of them had children, and given the happiness Sylvia shared with her sisters growing up, she'd always assumed she'd have kids of her own one day. The timing, however, was off. They were getting older, and their careers were demanding. They decided to continue their married life with just the two of them.

Despite NASA's budgetary troubles, CRAF's demise offered an opportunity. JPL could save a different mission: a return trip to Saturn. The spared project was named

Saturn Orbiter Titan Probe, or SOTP, and would explore the rings of Saturn, peek at its atmosphere, and probe its moons to determine their composition. The mission would collaborate with the European Space Agency. Founded in 1975, the ESA, whose headquarters are in Paris, is composed of twenty-two member states. As the Soviet Union had begun to cooperate more with the ESA, the old flames of competition were stoked. The United States wouldn't be second, not even in partnership. NASA would build the orbiter while the ESA would build the probe.

The SOTP spacecraft looked familiar to the women. Its three-axis design was reminiscent of the successful Mariner and Voyager missions. But the scale of the ship was unparalleled. At nearly four times the size of Voyager, it was the largest interplanetary spacecraft yet constructed by NASA: 22 feet long with a 13-foot-high antenna. With wide eyes, the engineers watched the giant spacecraft come together in the JPL assembly facility. Soon, the mission received its official name: the orbiter was rechristened Cassini while the ESA probe was named Huygens.

Sylvia worked on Cassini with her feelings still raw from the loss of her comet/asteroid mission. The engineers were plotting a roundabout route to the ringed planet, using gravity assist to carry the ship. It would encircle Venus twice before swinging around Earth and Jupiter, then being flung off to Saturn.

It wasn't the only collaboration NASA had with the ESA. After years of delays, budget setbacks, and then the Challenger disaster, the Hubble Telescope made its way into space, riding the back of the space shuttle Discovery, on April 24, 1990. A month later the telescope opened its eyes and took its first picture. While Hubble had better resolution than ground-based telescopes, that first image didn't meet anyone's expectations. Astronomers operating it from the Space Telescope Science Institute at Johns Hopkins University immediately knew something was amiss. They soon discovered that the telescope had a flaw in its nearly eight-foot-wide primary mirror. To fix the problem, astronauts serviced Hubble, and soon afterward, the space telescope began sending back breathtaking images, some of which were familiar to the women. Those of the planets showed features recognizable from the old Mariner missions. As Helen and Barbara gazed at the thick sulfuric acid clouds of Venus

photographed by Hubble, they were reminded of their first peeks at the planet with
Mariner 2 in 1962, and the excitement they
had felt witnessing the first flyby of another
planet.

Barbara was now working on a return to
Venus in a mission named Magellan. JPL
scientists wanted to understand why the
planet, which should be the most like Earth,
given its distance from the sun, was a bar-
ren wasteland. It had been ten years since
the launch of the last planetary probes, the
Voyagers. With the NASA budget limping
along, Magellan was constructed mostly out
of odds and ends lying around the lab from
previous missions. Their goal was to map as
much of the planet as possible. As part of
the sequence design team, Barbara was writing software for the ship. She was working
on the program that would send the spacecraft orbiting the planet, connected to the
DSN as it flew.

Barbara had a reputation for meticulous
programming. She was trying to improve
the efficiency of one of the Magellan programs when Bob Wilson, a supervisor, told
her, "You don't have to hone it anymore.
The program works just fine." Her years of
experience had taught her to be fastidious.
Helen was right beside her, working on

software that connected the shuttle launch to the planetary launch. At the same time she was amazed at the new computer she had for the job. Helen couldn't believe how slim and light her IBM PC Convertible laptop was. It weighed only thirteen pounds, so she could bring her work with her wherever she went.

On April 28, 1989, the team gathered for the launch. As the shuttle counted down, they looked around at one another. There were no peanuts. Dick Wallace, the engineer who started the tradition during Ranger 7, had forgotten this time. They were scientists and tried not to be superstitious, but the oversight put them all on edge. The peanuts had been handed out for nearly every launch since 1964. At T minus 31 seconds, the countdown stopped. An electrical issue had cropped up, and the launch was canceled. The room collectively took a deep breath. A week later, on May 4, the launch restarted. This time Wallace had made peanuts a top priority. Barbara and the other engineers, now fortified, watched the rocket blast off successfully. They were on their way back to Venus.

Magellan arrived at Venus in August 1990. The mission was going just as planned, a sign of how well the group worked together.

Now the ship was orbiting Venus, using radar imaging to map out as much of the surface as possible. Barbara hoped their programming would be a success and their view of Venus more detailed than ever before.

On a mild day in April 1991, the lights were turned off but the sun still shone. Barbara smiled as Al Nakata, a mission manager, and the Magellan team sang "Happy Birthday." A cake decorated with stars and aglow with candles sat before her. Barbara closed her eyes and let wishes float through her mind before settling on the right one. She blew out the candles and hoped it would come true. Despite the ever-increasing size of JPL, now the largest employer in Pasadena with more than five thousand employees, the lab clung to its close-knit community feeling.

Barbara delighted in the Magellan team. They were dear to one another, their friendships glued together with the sugary icing of birthday cakes. It was a small thing, remembering birthdays, yet after decades of working on missions, she knew that it was the sign of a strong team and a great project manager.

Over the years Barbara had spent many of her birthday wishes trying to sway the fates in favor of her missions. They hadn't all worked out. The next project, the Mars Observer, would be one of the most painful. The mission started out with every chance of success — with one exception: they forgot to pass out the peanuts. The ship blasted off from Cape Canaveral in September 1992. Even as Barbara watched, she knew her days of watching launches were coming to a close. She was getting older and beginning to think about retirement. It had been seventeen years since she worked on Viking, the previous mission to Mars, and everyone was anxious to return. Helen and Barbara had worked side by side, developing the graphic display software for the mission. There was so much they still wanted to understand about the planet, and Observer would give them a glimpse of its climate, geology, and gravitational field.

Yet Barbara wouldn't be there to see the results. After putting in the hard work of programming, she was leaving the project in capable hands. In April 1993 she retired, forty-five years after she started at JPL. Packing up her office was like opening up a time capsule. Mementos from all of JPL's missions lined the walls. She boxed up pictures from Voyager, a landscape of Venus taken by Magellan, and numerous achievement awards, then headed to her farewell luncheon, where all her friends were gathering. She took a last look and swallowed, holding the tears back. *This isn't a real goodbye,* she told herself. *I'll be back.* She knew that even in retirement she wouldn't be able to stay away, especially from Helen, Sue, and Sylvia.

Four months later, Barbara got the news. The Mars Observer had disappeared. Two days before it was supposed to enter the Red Planet's orbit, it simply dropped off the map. While the engineers debated theories — the most popular being that the fuel line had ruptured, causing the ship to spin and enter "contingency mode," a state of reduced communications — there would never be an answer. The ship was simply gone. The mission was a complete failure. While newspaper headlines lambasted NASA for wasting $813 million on a vanishing hunk of metal, Barbara wept over the hours of work they had put in.

A year later it was Helen's turn to retire. She was ready to go; there were no regrets. The room swelled as engineers from decades of JPL's history, even some from the 1950s, came to share their memories in tribute. Everyone loved Helen. She smiled at the crowd of familiar faces and warmly

431

embraced Dennis Tito, a former engineer at JPL turned billionaire space tourist, who had come to celebrate his favorite human computer. In the heat of the late afternoon they talked about old times, no trace of tears on their cheeks, since they knew that the friendships they formed would long outlive their careers in the lab.

Sylvia, younger than her friends, attended Barbara's and Helen's retirement parties with a heavy heart. She would miss them. Yet her work at JPL was shifting. Sylvia had been applying for new positions within the lab and was now excited to step into her dream job: project manager in the Mars exploration program.

She was gleeful about the planned expansion of the program. She wouldn't take her position until after the Mars Surveyor mission of 1998, but the intervening years were going to be busy. As part of the program, JPL would first set up a communications network on the planet and then send rovers down to the surface. Sylvia watched the rovers being built in the lab and going through their rigorous training program. In a rocky, dusty playground built at JPL to simulate the Martian surface, the little robots learned to stand up from their squatting position, straightening themselves out to about a foot tall. Instead of using rockets to land safely on the surface, the team was designing an innovative system using parachutes and airbags to achieve a soft landing. Everyone cheered when the rover survived a bounce as high as a ten-story building.

JPL launched the Mars Pathfinder, armed with airbags, in December 1996. The mood was tense; after all, it had been two decades since a successful Mars mission. The loss of the Mars Observer had extended the long lull in Martian exploration. Russia had similarly struggled in getting to the Red Planet. Phobos, their program to Mars and its moons, had failed in 1988. Mars missions have a history of disappointment; to date, approximately two-thirds of them have ended in failure.

By July 1997, NASA's ship arrived at the planet. Sylvia held her breath as the parachute deployed and the Mars lander and rover softly sank to the surface. Only eight seconds before landing, the airbags puffed out, the whole apparatus measuring 17 feet wide. They enfolded the equipment as it hit the surface of the distant planet and bounced 40 feet in the air. After fifteen more bounces, the lander rolled to a stop, its airbags retracted, and its solar panels fanned out like the petals of a flower. In celebration, Sylvia proudly had her picture taken with a duplicate of the rover's giant airbags.

The lander, named the Carl Sagan Memorial Station, started relaying information and images back to Earth while the rover started to roam. The first of its kind on Mars, the rover was named Sojourner, after the abolitionist Sojourner Truth. At only twenty-five pounds, the robot started to cruise the Martian landscape, analyzing rocks with an X-ray spectrometer. It found that the rocks had higher levels of silica than expected. Martian meteorites, the only samples from Mars we have so far, are basalts, a type of volcanic rock relatively low in silicon and high in iron and magnesium. Because basalts are so common on Earth, the moon, and among Martian meteorites, geologists expected Pathfinder to find them as well. Instead, the high silica content indicated that a different type of volcanism might have taken place on Mars's surface, a type that typically occurs in the presence of water on Earth. Such findings only whetted appetites back home for more data.

Sojourner lasted eighty-five sols, short for "solar days" on Mars, which are slightly longer than Earth's at twenty-four hours, thirty-nine minutes. It was far longer than the seven sols planned for the mission. Eventually, Sojourner lost communication with Earth, likely due to depleted batteries.

Luckily the JPL team knew they were going back. In December 1998 and January 1999, the Surveyor mission launched. It was composed of two spacecraft: the Mars Climate Orbiter and the Mars Polar Lander. The Climate Orbiter would measure the weather and double as a communications satellite for the next generation of rovers sent down to the surface. The Polar Lander would launch the next month, landing on the planet's south pole and studying its composition. The south pole, with its white cap, was seen as a promising place to find water on the planet.

The engineers watched the trajectory of the Orbiter closely, correcting the spacecraft's path through space. That's where the trouble started. The numbers taken from the ground didn't match that of the ship. They soon found out why. The ship's software used the metric system, whereas the ground computers were programmed to use the far less common imperial pound seconds. Although NASA had been using the metric system exclusively since 1990, the ground computers sending navigation commands for the orbiter's thrusters were coming from a private contractor, Lockheed Martin. The company sent their commands in the unusual English unit of measurement while the ship, programmed by JPL, used newton seconds. The result was that they were underestimating the impact of the thrusters on the ship by a factor of 4.45. With their measurements off for an embarrassing reason, the engineers had to keep making little corrections to the ship's path, far more than they had planned. Once it reached Mars, the spacecraft would start its engine to make one big push into orbit before putting on the brakes and gradually losing speed. At least that was the plan. Sylvia watched nervously as the ship fired up its engine. It was coming in too fast and too low. Then, just like the Observer before it, it disappeared. It had likely dipped down into the atmosphere before leaving Mars to circle the sun.

The Polar Lander suffered a similar fate. Its signal vanished after the ship arrived at the Red Planet. As the days passed, Sylvia began to give up all hope that the lander would be located. Its demise was likely due to a software bug that caused the engines to shut down prematurely. Sylvia's shock turned into sorrow. The mission was a complete failure. Worse yet, the mishap made the future of Mars missions shaky. With so many unknowns, NASA canceled the Mars Lander scheduled for 2001. It made Sylvia nervous to be taking her position as manager in the wake of the catastrophe, especially since JPL had previously planned to increase the number of Mars missions. About every two years, the planets lined up and the door to Mars opened. If they wanted to seize each opportunity, they had to decide how to explore Mars, by probe or by rover, and how to reconcile their scientific goals with limited budgets.

Investigating the mishaps that had been their downfall, Sylvia and her team pushed on. They needed more testing and more teamwork for their missions, and she wanted to help create that culture in the lab. They planned a future for the Mars missions, focusing on a new generation of Mars exploration rovers. During one of these meetings Donna Shirley, the manager of the Mars Exploration Program and one of Sylvia's supervisors, looked around the room. All of the engineers at the table were women. It was the first time Donna could remember such a thing happening. *The times they are a-changin',* she thought. The engineers were considering using nimble robots that would one day drill into the

Martian surface, collect samples, and send them back to Earth. They would probe the geologic history and hopefully unearth evidence of life on the planet.

Under Sylvia's guidance, the Mars program office reeled off a string of successes. In 2004, the Spirit and Opportunity rovers bounced down on the planet, again protected by airbags. The airbags got in the way for Spirit after it landed. The poor rover couldn't break free of the meddlesome things, and the engineers at JPL had to spin it around before driving off a side ramp. Finally freed, Spirit dug into the soil and took the first microscopic image from the surface of another planet.

Opportunity, on the other hand, had fantastic luck right out of the gate. The rover stumbled onto evidence, nestled in the rocks, that salty water deep enough to splash in had once covered them. Using a microscope at the end of its arm, the rover returned an image of tiny round spheres that JPL called blueberries. The berries were filled with the mineral hematite in a crystal pattern that on Earth forms only in water. Watching the rovers roam, Sylvia felt as if she were watching a piece of herself crossing the Martian dirt. Both rovers sent back stunning panoramic images of Mars. The design goal for the rovers was one year of operation, far more than Sojourner's three-month voyage. The rovers far surpassed Sylvia's goal. Spirit wandered the planet for five years before losing a wheel in the soft soil; Opportunity continues to roam Mars, a decade after it started. And a newcomer has joined the rovers: Curiosity, which landed in 2012.

While robots roamed Mars, a new group of women were taking over at JPL. The cohort hired and trained by Helen, Barbara, and Sue had spread out around the campus and, in turn, hired women of their own. The proportion of female engineers at the lab increased from 9 percent in 1984 to 15 percent in 1994. Today more women are employed at JPL, in all positions, than at any other NASA center. It's an achievement made possible by Macie and Helen and their tireless campaigns to hire women over the course of fifty years. The expansion of women's roles at JPL stands in sharp contrast to trends in the rest of the country. In 1984, 37 percent of computer-science graduates were women; today that number is at 18 percent.

You can write a lot of programs in five decades. The code that Sylvia, Helen, Margie, Sue, Barbara, and their colleagues wrote would continue to work its way into space-craft, navigation systems, climate studies, and Mars rovers. It would get spliced up and repurposed, pasted into different missions, sent out into space, driven on far-off planets, and even brought back to Earth, taking on a life of its own long after the women departed. The code would even inform our missions today, from the Mars Curiosity rover that has been exploring Mars since 2012, to the Cassini orbiter that has been swinging around Saturn since 2004, to future Earth-orbiting instruments designed to study our own world.

When Helen left, she was the last of her kind. The group of women once known as computers were no more. In their place a new generation of women with even more power and responsibility had taken their places. The sunny room in Building 122 where Barbara and Helen forged their careers as part of a committed all-female team was now dark, the old wooden desks long replaced by particleboard and plastic furniture.

Sylvia, who bridged the gap as the last of the computers and the first of the new generation, left the lab in 2008, after forty years. Fiercely loved by her nephews and nieces, she never had children of her own.

Sylvia was able to see part of her beloved canceled comet mission resurrected in a project called Rosetta. The mission is part of her heritage at JPL, an attempt to catch a comet as it falls through the sky. Launched in 2004 by the ESA in collaboration with JPL, the ship's Philae lander touched down on comet 67P/Churyumov-Gerasimenko on November 12, 2014. As it sends back data, thanks to the DSN, it's documenting the comet's rising activity as it nears the sun.

Sue remains at JPL. She's worked at the lab for fifty-eight years and won't retire until she sees her latest mission, Juno, succeed in orbiting Jupiter, which should happen in July 2016.

Soft light sparkled onto the archways and tall columns of the opulent Caltech Athenaeum. It was an occasion like none other at JPL: the fiftieth anniversary of Explorer 1. On a January night in 2008, the institute celebrated the fateful day the first American satellite left Earth's atmosphere. Sadly, when making up the guest list for the anniversary, JPL forgot some important names. Five decades earlier, Barbara and Margie had sat in the control room and tracked the satellite as it flew through the sky, but in 2008, they were in their homes in Pasadena, just a few miles away from the celebration. They are two of the last people who remember JPL's control room that night, and their work formed our first steps into space.

Their legacy stretches into the unknown. The Voyagers are reaching far into deep, dark space. On February 14, 1990, Voyager 1 looked over its shoulder to take some final pictures, now known as the *Family Portrait*. Taken at the suggestion of Carl Sagan, it is a series of photos that show our sun and six planets of our solar system. *Pale Blue Dot,* one of these photos (a composite of three images), became famous because, when viewed at a distance of four billion miles, Earth is less than a pixel in size, a small speck of blue surrounded by the vastness of the universe. Yet within that tiny dot, swirling in a ray of sunlight, lies all known life. With one last look at its home, the little probe left the solar system and entered interstellar space. It is traveling farther than any man-made object ever has. But it wasn't just made by men.

Enclosed in aluminum, a treasure lies within Voyager's memory banks. Written on only forty kilobytes of memory, thousands of times less than what an iPhone holds, are programs first handwritten with pencil and paper by an extraordinary group of women. The programs represent only a slice of their work but were constructed at the pinnacle of their careers. Those programs are remnants soaring amid the space dust. They are the legacy of women written in the stars.

EPILOGUE

I pass through the security gate and into the visitors' parking lot. There are deer nibbling away at the grass, not at all frightened of the humans walking nearby. It's just how Barbara described it. Yet the rest of the lab is different than I imagined, smaller somehow. The buildings are nestled close together and the courtyard is full of young people enjoying the California sunshine. It doesn't feel like a government installation, but more like a college campus.

However, appearances are deceiving; once I enter the buildings, the complexity of the science performed within becomes apparent. Along with a group of seventeen women, I watch as rovers play tag in a rocky playground and spacecraft are assembled in a huge, clean hangar that, according to my companions, hasn't changed much over the decades. I'm traveling with a group of women who are not strangers to the lab.

They are the computers, the first women of JPL. My companions are Barbara Paulson, Joanie Jordan, Kathryn Thuleen, Georgia Dvornychenko, Virginia Anderson, Janet Davis, Helen Ling (accompanied by her daughter, Eve), Sylvia Miller, Victoria Wang, Margie Brunn, Caroline Norman, Lydia Shen, Linda Lee, Marie Crowley, Nancy Key, and Sue Finley. We have gathered for a reunion, and some of the women have traveled across the country to be here.

From the moment I met them, it was obvious they are not just former co-workers, but also close friends. They groan as they point out Building 11, remembering how uncomfortable the concrete-walled computer room was with no heat or air-conditioning. Then they look over at the outdated test pits, no longer in use, and reminisce about those ear-shattering small-motor tests. I watch Barbara and Helen. They have spoken tens of thousands of times, in settings both formal and casual, yet today seems special. It's been years since they last saw each other.

Helen resides in an assisted-living facility nearby, and her children, especially Eve, take care of her. Her husband, Arthur, retired five years before she did and started taking care of their grandchildren. Patrick, their son, learned programming from Helen, who taught him BASIC and FORTRAN and inspired him to study computer science. Eve excelled in swimming, making it all the way to a qualifying round in tryouts for the U.S. Olympic swim team. Since Arthur passed away, Helen relies on Eve, who takes tender care of her and loves to bake for her.

In 2003, Barbara's husband, Harry, was suffering from cancer. He was in hospice when Barbara swayed with sudden vertigo and flailed wildly around, unable to get her bearings. She'd never experienced anything like it before or since. She was finally able to right herself, but the doctors worried that she might have had a stroke. Their daughters, Karen and Kathy, were living in Iowa when they received the news, and they rushed back home to take care of her. As it turned out, Barbara was fine, but Harry was in decline. The girls spent one last week with their dad before he passed away. The father who snuggled them in blankets, changed their diapers, and loved them dearly was gone. Barbara's unexplained case of vertigo was an undeniable gift to the girls, giving them that last week. After Harry passed, Barbara moved out to Iowa to be closer to Kathy and Karen. She's never stopped being busy with her church, friends, and family. She recently became a great-grandmother.

Despite her years, Margie still looks like the baby of the group. Her eyes twinkle like a twenty-year-old's when she remembers her days at JPL. She's unmarried but is surrounded by the spectrum of life: taking care of her ninety-seven-year-old mother and sometimes caring for several young children. She remembers how much a good babysitter meant to her during her working days.

Sylvia's retirement has been an active one. She and Lanny travel frequently. At her retirement party, after her friends sang her praises, she said, "I didn't realize I walked on water!" Although she is incredibly modest, her work at JPL lives on, an integral part of our robotic exploration of Mars.

Sue travels quite a bit as well, although in her case it's essential to her job. As part of her work on the DSN, she's been around the world, including Australia, Spain, and Greenland. Traveling to research stations means she's often out of the country when missions are receiving attention from the press. "They're always focused on the control room at JPL. The people really doing the work don't get on TV," she remarks. She's seen the lab change in unusual ways, not all of them for the better. In 2008, the fiftieth anniversary of her starting at the lab, JPL changed the rules and dictated that all engineers were required to hold advanced degrees. Because Sue never finished college, they took away her salaried position and switched her to an hourly rate. However, once administrators saw how much overtime she was getting, they made an exception and switched her back. Sue is NASA's longest-serving woman. She remains a software tester and subsystem engineer at JPL who loves her work and keeps a cache of old graphing paper for hand-plotting trajectories. You never know.

During our tour of JPL, we walk past a model of Explorer 1. Barbara and Margie look at the model admiringly. The real thing crashed into the Pacific Ocean on March 31, 1970, while they still worked at JPL. As the women's eyes fasten on the tall, slim satellite, their memories come rushing back. I'm privileged to be here to hear them.

At the end of the weekend, under a full moon, they say good-bye. Among the hugs and kisses, the happy well-wishes between friends who remain close despite the passing of the decades, I hear words that stand out sad and solemn: "This is the last time we'll see each other." Buried in those final good-byes are friendships far more powerful than any rocket engine.

ACKNOWLEDGMENTS

I am incredibly grateful to the many women, all current and former employees at JPL, who spoke with me for this project. They are unsung heroes, without whom we wouldn't have an American space program. I am so thankful for the many hours they and their families have spent sharing their stories and documenting their experiences. I wish I had space to include all their stories here, but certainly every interview was a vital part of the project and ultimately informed the book.

There are a few women who sacrificed an extraordinary amount of their time to help me. One is Barbara Paulson. It took me twelve tries to find the right one by that name, but I am very lucky to have finally reached her. Without her sharp memory, quick wit, and friendly attitude, I would have never been able to write this book. I am thankful to her and her wonderful family, especially her daughters, Karen Bishop and Kathleen Knutson, for their invaluable assistance. Similarly, this book would not have been possible without Sylvia and Lanny Miller. Sylvia spent considerable time speaking with me, helping me obtain the right contacts, and sending me useful articles and photographs. In addition, Susan Finley's knowledge was essential; Sue sacrificed many hours, both on the telephone and in person, to help me. I also especially thank Eve and Helen Ling. Eve has been a key resource for the book, and I am so glad for her efforts and her incredible baking prowess.

Many thanks to the "rocket boys," especially Roger Bourke, Charley Kohlhase, Bill McLaughlin, Dick Wallace, and Frank Jordan, a group of retired JPL engineers whose history-changing work is deserving of far greater recognition than it has received and whose memories and assistance have been invaluable.

Without my incredible agent, Laurie Abkemeier, this book would never have existed. I am so thankful for her support, wisdom, and masterful editing. No matter the question, Laurie always has the right answer.

I am very grateful for my amazing editor, Asya Muchnick. She has transformed a manuscript riddled with repetitions and errors into something special. Her fervor for science, and skill with the written word, have been indispensable. I'm indebted to Jayne Yaffe Kemp and Deborah Jacobs, whose invaluable skills have improved the manuscript immensely. Thanks also to Genevieve Nierman for her critical contributions. I am very lucky to have the team at Little, Brown and Company, who have been wonderfully enthusiastic and whose expertise has been essential.

Many other people helped me with this book. The archivists at Caltech and the Jet Propulsion Laboratory have gone above and beyond to assist me. Many thanks are due to the indefatigable Julie Cooper, who has spent endless hours aiding my research, finding photographs, and arranging tours. Archivist Dudee Chang and historian Erik Conway have aided my research enormously. Special thanks to Sara Tompson, who helped arrange a special evening for the women who worked as computers at JPL. Thanks to P. Thomas Carroll, whose research and personal assistance were essential.

I have been lucky to have perceptive readers on this project, particularly planetary science superstar, historian, and talented writer-editor Dr. Meg Rosenburg; the astute Dr. Jeffrey Cooke, an extragalactic observational astronomer at the Centre for Astrophysics and Supercomputing at Swinburne University of Technology in Australia; and Julie Cooper, a gifted historian at JPL. Their insight and intelligence have been instrumental in shaping this manuscript.

Thanks to the Little Turkeys, especially Erika Hilden, Autumn Brucha, Shelly McGill, Amy Blackwell, Kristin Rascon, Valerie Levitt Halsy, Clare Rice, Rachael Nelson, Laurie Weeks, Mande Norman, Amy McCain, Kiersti Pilon, Karlyn Goodman, Amanda Schuster, Lisa Brinks Funari, Erica Virginia Johansen, Rosie Forb, Callie Slama, Andrea Alexander, and Holly Button.

Many friends and family have helped with this work, including Marco Katz and Betsy Boone; Joyce Boone and the deeply missed John Boone; Eva Grundgeiger; Ruby Frances Holt; Sheldon Katz; Rose Grundgeiger; Rachael and Gerry Coakley; Elizabeth Keane and Sean Cashman; Cynthia Boyle; Sarah Eliott and Jill Rubinstein; Chrissy Grant; Mrs. Jerome and Mrs. Cronin; J. A. and Joline MacFarland; Elizabeth Shaw; Emlyn Jones; Tim Flanagan; Amy Cantor and Scott Ambruster; Jennifer and Payson Thompson; Scott and Shea Holt. I couldn't have written this book without the support and love Claire and Jerry McCleery gave me during a critical research trip; similarly, special thanks to my wonderful father-in-law, Ken Holt, who provided extra help and whose encouragement has been instrumental.

To the most important people in my life: my husband, Larkin Holt, and our inspirational daughters, Eleanor Frances and Philippa Jane.

NOTES

Research for this book primarily consisted of first-person interviews I conducted between 2011 and 2015. When possible, events reported in interviews have been confirmed by archival material. Interviews were conducted with the women who worked as computers at JPL, their families, the engineers at JPL they worked closely with, other researchers in the lab, and staff currently working at JPL. When writing about women and men who have passed away, I relied on the memories of friends and family and used documents such as letters and diary pages to re-create scenes. Many interviews, while not directly used in the final book, have been instrumental in informing the overall picture of life and work at JPL.

Interview subjects include: Virginia Anderson, Virginia Prettyman Bertrando, Roger Bourke, Margaret Brunn, Marie Crowley,

Janet Davis, Georgia Dvornychenko, Susan Finley, Barbara Gaffney, Roberta Headley, Joan and Frank Jordan, Nancy Key, Charles Kohlhase, Cristyne Lawson, Linda Lee, Eve Ling, Helen Ling, Bill McLaughlin, Sylvia Miller, Marcia Neugebauer, Caroline Norman, Barbara Paulson, Phil Roberts, Lydia Shen, Donna Shirley, Janine Bordeaux Smith, Patricia Canright Smith, Kathryn Thuleen, and Victoria Wang.

In addition, many interviewees provided historical materials, including mission reports, correspondence, photographs, and journal excerpts.

The following collections at the JPL Archives were utilized: Analog-Computing Facility at JPL; Director's Projects Review: Agendas; Earth–Mars Trajectory Calculation Collection; Flight Command and Data Management Collection; Frank Malina Collection; Galileo S-Band and X-Band Telemetry Parameters Computations Collection; Historical Biography Collection; History Collection; Hsue-Shen Tsien: articles, photos, 1939–1970; JPL Annual Reports; JPL Bulletins: 1944–1958; JPL Computational Mathematics Collection; JPL Computer Group Memoranda Collection; JPL Personnel Lists; Mariner Mars Aperture Collection; Mars Pathfinder Assembly;

458

Navigations Systems Records; Operations History of the JPL Electronic Differential Analyzer for 1952; photo albums, newsletters (*GALCIT-EAR, Lab-Oratory, Universe*); Records of the Flight Office; Robert Droz Collection; SEASAT artwork; Solid Propellant Engineering Section Records; Spacecraft Configuration Testing Collection; Test and Launch Operations Collection; transcript of interview with Charles Kohlhase, 2002; transcript of interview with Charles Terhune, 1990; transcript of interview with Gerald Levy, 1992; transcript of JPL press conference regarding the recent launch of Sputnik I; Viking Lander Camera Test Collection; Viking Project Records; Voyager Computer Command Subsystem Document Collection; Walter Powell Collection.

Dialogue is reported either directly from author interviews or re-created based on interviews and archival material, particularly meeting minutes, lab notebooks, letters, and oral histories.

Launch Day

Personal anecdotes come from author interviews. Details on the launch of Explorer 1 can be found in Matthew A. Bille and Erika Lishock, *The First Space Race: Launching the World's First Satellites* (College Station: Texas A&M University Press, 2004).

Chapter 1: Up, Up, and Away

All personal anecdotes obtained from census data, personal correspondence, oral histories, author interviews with JPL employees, and archival material, including photographs, meeting minutes, and newsletters.

Information about the Suicide Squad and the early history of JPL can be found in Frank Malina, "The Rocket Pioneers: Memoirs of the Infant Days of Rocketry at Caltech," *Engineering and Science* 31(5) (1968); Malina, "Memoir on the GALCIT Rocket Research Project, 1936–1938," *Smithsonian Annals of Flight* 10 (1974); Malina, "The Jet Propulsion Laboratory: Its Origin and First Decade of Work," *Spaceflight* 6(5) and 6(6) (1964); oral-history interview of Malina by Mary Terrall, December 14, 1978, Caltech Archives; Chris Gainor, *To a Distant Day: The Rocket Pioneers* (Lincoln: University of Nebraska Press, 2008); and Erik M. Conway, "From Rockets to Spacecraft: Making JPL a Place for Planetary Science," *Engineering and Science* 70(4) (2007).

The number of industrial establishments

in Pasadena totaled only 159 in 1929 and decreased even further, to 83 in 1933, as reported on the City of Pasadena website (http://ww2.cityofpasadena.net/history/ 1930-1950.asp, accessed December 2014).

A history of women in computing, including the women who worked in early astronomy and those who were hired as part of the WPA, can be found in David Alan Grier, *When Computers Were Human* (Princeton, NJ: Princeton University Press, 2007), and Grier, "The Math Tables Project of the Works Project Administration: The Reluctant Start of the Computing Era," *IEEE Annals of the History of Computing* 20(3) (1998): 33–50.

Fritz Zwicky is quoted as saying "You're a bloody fool," etc., in an oral-history interview of Malina by Mary Terrall, December 14, 1978, Caltech Archives. It's important to note that soon afterward, Zwicky supported Malina and his work, eventually becoming a consultant at JPL.

MIT's Vannevar Bush is quoted as saying "I don't understand how a serious scientist or engineer can play around with rockets" in G. Pascal Zachary, *Endless Frontier: Vannevar Bush, Engineer of the American Century* (New York: Free Press, 1997).

Further details about the development of

jet engines can be found in Sterling Michael Pavelec, *The Jet Race and the Second World War* (Westport, CT: Praeger, 2007).

Information about Malina from the Frank Malina Collection, JPL Archives. His FBI files and personal correspondence are available at the Library of Congress.

Jerome Hunsaker is quoted as saying "Von Kármán can take the Buck Rogers job" in Malina, "Origins and First Decade of the Jet Propulsion Laboratory," in Eugene M. Emme, ed., *The History of Rocket Technology: Essays on Research, Technology, and Utility* (Detroit: Wayne State University Press, 1964).

Discussion of JATO technology can be found in J. D. Hunley, *Preludes to U.S. Space-Launch Vehicle Technology: Goddard Rockets to Minuteman III* (Gainesville: University Press of Florida, 2008).

Details of the Ercoupe flight schedule and results can be found in Malina, "Results of Flight Tests of the Ercoupe Airplane with Auxiliary Jet Propulsion Supplied by Solid Propellant Jet Units: Report," 1941, JPL Archives History Collection. The documents in this collection include original notebooks that mention Barbara Canright's contributions as well as the quote from Jack Parsons, "The pilot deserves credit for his willingness to continue flight test as soon as the airplane was repaired."

A description of Ercoupe planes being sold at Macy's department store can be found in Paul Glenshaw, "Buy Your Plane at Penney's," *Air & Space Smithsonian,* November 2013.

Eleanor Roosevelt said, "We know what we have to face, and we know that we are ready to face it" as part of her weekly radio broadcast on December 7, 1941.

Description of the Douglas A-20A bomber experiments can be found in J. D. Hunley, *The Development of Propulsion Technology for U.S. Space-Launch Vehicles, 1926–1991* (College Station: Texas A&M University Press, 2013).

Details about Melba Nead, Freeman Kincaid, Macie Roberts, and Virginia Prettyman can be found in "Reminiscences of California Institute of Technology Guggenheim Aeronautical Laboratory, GALCIT No. 1, later JPL," memo from Nead to Kyky Chapman, JPL Archives History Collection.

Walt Powell's attack on Malina with a hatchet is described in Powell's comments on Malina's memoir, Walter Powell Collection, JPL Archives. Malina's memoir also includes a discussion of how von Kármán chose a successor for JPL and the role of

Clark Millikan.

A biography of Jack Parsons, which relates how Parsons got the idea for an asphalt-based propellant by watching a construction crew mix molten asphalt, can be found in John Carter, *Sex and Rockets: The Occult World of Jack Parsons* (Port Townsend, WA: Feral House, 2005).

A technical description of Jack Parsons's asphalt-based propellant, also known as GALCIT 61-C, including the calculations used to test it, can be found in "The Preparation and Some Properties of an Asphalt Base Solid Propellant GALCIT 61-C," GALCIT Report No. 22, JPL Archives History Collection.

Macie's promotion to "acting head of the computing group" was announced in a memo to the lab on September 3, 1946.

A description of the Rose Parade in the 1940s and of the mandatory tryouts required by women's physical education classes at Pasadena Junior College can be found in Kim Kowsky, "Parade Passed Her By: In 1942, a Rose Princess Could Only Wave Good-bye to Her Dreams," *Los Angeles Times,* December 27, 1992.

Chapter 2: Headed West

All personal anecdotes and family history obtained from author interviews.

China's role in World War II is discussed in Rana Mitter, *Forgotten Ally: China's World War II, 1937–1945* (New York: Houghton Mifflin Harcourt, 2013).

More information about the Flying Tigers can be found in Daniel Ford, *Flying Tigers: Claire Chennault and His American Volunteers, 1941–1942* (New York: HarperCollins, 2007).

The boom in jobs in the aerospace industry in the 1940s is reported in Robert A. Kleinhenz et al., "The Aerospace Industry in Southern California," prepared for the Los Angeles Economic Development Corporation, 2012.

The U.S. aircraft industry rose from the forty-first-largest industry in the world to the first between 1939 and 1945, as reported in Roger E. Bilstein, *The American Aerospace Industry* (New York: Twayne, 1996).

Chapter 3: Rockets Rising

All personal anecdotes and family history obtained from author interviews.

Barbara signed the hundredth Corporal in 1955. The rocket launched from White

Sands on April 28, 1955. William Pickering described the event in a JPL Stories presentation in the JPL library, January 2001.

Descriptions of the Corporal, WAC Corporal, and the Bumper WAC can be found in Frank H. Winter, *Rockets into Space* (Cambridge, MA: Harvard University Press, 1990); A. Bowdoin Van Riper, *Rockets and Missiles: The Life Story of a Technology* (Baltimore: Johns Hopkins University Press, 2007); and Mike Gruntman, *Blazing the Trail: The Early History of Spacecraft and Rocketry* (Reston, VA: American Institute of Aeronautics and Astronautics, 2004).

A history of the name of the WAC Corporal, including the alternate definitions "Without Altitude Control" and "Women's Army Corps," can be found in Simon Naylor and James R. Ryan, eds., *New Spaces of Exploration: Geographies of Discovery in the Twentieth Century* (London: I. B. Tauris, 2010).

The description of the White Sands Proving Ground obtained from personal interviews and correspondence. A description of the antics that occurred there can be found in M. G. Lord, *Astro Turf: The Private Life of Rocket Science* (New York: Walker, 2006). The physical beauty of the site and its use in the Trinity test are noted in Rose Houk and Michael Collier, *White Sands National Monument* (Tucson, AZ: Western National Parks Association, 1994).

The January 1949 snowstorm is described in Stephen B. Johnson, "In 1949, the Snowman Socked Los Angeles," *Los Angeles Times,* January 11, 2013.

Results of Corporal and Bumper WAC tests are documented in the official government report, James W. Bragg et al., "Development of the Corporal: The Embryo of the Army Missile Program," Army Missile Command (Huntsville, AL: April 1961).

The V-2 rocket's flight over El Paso and its crash in Juarez were described in "V-2 Rocket, Off Course, Falls Near Juarez," *El Paso Times,* May 30, 1947.

A history of what would later be Cape Canaveral, and its origins in Cocoa Beach, can be found in Tony Long, "July 24, 1950: America Gets a Spaceport," *Wired,* July 24, 2009.

Information about Coralie Pearson's role in helping the Bumper WAC to launch was obtained through author interviews. A description of the launch on February 24, 1949, and technical considerations of the Bumper WAC can be found in J. D. Hunley, *Preludes to U.S. Space-Launch Vehicle Tech-*

nology: Goddard Rockets to Minuteman III (Gainesville: University Press of Florida, 2008).

The USSR's first atomic bomb, code-named First Lightning, is described in Andrew Krepinevich and Barry Watts, *The Last Warrior: Andrew Marshall and the Shaping of Modern American Defense Strategy* (New York: Basic Books, 2015).

Hsue-Shen Tsien is the name used in the United States, though Tsien was known as Qian Xuesen in China. His history is documented in Iris Chang, *Thread of the Silkworm* (New York: Basic Books, 1995). His FBI record was obtained using the Freedom of Information Act. Tsien was still considered a spy by the U.S. government in 1999, as reported in the U.S. House of Representatives Report 105–851, "Report of the Select Committee on U.S. National Security and Military/Commercial Concerns with the People's Republic of China, Submitted by Mr. [Christopher] Cox of California, [Committee] Chairman," January 3, 1999, 105th Congress, second session.

Frank Malina's troubles with the FBI and self-imposed exile to France are documented in his FBI files.

Description of the Corporal convoy, including its sixteen-mile length, can be found in Stephen B. Johnson, *The Secret of Apollo: Systems Management in American and European Space Programs* (Baltimore: Johns Hopkins University Press, 2006).

Chapter 4: Miss Guided Missile

All personal anecdotes and family history obtained from author interviews.

JPL's budget doubled to $11 million and the lab's personnel subsequently grew, as described in Clayton R. Koppes, *JPL and the American Space Program: A History of the Jet Propulsion Laboratory* (New Haven, CT: Yale University Press, 1982).

Multiple advertisements for computers were made by JPL in the 1950s and posted in area universities, as documented in archives of the lab's newsletter *Lab-Oratory.*

The changing African-American population in Los Angeles is described in Charles A. Gallagher and Cameron D. Lippard, eds., *Race and Racism in the United States: An Encyclopedia of the American Mosaic* (Santa Barbara, CA: Greenwood, 2014).

Tract housing replacing orange groves in Southern California is documented in "Tract Housing in California, 1945–1973: A Context for National Register Evaluation," prepared by the California Department of Transportation (Sacramento, CA: 2011).

The hiring of Firestone Tire and Rubber Company as a contractor for production of the Corporal, and JPL's growing frustration over its lack of consistency, are described in Stephen B. Johnson, *The Secret of Apollo: Systems Management in American and European Space Programs* (Baltimore: Johns Hopkins University Press, 2002).

The history of Harry James Pool and his burning star can be found in P. Thomas Carroll, "Historical Origins of the Sergeant Missile Powerplant," in Kristan R. Lattu, ed., *History of Rocketry and Astronautics: Proceedings of the Seventh and Eighth History Symposia of the International Academy of Astronautics, 1973–1974* (San Diego: Univelt, 1989).

The twelve successive Sergeant rocket explosions and the intrinsic problems with the burning star were described in Roger D. Launius and Dennis R. Jenkins, eds., *To Reach the High Frontier: A History of U.S. Launch Vehicles* (Lexington: University Press of Kentucky, 2002).

More information about the Fibonacci sequence can be found in Alfred S. Posamentier and Ingmar Lehmann, *The (Fabu-*

lous) Fibonacci Numbers (Amherst, NY: Prometheus Books, 2007).

The history of the IBM 701 can be found in Paul E. Ceruzzi, *Beyond the Limits: Flight Enters the Computer Age* (Cambridge, MA: MIT Press, 1989), and Emerson W. Pugh, *Building IBM: Shaping an Industry and Its Technology* (Cambridge, MA: MIT Press, 1995).

Janez Lawson and Elaine Chappell were both sent to the IBM training school, as reported in JPL's *Lab-Oratory* newsletter, February 1953.

Remembrances of hearing magnetic-tape audio recordings during World War II are from John T. Mullin, "Creating the Craft of Tape Recording," *High Fidelity,* April 1976, 62–67.

More information on how magnetic tape holds data can be found in H. Neal Bertram, *Theory of Magnetic Recording* (New York: Cambridge University Press, 1994).

Thomas Watson Jr. told IBM stockholders on April 18, 1952, "As a result of our trip, on which we expected to get orders for five machines, we came home with orders for eighteen," as recorded in Susan Ratcliffe, ed., *Oxford Treasury of Sayings and Quotations* (Oxford, England: Oxford University Press, 2011).

Accidents at JPL during the 1950s were described by former staff in author interviews; little documentation exists.

The inertial guidance system of the Sergeant is described in Koppes, *JPL and the American Space Program*.

Leslie Greener, *Moon Ahead* (New York: Viking Press, 1951).

Opposition to desegregation in Pasadena in 1950 and the consequences for the school superintendent are reported in Adam Laats, *The Other School Reformers: Conservative Activism in American Education* (Cambridge, MA: Harvard University Press, 2015).

Janez Lawson's marriage to Theodore Bordeaux was announced in the *California Eagle,* September 2, 1954.

Chapter 5: Holding Back

All personal anecdotes and family history obtained from author interviews.

An excellent biography of Wernher von Braun is by Michael J. Neufeld, *Von Braun: Dreamer of Space, Engineer of War* (New York: Alfred A. Knopf), 2008.

Von Braun's relationship with Walt Disney is described in Mike Wright, "The Disney–Von Braun Collaboration and Its Influence on Space Exploration," in Daniel Schenker et al., eds., *Selected Papers from the 1993*

Southern Humanities Conference (Huntsville, AL: Southern Humanities Press, 1993).

"Man Will Conquer Space Soon" was a series of articles in *Collier's* from 1952 to 1954. Von Braun contributed eight articles to the series, including "Crossing the Last Frontier," March 22, 1952.

Von Braun's reputation for arrogance and the jealousy he provoked in American scientists are described in Drew Pearson and John F. Anderson, *U.S.A. — Second-Class Power?* (New York: Simon and Schuster, 1958).

The quote "extensive cosmic ray studies be deferred until a satellite rocket can be produced" is from William Pickering, "Study of the Upper Atmosphere by Means of Rockets," JPL Publication No. 15, June 20, 1947.

Plans for the International Geophysical Year are described in "Proposed United States Program for the International Geophysical Year, 1957–1958," National Academy of Science, National Research Council, 1956.

Personnel records at the JPL Archives were used to calculate the average number of hires in the computing department.

Details about Project Orbiter and the

competition with Vanguard can be found in Dwayne A. Day, "New Revelations About the American Satellite Programme Before Sputnik," *Spaceflight* 36(11) (1994): 372–373; Constance McLaughlin Green and Milton Lomask, *Vanguard: A History* (Washington, DC: U.S. Government Printing Office, 1970); Roger D. Launius et al., eds., *Reconsidering Sputnik: Forty Years Since the Soviet Satellite* (London: Routledge, 2013); Pickering with James H. Wilson, "Countdown to Space Exploration: A Memoir of the Jet Propulsion Laboratory, 1944–1958," in R. Cargill Hall, ed., *History of Rocketry and Astronautics* (San Diego: Univelt, 1986).

The conditions of the vacuum of space are described in Andrew M. Shaw, *Astrochemistry: From Astronomy to Astrobiology* (Chichester, England: John Wiley, 2006).

The challenges with leaving the atmosphere are explained in Paul A. Tiper and Gene Mosca, *Physics for Scientists and Engineers,* 6th ed. (New York: W. H. Freeman, 2007).

The science of multistage rocketry, including the necessary speed and direction to achieve escape velocity and enter orbit, is explained in George P. Sutton and Oscar Biblarz, *Rocket Propulsion Elements* (Hoboken, NJ: John Wiley, 2009).

A history of Redstone and the Army Ballistic Missile Agency can be found in T. Gary Wicks, *Huntsville Air and Space* (Charleston, SC: Arcadia, 2010).

How Project Vanguard was chosen over Project Orbiter is described in Green and Lomask, *Vanguard*.

A history of Hotel Del Coronado can be found in Donald Langmead, *Icons of American Architecture: From the Alamo to the World Trade Center* (Santa Barbara, CA: Greenwood, 2009).

Jupiter-C is described in Clayton R. Koppes, *JPL and the American Space Program: A History of the Jet Propulsion Laboratory* (New Haven, CT: Yale University Press, 1982); Abigail Foerstner, *James Van Allen: The First Eight Billion Miles* (Iowa City: University of Iowa Press, 2009); Roger D. Launius and Dennis R. Jenkins, eds., *To Reach the High Frontier: A History of U.S. Launch Vehicles* (Lexington: University Press of Kentucky, 2002); Asif A. Siddiqi, *The Red Rockets' Glare: Spaceflight and the Soviet Imagination, 1857–1957* (New York: Cambridge University Press, 2010); and James M. Grimwood and Frances Strowd, "History of the Jupiter Missile System,"

Report of U.S. Army Missile Command, July 27, 1962.

Microlock is explained in David Christopher Arnold, *Spying from Space: Constructing America's Satellite Command and Control Systems* (College Station: Texas A&M University Press, 2008), and in H. L. Richter Jr. et al., "Microlock: A Minimum-Weight Radio Instrumentation System for a Satellite," JPL Publication No. 36, April 17, 1958.

Chapter 6: Ninety Days and Ninety Minutes

All personal anecdotes and family history obtained from author interviews.

Pickering's experiences in Washington, D.C., when Sputnik launched are described in Douglas J. Mudgway, *William H. Pickering: America's Deep Space Pioneer* (Washington, DC: National Aeronautics and Space Administration, 2008).

The challenges of reentry are described in José Meseguer et al., *Spacecraft Thermal Control* (Oxford, England: Woodhead, 2012).

The clunky design of nose cones for reentry is explained in Andrew Chaikin, "How the Spaceship Got Its Shape," *Air & Space*

Smithsonian, November 2009.

Disappointment over the shutdown of Jupiter-C, or Juno, is described in Clayton R. Koppes, *JPL and the American Space Program: A History of the Jet Propulsion Laboratory* (New Haven, CT: Yale University Press, 1982).

Burns incurred from nitric acid are described in L. Kolios et al., "The Nitric Burn Trauma of the Skin," *Journal of Plastic, Reconstructive and Aesthetic Surgery* 63(4) (2010).

A history of Sputnik can be found in Paul Dickson, *Sputnik: The Shock of the Century* (New York: Walker, 2007), and Yanek Mieczkowski, *Eisenhower's Sputnik Moment: The Race for Space and World Prestige* (Ithaca, NY: Cornell University Press, 2013).

Von Braun's conversation, beginning with "Vanguard will never make it," with Medaris and McElroy the evening that Sputnik's launch was announced is reported in William E. Burroughs, *This New Ocean: The Story of the First Space Age* (New York: Random House, 1998).

President Eisenhower's role in Jupiter-C and Explorer is explained in Yanek Mieczkowski, *Eisenhower's Sputnik Moment: The Race for Space and World Prestige* (Ithaca,

NY: Cornell University Press, 2013).

Project Red Socks is described in Paolo Ulivi and David M. Harland, *Lunar Exploration: Human Pioneers and Robotic Surveyors* (London: Springer, 2004); R. Cargill Hall, *Lunar Impact: The NASA History of Project Ranger* (Mineola, NY: Dover, 2010); and Jay Gallentine, *Ambassadors from Earth: Pioneering Explorations with Unmanned Spacecraft* (Lincoln: University of Nebraska Press, 2009).

Daily health reports were issued by the Soviet government claiming that the dog cosmonaut Laika was healthy and, later, that it was euthanized in space. In 2002, it was revealed that Laika died a few hours into the flight, due to overheating (temperatures inside Sputnik 2 were over 120 degrees Fahrenheit). More information can be found in Jennifer Latson, "The Sad Story of Laika, the First Dog Launched into Orbit," *Time,* November 3, 2014.

Vanguard's initial failure and subsequent success are described in Constance McLaughlin Green and Milton Lomask, *Vanguard: A History* (Washington, DC: U.S. Government Printing Office, 1970).

Kennedy warned, "The nation was losing the satellite-missile race with the Soviet Union because of . . . complacent miscalculations," etc., as quoted in Zuoyue Wang, *In Sputnik's Shadow: The President's Science Advisory Committee and Cold War America* (New Brunswick, NJ: Rutgers University Press, 2009).

The launch of Explorer 1, including accounts of the Teletypes between Cape Canaveral and JPL and the subsequent press conference, is described in Matthew A. Bille and Erika Lishock, *The First Space Race: Launching the World's First Satellites* (College Station: Texas A&M University Press, 2004).

Von Braun is quoted as saying "She is eight minutes late" in Erik Bergaust, *Wernher von Braun: The Authoritative and Definitive Biographical Profile of the Father of Modern Space Flight* (Washington, DC: National Space Institute, 1976).

Chapter 7: Moonglow

All personal anecdotes and family history obtained from author interviews.

The early days of NASA are documented in Thomas Keith Glennan, *The Birth of NASA: The Diary of T. Keith Glennan* (Washington, DC: National Aeronautics and Space Administration, 2009).

Early plans made at JPL to explore the

solar system soon after NASA's formation, as well as the history of the Pioneer missions, are described in Clayton R. Koppes, *JPL and the American Space Program: A History of the Jet Propulsion Laboratory* (New Haven, CT: Yale University Press, 1982), and Mark Wolverton, *The Depths of Space: The Story of the Pioneer Planetary Probes* (Washington, DC: Joseph Henry Press, 2004).

"Mars and Beyond" was an episode of *Disneyland* that aired on December 4, 1957.

The IBM 704 is described in Paul E. Ceruzzi, *Computing: A Concise History* (Cambridge, MA: MIT Press, 2012).

Luna 1 was also known as Mechta and was the fourth launch of the series, although the first that was successful. It was named by the famous Soviet rocket engineer Sergei Korolev and then renamed by the government. It is still circling the sun. More information on both the Luna and Pioneer missions can be found in Tom McGowen, *Space Race: The Mission, the Men, the Moon* (New York: Enslow, 2008).

The transfer of 157 employees from the navy's Vanguard team and the phasing out of von Braun's group at ABMA are described in Virginia P. Dawson and Mark D. Bowles, eds., *Realizing the Dream of Flight*

(Washington, DC: National Aeronautics and Space Administration, 2005), and Howard E. McCurdy, *Space and the American Imagination* (Baltimore: Johns Hopkins University Press, 2011).

The history of what would become the Deep Space Network can be found in William A. Imbriale, *Large Antennas of the Deep Space Network* (Hoboken, NJ: John Wiley, 2003).

Chapter 8: Analog Overlords

All personal anecdotes and family history obtained from author interviews.

The shutdown of Project Vega and subsequent plans made at JPL are described in Clayton R. Koppes, *JPL and the American Space Program: A History of the Jet Propulsion Laboratory* (New Haven, CT: Yale University Press, 1982), and Stephen J. Pyne, *Voyager: Exploration, Space, and the Third Great Age of Discovery* (New York: Viking, 2010).

Project Mariner is described in Franklin O'Donnell, "The Venus Mission: How Mariner 2 Led the World to the Planets," JPL/California Institute of Technology, 2012; Robert Van Buren, *Mariner Mars 1964 Handbook,* JPL, 1965; and Koppes, *JPL and the American Space Program.*

A history of Project Mercury can be found in M. Scott Carpenter et al., *We Seven* (New York: Simon and Schuster, 1962), and John Catchpole, *Project Mercury: NASA's First Manned Space Programme* (London: Springer, 2001).

The letter quoted from von Braun to Pickering is also documented in Michael J. Neufeld, *Von Braun: Dreamer of Space, Engineer of War* (New York: Alfred A. Knopf), 2008.

Alan Shepard's orbit is described in Colin Burgess, *Freedom 7: The Historic Flight of Alan B. Shepard, Jr.* (New York: Springer, 2014).

That the Vostok was designed to survive a week while the Mercury capsule could barely survive twenty-four hours is explained in Scott Carpenter and Kris Stoever, *For Spacious Skies: The Uncommon Journey of a Mercury Astronaut* (Orlando, FL: Harcourt, 2002).

The Atlas-Agena rocket is described in Lewis Research Center, ed., *Flight Performance of Atlas-Agena Launch Vehicles in Support of the Lunar Orbiter Missions III, IV, and V* (Washington, DC: National Aeronautics and Space Administration, 1969).

The Ranger failures are detailed in David M. Harland, *NASA's Moon Program: Paving the Way for Apollo 11* (New York: Springer, 2009); Koppes, *JPL and the American Space Program;* and R. Cargill Hall, *Project Ranger: A Chronology* (Pasadena, CA: JPL/California Institute of Technology, 1971).

The thrilling 1960 World Series is chronicled in Michael Shapiro, *Bottom of the Ninth: Branch Rickey, Casey Stengel, and the Daring Scheme to Save Baseball from Itself* (New York: Henry Holt, 2010).

In 1960, 25 percent of married mothers with children under the age of eighteen entered the workforce, as reported in Sharon R. Cohany and Emy Sok, "Trends in Labor Force Participation of Married Mothers of Infants," *Monthly Labor Review,* February 2007.

Birth control became available in 1960 in the United States, as described in James Reed, *The Birth Control Movement and American Society: From Private Vice to Public Virtue* (Princeton, NJ: Princeton University Press, 2014).

A history of FORTRAN, along with descriptions of how early keypunch computers worked and the IBM 1620, can be found in

Paul E. Ceruzzi, *A History of Modern Computing,* 2nd ed. (Cambridge, MA: MIT Press, 2003).

Grace Murray Hopper's story is told in her biography, Kathleen Broome Williams, *Grace Hopper: Admiral of the Cyber Sea* (Annapolis, MD: Naval Institute Press, 2013).

Lois Haibt is quoted as saying, "Nobody knew anything," etc., when asked about compilers, in Lois Haibt, an oral-history interview conducted August 2, 2001, by Janet Abbate, Institute of Electrical and Electronics Engineers History Center, Hoboken, NJ, U.S.A. (http://ethw.org/Oral-History:Lois_Haibt).

The IBM 1620's nickname of CADET was facetiously said to stand for "Can't Add, Doesn't Even Try" because it had no digital circuit that performed addition functions, which meant that operators had to look up their answers in tables instead, as described in Richard Vernon Andree, *Computer Programming and Related Mathematics* (Hoboken, NJ: John Wiley, 1966).

A missing bar in the program was partly responsible for the Mariner accident, as reported in Ceruzzi, *Beyond the Limits: Flight Enters the Computer Age* (Cambridge, MA: MIT Press, 1989). Arthur C. Clarke mistakenly said that Mariner 1 was "wrecked by the most expensive hyphen in history" in *The Promise of Space* (New York: Berkley, 1955), and similar reports have been made elsewhere. Ceruzzi explains how the Mariner 1 failure was a "combination of a hardware failure and software bug."

Material about the Mercury 7 and the Saturn rocket can be found in Richard W. Orloff and David M. Harland, *Apollo: The Definitive Sourcebook* (New York: Springer, 2006).

The Cuban missile crisis is described in Sheldon M. Stern, *The Cuban Missile Crisis in American Memory: Myths Versus Reality* (Palo Alto, CA: Stanford University Press, 2012). Both this book and the Kennedy Presidential Library website (http://www.jfklibrary.org/JFK/JFK-in-History/Cuban-Missile-Crisis.aspx) describe the presence of Jupiter missiles in Turkey. However, the role that the missiles played in the crisis wasn't revealed to the American public until 1987.

Pythagoras, the Greek mathematician, is credited with the saying "There is geometry in the humming of the strings. There is music in the spacing of the spheres." Bill Pickering told the newspaper reporters, "Listen to the music of the spheres." His words were repeated in many newspaper columns, including Philip Dodd, "Rendezvous with Venus a Success!," *Chicago Daily Tribune,* December 15, 1962.

Mariner's float in the 1963 Rose Parade is described in David S. Portree, "Centaurs, Soviets, and Seltzer Seas: Mariner 2's Venusian Adventure (1962)," *Wired,* December 20, 2014.

Chapter 9: Planetary Pull

All personal anecdotes and family history obtained from author interviews.

Abe Silverstein said, "I was naming the spacecraft like I'd name my baby" when speaking of Apollo, as quoted in Charles A. Murray and Catherine Bly Cox, *Apollo: The Race to the Moon* (New York: Simon and Schuster, 1989).

The Mariner Mars mission is described in Edward Clinton Ezell and Linda Neuman Ezell, *On Mars: Exploration of the Red Planet, 1958–1978 — The NASA History* (Mineola, NY: Dover, 2009); Clayton R. Koppes, *JPL and the American Space Program: A History of the Jet Propulsion Laboratory* (New Haven, CT: Yale University Press, 1982); *Mariner-Mars 1964: Final Project Report,* JPL, 1968; and Dennis A. Tito, "Trajectory

Design for the Mariner-Mars 1964 Mission," *Journal of Spacecraft and Rockets* 4(3) (1967): 289–296.

Venus possibly has no magnetic field because the core is either completely solid or completely liquid. On Earth, the phase boundary in the interior also releases heat, driving convection as the inner core expands in size, approximately 1 millimeter a year. However, it's unknown whether this effect can drive a geodynamo by itself. Models of Venus's core predict that it is at least partially liquid, given its size and heat budget, although the actual state is unknown. Slow rotation of a planet has other interesting effects, such as uneven solar heating and unusual atmospheric dynamics. A discussion of the magnetic field on Venus can be found in Frederic W. Taylor, *The Scientific Exploration of Venus* (New York: Cambridge University Press, 2014).

More information on the Coriolis effect can be found in Graham P. Collins, "Coriolis Effect," *Scientific American,* September 1, 2009.

The problems with heat sterilization affecting the operation of the spacecraft are described in R. Cargill Hall, *Lunar Impact: The NASA History of Project Ranger* (Mineola, NY: Dover, 2010). The Mariner Mars missions were not heat-sterilized, as specified in *Mariner-Mars 1964,* JPL.

The live feed of Ranger 6 that got switched to "Spray on Avon cologne mist and walk in fragrant beauty," James Webb's saying "One more flight. You've got only one more flight," and Pickering's quote at the Miss Guided Missile contest — "We're going to fix this. We're going to make it work" — are detailed in Jeffrey Kluger, *Moon Hunters: NASA's Remarkable Expeditions to the Ends of the Solar Systems* (New York: Simon and Schuster, 2001).

A 43 percent drop in the number of switchboard operators between 1947 and 1960 was reported by the U.S. Bureau of Labor Statistics in 1963.

Computer jobs being cut at NASA centers is reported in Sheryll Goecke Powers, "Women in Flight Research at NASA Dryden Flight Research Center from 1946 to 1995," National Aeronautics and Space Administration History Office, 1997.

The history of peanuts at JPL is explained in Associated Press, "Peanuts: Rocket Scientists' Lucky Charm," *Lodi (California) News-Sentinel,* December 3, 1999.

The debate over lunar landing sites is reported in Hall, *Lunar Impact,* and Paolo Ulivi and David M. Harland, *Lunar Explora-*

tion: Human Pioneers and Robotic Surveyors (London: Springer, 2004).

Eugene Shoemaker's push to take images at the moon's terminator for Ranger 8 is described in David H. Levy, *Shoemaker by Levy: The Man Who Made an Impact* (Princeton, NJ: Princeton University Press, 2002).

Problems with the shroud covering Mariner 3 and the eventual solution are described in John S. Lewis and Ruth A. Lewis, *Space Resources: Breaking the Bonds of Earth* (New York: Columbia University Press, 1987).

Percival Lowell published three books about Mars. He describes the canals extensively in *Mars and Its Canals* (New York: Macmillan, 1906).

Fred Billingsley, one of the engineers the computers worked with, first published the word *pixel,* short for "picture element," in 1965. The early days of digital-image processing and JPL's pioneering role are described in James Tomayko, *Computers in Spaceflight: The NASA Experience* (Washington, DC: National Aeronautics and Space Administration, 1988).

"Mars is probably a dead planet" is from the editorial "The Dead Planet," *New York Times,* July 30, 1965.

Twenty percent of married women with

children under the age of six participated in the labor force, as reported in Committee on Finance, *Child Care Data and Materials,* U.S. Senate, 1974.

The Mariner findings, including the poles and gravitational field, are described in Ezell and Ezell, *On Mars.*

The Surveyor program is explained in Koppes, *JPL and the American Space Program.*

Pickering recounts hearing "Oh, by the way, we're live all over the world" from a member of the media, in an oral-history interview with Mary Terrall, November 7–December 19, 1978, Caltech Archives.

The Apollo 1 disaster, including the quote "Fire! We've got a fire in the cockpit!," is chronicled in David J. Shayler, *Disasters and Accidents in Manned Spaceflight* (London: Springer, 2000).

The history of pantyhose is recounted in Joseph Caputo, "50 Years of Pantyhose," *Smithsonian,* July 7, 2009.

The Apollo 6 mission is described in Richard W. Orloff and David M. Harland, *Apollo: The Definitive Sourcebook* (New York: Springer, 2006).

Chapter 10: The Last Queen of Outer Space

All personal anecdotes and family history obtained from author interviews.

FORTRAN 66 is described in Dennis C. Smolarski, *The Essentials of FORTRAN* (Piscataway, NJ: Research and Education Association, 1994).

The story of Apollo 11 is recounted in Charles A. Murray and Catherine Bly Cox, *Apollo: The Race to the Moon* (New York: Simon and Schuster, 1989).

The Mariner missions and their findings are described in Edward Clinton Ezell and Linda Neuman Ezell, *On Mars: Exploration of the Red Planet, 1958–1978 — The NASA History* (Mineola, NY: Dover, 2009). Mariner 5 was originally a backup for 4 but was modified to go to Venus instead.

The telemetry system that Margie worked on is described in R. C. Tausworthe et al., "A High-Rate Telemetry System for the Mariner Mars 1969 Mission," JPL Technical Report 32–1354, 1969.

The dust storm that was mistaken for vegetation and a Martian spring is explained in William Sheehan and Stephen James O'Meara, *Mars: The Lure of the Red Planet* (Amherst, NY: Prometheus Books, 2001).

The effect of Mars on literature is described in Robert Crossley, *Imagining Mars: A Literary History* (Middletown, CT: Wesleyan University Press, 2011).

Invaders from Mars premiered in 1953, and *The Day Mars Invaded Earth* came out in 1963.

The Grand Tour, as well as the origins of what would become known as Voyager and its trajectory, is described in Stephen J. Pyne, *Voyager: Exploration, Space, and the Third Great Age of Discovery* (New York: Viking, 2010), and Ben Evans with David M. Harland, *NASA's Voyager Missions: Exploring the Outer Solar System and Beyond* (London: Springer-Verlag, 2004).

The cancellation of the Grand Tour is discussed in Edward C. Stone, "Voyager, the Space Triumph That Almost Wasn't," *Los Angeles Times,* February 18, 2014.

A description of the Women's Strike for Equality and the quote "I don't know what these women are thinking of," etc., are found in Catherine Gourley, *Ms. and the Material Girls: Perceptions of Women from the 1970s Through the 1990s* (Minneapolis: Lerner, 2007).

Giuseppe Columbo's role in Mariner 10 is described in Robert S. Kraemer, *Beyond the Moon: A Golden Age of Planetary Explora-*

tion, 1971–1978 (Washington, DC: Smithsonian Institution Scholarly Press, 2000).

The percentage of women receiving engineering degrees in 1970 is published by the National Center for Education Statistics, Statistical Analysis Report, 2013.

Caltech opening its doors to undergraduate women in 1970 is reported on the Caltech alumni website (http://www.alumni.caltech.edu/news/2014/5/12/remembering-a-milestone) and in Amy Sue Bix, *Girls Coming to Tech!: A History of American Engineering Education for Women* (Cambridge, MA: MIT Press, 2014).

Chapter 11: Men Are from Mars

All personal anecdotes and family history obtained from author interviews.

The results of Mariner 10's mission are reported in James A. Dunne and Eric Burgess, *The Voyage of Mariner 10: Mission to Venus and Mercury* (Washington, DC: National Aeronautics and Space Administration, 1978).

Telemetry from Mariner Venus/Mercury 1973 is described in J. T. Hatch and J. W. Capps, "Real-Time High-Rate Telemetry Support of Mariner 10 Operations," JPL DSN Progress Report 42–23, 1974, and Bruce Murray and Eric Burgess, *Flight to*

Mercury (New York: Columbia University Press, 1977).

Mariner 10 did detect a tenuous atmosphere on Mars, one unlike typical thick planetary atmospheres. Mercury's atmosphere is considered an exosphere, in which the density is so low that the molecules don't behave like a gas anymore. Further information can be found in A. L. Broadfoot et al., "Mariner 10: Mercury Atmosphere," *Geophysical Research Letters,* 3(10) (1976).

Sylvia's paper, which she co-wrote with Roger D. Bourke, Ralph F. Miles Jr., Paul A. Penzo, and Richard A. Wallace, and which bears her name, Sylvia L. Van Dillen, is "Mariner Jupiter/Saturn 1977: The Mission Frame," *Astronautics and Aeronautics,* November 1, 1972.

The *Blue Marble* photo of Earth was taken during Apollo 17, as explained in Don Nardo, *The Blue Marble: How a Photo Revealed Earth's Fragile Beauty* (Mankato, MN: Capstone), 2014.

Nixon's formative role in NASA is explored in John M. Logsdon, *After Apollo?: Richard Nixon and the American Space Program* (New York: Palgrave Macmillan, 2015).

Perspective on the German Amerika

Bomber proposal can be found in Alan Axelrod, *Lost Destiny: Joe Kennedy Jr. and the Doomed WWII Mission to Save London* (New York: St. Martin's, 2015).

The history of Skylab is recounted in Pamela E. Mack, ed., *From Engineering Science to Big Science: The NACA and NASA Collier Trophy Research Project Winners* (Washington, DC: National Aeronautics and Space Administration History Division, 1998).

The Soyuz 11 disaster is recalled in John F. Burns, "Emerging New Details Indicate Soyuz Trouble," *New York Times,* December 14, 1982, and "The Crew That Never Came Home: The Misfortunes of Soyuz 11," *Space Safety,* April 28, 2013.

The ability of SEASAT to detect submarines is detailed in William J. Broad, "U.S. Loses Hold on Submarine-Exposing Radar Technique," *New York Times,* May 11, 1999.

The Viking mission, including the quote from Harold Masursky, "Computers are just like wearing shoes," etc., is described in Edward Clinton Ezell and Linda Neuman Ezell, *On Mars: Exploration of the Red Planet, 1958–1978 — The NASA History* (Mineola, NY: Dover, 2009).

Considerations affecting the trajectory of

the Viking mission are explained in Douglas J. Mudgway, "Viking Mission Support," JPL Technical Report 32–1526, 1976.

The landing of Viking 2 is described in Walter Sullivan, "Viking 2 Lander Settles on Mars and Sends Signal," *New York Times,* September 4, 1976.

The use of the DSN for tracking Viking is explained in F.H.J. Taylor, "Deep Space Network to Viking Orbiter Telecommunications Performance During the Viking Extended Mission, November 1976 through February 1978," JPL DSN Progress Report 42–25, 1978.

The story of how Voyager got its name is explained by Charley Kohlhase in David W. Swift, *Voyager Tales: Personal Views of the Grand Tour* (Reston, VA: American Institute of Aeronautics and Astronautics, 1997).

Voyager's "anxiety attack" and launch malfunctions are described in Bruce Murray, *Journey into Space: The First Thirty Years of Space Exploration* (New York: W. W. Norton, 1990).

Chapter 12: Look Like a Girl
All personal anecdotes and family history obtained from author interviews.

The Voyager mission is described in Stephen J. Pyne, *Voyager: Exploration, Space, and the Third Great Age of Discovery* (New York: Viking, 2010), and Dan Vergano, "Voyager," *National Geographic,* August 18, 2014, which also includes Bradford Smith's quote, "You count them."

The problem of Voyager 2's stuck platform and its subsequent solution by the accidental command of a flight engineer are reported in Associated Press, "Accident Frees Voyager 2 Camera; Now, Will It Work?," *Miami News,* August 27, 1981.

Details of the Challenger disaster are described in Diane Vaughan, *The Challenger Launch Decision: Risky Technology, Culture and Deviance at NASA* (Chicago: University of Chicago Press, 1997), and "Report to the President by the Presidential Commission on the Space Shuttle Challenger Accident," June 6, 1986.

Roger Boisjoly wrote in a memo on July 31, 1985, National Archives, identifier 596263: "It is my honest and very real fear that if we do not take immediate action to dedicate a team to solve the problem with the field joint having the number one priority, then we stand in jeopardy of losing a flight along with all the launch pad facilities."

The role of Boisjoly and Allan J. McDonald in the Challenger disaster is explained in David E. Sanger, "A Year Later, Two Engineers Cope with Challenger Horror," *New York Times,* January 28, 1987.

The history of the microprocessor can be found in Robert Slater, *Portraits in Silicon* (Cambridge, MA: MIT Press, 1989).

The role of Jack Kilby in the development of the microchip is described in T. R. Reid, *The Chip: How Two Americans Invented the Microchip and Launched a Revolution* (New York: Simon and Schuster, 1985).

A history of the Altair 8800 can be found in Robert M. Collins, *Transforming America: Politics and Culture During the Reagan Years* (New York: Columbia University Press, 2009).

Stephen Wozniak is quoted as saying, "The whole vision of a personal computer popped in my head," etc., in Walter Isaacson, *Steve Jobs* (Simon and Schuster, 2011).

The antenna failure on Galileo is explained in J. George et al., "Galileo System Design for Orbital Operations," Digital Avionics Systems Conference, Phoenix, Arizona, 1994, and Jean H. Aichele, ed., "Galileo, the Tour Guide: A Summary of the Mission to Date," JPL Progress Report D–13554, 1996.

More information on the Galileo mission

can be found in David M. Harland, *Jupiter Odyssey: The Story of NASA's Galileo Mission* (London: Springer, 2000), and Daniel Fischer, *Mission Jupiter: The Spectacular Journey of the Galileo Spacecraft* (New York: Springer-Verlag, 2001).

The CRAF project and its budget considerations are discussed in Roger D. Launius, ed., *Exploring the Solar System: The History and Science of Planetary Exploration* (New York: Palgrave Macmillan, 2013), and Peter J. Westwick, *Into the Black: JPL and the American Space Program, 1976–2004* (New Haven, CT: Yale University Press, 2007).

More information on Cassini can be found in Michael Meltzer, *The Cassini–Huygens Visit to Saturn: An Historic Mission to the Ringed Planet* (Cham, Switzerland: Springer International Publishing, 2015).

The Magellan mission is described in Westwick, *Into the Black*.

More detail about the Mars missions can be found in Erik M. Conway, *Exploration and Engineering: The Jet Propulsion Laboratory and the Quest for Mars* (Baltimore: Johns Hopkins University Press, 2015).

The metric-system mix-up that doomed the Mars climate orbiter is explained in "Mars Climate Mishap Investigation Board

Phase I Report," November 10, 1999, and "Report on the Loss of the Mars Climate Orbiter Mission," EDS–D18441, November 11, 1999.

The Polar Lander's demise is detailed in Bruce Moomaw and Cameron Park, "Was Polar Lander Doomed by Fatal Design Flaw?," *SpaceDaily,* February 16, 2000.

More information on the Mars rovers can be found in Stephen Squyres, *Roving Mars: Spirit, Opportunity, and the Exploration of the Red Planet* (New York: Hyperion, 2005), and Rod Pyle, *Curiosity: An Inside Look at the Mars Rover Mission and the People Who Made It Happen* (Amherst, NY: Prometheus Books, 2014).

In addition to a personal interview, Donna Shirley is quoted as saying, "Everything was going so smoothly and all of a sudden we realized it was all women," etc., in Kenneth Change, "Making Science Fact, Now Chronicling Science Fiction," *New York Times,* June 15, 2004.

Information about Sue's work on the Juno mission to Jupiter can be found in one of her papers, co-written with M. Soriano et al.: "Spacecraft-to-Earth Communications for Juno and Mars Science Laboratory Critical Events," Aerospace Conference, Institute of Electrical and Electronics

Engineers, Big Sky, Montana, 2012.

Voyager's nuclear battery and lifetime are explained in William J. Broad, "Voyager's Heartbeat Is Nuclear Battery," *New York Times,* August 26, 1989.

Carl Sagan named one of his books — *Pale Blue Dot: A Vision of the Human Future in Space* (New York: Random House, 1994) — after the last picture Voyager 1 took, a picture that was taken at his suggestion.

Epilogue

All personal anecdotes and family history obtained from author interviews.

A reunion of the women who worked as computers was held at JPL in October 2012.

ABOUT THE AUTHOR

Nathalia Holt is the author of *Cured: The People Who Defeated HIV* and a former Fellow at the Ragon Institute of Massachusetts General Hospital, MIT, and Harvard University. Her writing has appeared in the *New York Times*, the *Los Angeles Times*, *The Atlantic*, *Slate*, *Popular Science*, and *Time*. She lives in Boston.